THE ENERGY EQUATION

UNLOCKING THE HIDDEN POWER
OF ENERGY IN BUSINESS

THE ENERGY EQUATION

GREG BAKER

WILEY

Published by John Wiley & Sons, Inc., Hoboken, New Jersey.
Published simultaneously in Canada.

For general information on our other products and services or for technical support, please contact our Customer Care Department within the United States at (800) 762–2974, outside the United States at (317) 572–3993, or fax (317) 572–4002.

Wiley publishes in a variety of print and electronic formats and by print-on-demand. Some material included with standard print versions of this book may not be included in e-books or in print-on-demand. If this book refers to media such as a CD or DVD that is not included in the version you purchased, you may download this material at http://booksupport.wiley.com. For more information about Wiley products, visit www.wiley.com.

Library of Congress Cataloging-in-Publication Data is Available:
ISBN 9781119638681 (Hardcover)
ISBN 9781119638728 (ePDF)
ISBN 9781119638735 (ePub)

Cover Design: Wiley
Cover Image: © PeopleImages/Getty Images

Printed in the United States of America

V10015058_110519

Contents

Caption List

Preface

For several years now I've recognized that those of us working in companies, government agencies, and schools typically operate on a daily basis without direct visibility or awareness of large and important parts of our businesses. We make the best of this situation, but much is obscured from our view. As a result, common occurrences often go unexplained, including why some initiatives in business fail while others succeed, why some interactions create damaging animosity while others create productive harmony, and why some companies languish in their status quo while others reinvent themselves.

Yes, there have always been people willing to explain these things, but, for me, those explanations have been incomplete and overly focused on outcomes without explaining how and why things work, or don't work. The truth is that most of the time, we really don't know the details around why substantial business endeavors succeed any more than we know how or why they fail. Either way, our vision is obscured. We haven't been playing with a full deck, and many influential cards in the game have been out of sight and largely out of our awareness.

Challenged with this realization, my first journey was to figure out where and how to look for those missing cards and then use them to positively affect the outcome of the game. I discovered that the cards are different from business to business, much like organizational fingerprints, yet it is possible to follow the energy and discover the cards in any business. This path finding reveals a whole new world beneath the surface that provides deep insight into both problems and their solutions. With these revelations in hand, my next endeavor was figuring out how to communicate to others what seemed at first to be a very intangible topic. Obviously, that has taken the form of this book, and I'm happy to say that the resulting models, methods, and tools are all quite tangible and usable.

A friend asked me, "Why do you want to just give away your secrets?" I replied that I want to start a bigger conversation. I really think the business world needs this right now. So I offer this book to you. May it help you and your business, now and into the future. As you experience *The Energy Equation* and manage the (previously) hidden energy of yourself and your business, I hope you find it immensely useful, take it to heart, and become part of the bigger conversation.

Greg Baker
June 6, 2019

Chapter 1

The Dawn of a New Era in Business

In 2005 a friend showed me a book he had recently purchased called *The Hidden Messages in Water* by the renowned Japanese scientist Masaru Emoto. Using high-speed photography, Emoto discovered that crystals formed in frozen water reveal circumstances to which the water was exposed. For example, water from clear springs, when frozen, created beautiful, colorful, and complex snowflake patterns. Water that had been polluted formed incomplete, asymmetrical patterns with dull colors. Intrigued by this, Emoto took his research a step further by exposing water from pure springs to both positive and negative thoughts, words, and energy. For example, he wrapped pieces of paper with words on them around bottles of water and, following a period of exposure to the words, froze the water. Phrases like "Love and Gratitude" and "Thank You" had a positive effect on the water, producing beautiful, clearly formed crystals. Conversely, water samples exposed to words like "You fool!" and "You make me sick. I will kill you" formed no crystals at all. I was absolutely dumbfounded by these results. Although they made intuitive sense to me, it was striking to see the intangible effects of energy made tangible in a way that could not be denied or ignored. Emoto took his research into the realm of human interaction when he adopted a Japanese elementary school as his next test bed. He brought four samples of water from the same spring and instructed the children to treat each bottle differently.

1

To the first bottle they were to say "You're cute." To the second they were to say "You're beautiful." To the third they were to say "You fool." As for the fourth, they were told to completely ignore it. The children complied and the samples were then frozen. The first two—You're cute and You're Beautiful—produced amazingly beautiful crystals. The third—You fool— produced distorted crystals, and the fourth, which was ignored, produced the most distorted crystals of all. Now I was even more blown away as Emoto's research showed us a direct link between the actions and energies of people and their impact on water. Marveling at this documented evidence, all I could think about was how cavalier we as people have been about our own energy.

It was clear that energy, both positive and negative, was affecting the water on a molecular level. Emoto said it was all about vibration, a form of energy. Considering the fact that approximately 60% to 70% of the human body is water, he extrapolated that the energy around us and within us affects our health and well-being as well. Since I am a management consultant for organizations and businesses, I began to think about how energy plays out every day in the business arena. I wondered if I could somehow replicate Emoto's work and insights on energy flow within water to energy flow within organizations. Would it work, could I see it, understand its flow and effects, and change it if necessary? As doing so would be key to my success as a consultant and business owner, I applied myself with fervor.

When it comes to energy in our organizations, a big piece of the puzzle is making the invisible visible. We have seen examples of exactly how powerful and game changing such advancements can be. For example, on December 22, 1895, German physicist Wilhelm Roentgen, who is credited with the discovery of X rays, took an X-ray image of his wife's hand that showed a clear image of her bones as well as her wedding ring. Thus began the use of X-ray imaging in medicine—a way to see internal workings that could not be seen before. The practice of medicine evolved to incorporate this new field that we know today as radiology. Because physicians could quickly and noninvasively diagnose wounds and diseases, both their diagnoses and treatments were much more accurate and successful. In 1914 Marie Curie developed "radiological cars" to provide on-site X-ray imaging for wounded soldiers in World War I. This allowed battlefield surgeons to operate quickly and more accurately, saving thousands of lives that may have otherwise been lost. Looking back, one can imagine doctors' frustration before this imaging was available. There was a lot of poorly informed guesswork. The guesses and subsequent treatments were often misguided, causing further harm to patients, wasted time and money, and sometimes even death.

Since the emergence of modern organizations, business leaders and managers have endured circumstances similar to those faced by physicians prior to the advent of radiology. To put this into perspective, we go back before the modern organization to the 18th century with the rise of the Industrial Revolution and the development of production methods that allowed organizations to grow and scale. The focus of this era was on *execution* of mass production. "The goal was to optimize the outputs that could be generated from a specific set of inputs" (Gunther McGrath 2014). By the early 1900s, Adam Smith's concepts on topics such as the division of labor, specialization, and economic productivity reinforced the principles of mass production, adding support at the macroeconomic level. Although this First Industrial Revolution wouldn't last forever, both businesses and industrial nations prospered.

Many of our traditional management practices developed during this era and reflect its transactional input/output orientation. Efficiency, lack of variation, consistency of production, and predictability were emphasized while people were essentially viewed as cogs in the machine. Work on the factory floor could be easily seen, and management of people was a relatively simple matter of job definition, visible performance monitoring, and reward and/or punishment. Given the nature of work, managers focused on monitoring inputs and outputs; they felt little need to consider the experience of people within the process. The traditional practices that emerged were effective as long as the work of people and companies was openly visible, transactional, and consistently driven from the top.

By the mid-1900s, however, the focus of organizations began to shift toward what Rita Gunther McGrath (2014), a professor at Columbia Business School and a globally recognized expert on strategy, called *expertise*. In 1957 Peter Drucker, often called the father of management science, famously coined the phrase "knowledge work" (Drucker 1957, 69). He later suggested that "the most valuable asset of a 21st-century institution, whether business or non-business, will be its knowledge workers and their productivity" (Drucker 1999, ebook location 1804). In this era value was increasingly created by workers' use of information, a mode of work that was difficult or impossible to monitor visibly. As knowledge work grew in the United States, more and more work became "invisible" to managers. This shift in the nature of work marked the birth of the modern organization, when knowledge work began to grow and managers started to lose visibility into the internal workings of their businesses. Ultimately, knowledge work became pervasive and management visibility declined much further.

Today, our dilemmas go far beyond the simple opacity of knowledge work. The way people work with each other, and with technology, is undergoing a radical shift. Work has gone from organizationally defined and consistent to independently driven, networked, and self-adjusting. Whereas the work of mass production was designed to be static and predictable, work today incorporates tremendous variability and increasingly emphasizes personal and interpersonal human elements. How people interact and build business relationships is now center stage. How people experience their work and what they bring to the table personally has become a huge factor in determining work and business outcomes. Perhaps even Drucker couldn't have imagined the complexity of work today. Our dilemma is no longer limited to poor visibility; it has morphed into a severe limitation on our ability to understand and manage how things work in our businesses.

This dilemma exists because the way we manage our companies and people hasn't kept pace with the changes in the nature of work. That is why managers today face challenges similar to those faced by physicians prior to the development of radiology. Information about the internal workings of businesses is obscured and largely limited to what can be seen at the surface. In general, we see outcomes, good and bad, but too often we don't really understand why or how they came about. For example, a change initiative didn't stick. Most don't, actually, but why? Two managers and their departments are at odds with each other. Again, it happens all too often, but why? Everything just seems to take too long. Why? Business leaders and managers make do with largely uninformed views of how their businesses actually operate. They see outcomes, of course, and they also often see eruptions of conflict and breakdown. Most of this is surface-level diagnostics, or what I call surface-level management. Like their physician counterparts, well-meaning surface-level managers often misdiagnose, "solve" the wrong problems, fail to make the changes needed in their businesses, and sometimes even drive their businesses to the point of failure.

But what if leaders and managers had their version of radiology? What if they could see deeper into their organizations, understand their metabolisms with greater clarity, see how energy flows—or doesn't flow—see how things really work, accurately diagnose and solve problems, and bring about the kind of sustainable changes their businesses need? Before we get into energy, how it works and flows in organizations, I want to highlight the current course of business, including the four relevant and rising trends that I see day in, day out in the organizations that I consult. This course of business leaves our organizations vulnerable, exposed, and unprepared for the future. And these circumstances will only get worse until we start to make some fundamental changes in how we manage ourselves and our businesses.

The Current Course of Business

I want to acknowledge the many positive developments, innovations, and inventions that can and do happen in business every day. Business is a powerful force. However, in spite of these accomplishments, our current course of business is being driven by four very difficult trends. While each of these trends has a negative effect on business, it is the collision of these trends, the hideous and forceful way they interact, that constitutes our primary threat. Here are the four trends in a nutshell.

1. There has been a significant rise in internal conflict due largely to . . .
2. Tremendous external pressure to change our business models and retool our people. Many managers are . . .
3. Poorly equipped to understand the necessary changes, much less effectively manage through the changes, leading to . . .
4. Increased employee disengagement, anxiety, and fear.

Let's look at these four trends and the ways they interact in more detail to understand why this is such a pivotal time and why we need a new approach.

Our Current Path of Conflict

About nine years ago I wrote an article called "Don't Throw People Under the Bus." I wrote it because more and more people in business were being sacrificed and betrayed for the sake of retribution or to gain a competitive advantage. This ugliness had become so common that it had been given a name. Bus throwing was on the rise at all levels of our businesses, and I wanted to do something to help the problem. I was surprised by how much the article resonated with people and by the amount of online traffic it generated—and still generates to this day. But this popularity was also a disturbing indicator of just how prevalent conflict had become in our companies, government agencies, and educational institutions. I was coaching executives who were spending more time focusing inward, in an effort to survive brutal office politics, than they were spending on their jobs and customers. The frequency of people "bumping" (i.e., having interactions based in conflict) was on the rise as the pressure on businesses to fundamentally change major business processes from transactional assembly lines to collaborative efforts strained the skill sets of people who were much more comfortable with, and adept at, the old transactional methods. In addition, information overload and strained communications were exacerbating the problem.

In the years that have passed since I wrote the article, things have generally gotten worse. Conflict has become an epidemic, and it is by no means contained within the walls of our businesses. It has become a nagging part of customers' experience with many companies, no matter how much those companies try to hide it. Our traditional approaches are not solving this chronic problem, which is a growing cancer in our businesses. At a time when companies and agencies need to be more innovative, customer focused, effective, and capable of rapid ongoing transformation, they are distracted and lethargic from their own internal conflict.

The Change Dilemma

This distraction compromises our ability to change and adapt to an increasingly demanding business environment. Difficulty with change is not a new problem, of course, but it has been amplified in almost quantum proportions over the past 25 years. In the late 1980s, while working as a program manager at Science Applications International Corporation (SAIC), I read my first article on the top causes of change initiative failure. Since then I've read dozens if not hundreds of articles and books that each put forth their own list of reasons why roughly 70% of all change initiatives fail or significantly underperform. I have never been satisfied that these lists truly explained the problem; otherwise, we wouldn't be stuck at the 70% failure rate.

Meanwhile, advances in technology accelerate unabated, customers increasingly expect a good and more informed customer experience, and the management of supply chains is more complex, geographically dispersed, and time-sensitive than ever. Most business environments today are in a near-constant state of flux where agility is a matter of survival. While many managers share a common notion about what business agility is (i.e., "We can change what we need to change quickly and with relative ease"), there is little if any agreement on how it works or how one achieves it.

We have struggled with change and business agility for years with no apparent improvement. This lack of improvement is especially painful now, when we need business agility more than ever. Our traditional approaches are not solving our chronic lack of business agility.

The Fourth Industrial Revolution

Adding pressure to an already pressurized business environment is our recent entry into what Klaus Schwab, executive chairman of the World Economic Forum, has called the "Fourth Industrial Revolution," the age of robots, artificial intelligence, and rapidly accelerating technology. In their 2018 *Harvard Business Review* article, "Why So Many High Profile Digital Transformations Fail," Thomas Davenport and George Westerman describe high-profile failures among blue-chip companies including GE, Nike, Lego, P&G, and Ford. Perhaps the most pertinent question is: "Why would we expect the success rate of these digital transformation initiatives to be any better than other change initiatives?" In fact, they aren't. But whether the initiatives succeed or fail, the drive to digitize and incorporate new technology and business models adds a whole new set of reasons why business agility is essential.

Then there is the other side of the Fourth Industrial Revolution, the part where jobs and people will be displaced by machines and software, and those who remain in the workforce will need to work more effectively with both machines and people. Such displacement has happened before, as it did when heavy farm equipment started performing much of what was historically done via manual farm labor. However, we had more time to adjust for that and other historical displacements, and such advancements tended to be industry specific. The Fourth Industrial Revolution is happening very quickly and will affect every industry. Many workers will be displaced, but what about those who remain? Ironically, the risk for them is underutilization of the human asset. That may sound counterintuitive, as humans are becoming virtually obsolete in several job areas. Nevertheless, as many researchers suggest, we will still need humans in the workforce as this shift occurs. We just won't need them to do many of the things they have been doing. As people, we will be challenged to retool quickly and prepare for our uniquely human niche among technology. These challenges pose questions for all of us. What is the future role of people in business? What skill sets will be more important as this future unfolds?

In July 2016 ManpowerGroup commissioned a quantitative global study on the skills that would be needed in the new, more automated world. The resulting paper, "The Skills Revolution: Digitization and Why Skills and Talent Matter," states: "Creativity, emotional intelligence and cognitive flexibility are skills that will tap human potential and allow people to augment robots, rather than be replaced by them" (p. 5).

Other expert opinions are consistent with this finding. For example, Stuart Russell, professor of computer science at the University of California, Berkeley, and a member of the World Economic Forum's Council on the Future of Artificial Intelligence and Robotics, participated in a 2017 World Economic Forum podcast titled "A Glimpse into the Future: Widespread Artificial Intelligence." When asked about the future role and skill sets of people, Russell summed it up well when he said that people "will need to provide high-quality interpersonal services."

Interpersonal services are understood here to be uniquely human endeavors requiring skills such as creativity, emotional intelligence, and cognitive flexibility. They are uniquely human because they are not things that are easily programmable, if at all. They probably will never be truly replicated by technology. But what exactly are interpersonal services? Both words in the term are important. "Interpersonal" relates to relationships and communication among people. "Services" are about helping others and doing work. Put it together and we are doing helpful work by interacting with others in a human *collaboration*. Robots and artificial intelligence (AI) cannot do this well. Therefore, this collaboration will likely become our new human niche at work. This is where we as people will have the opportunity to bring the best of ourselves to work. The rest is subject to automation.

Fortunately for people who want to work and make a living, many jobs embed interpersonal services. For example, direct customer service, selling, working as part of a team, professional services, and a host of other jobs involve considerable interpersonal collaboration. The challenge will be for us to become better and better at providing interpersonal services and interacting with coworkers. Automation without people will not be enough. We need people to do what is uniquely human while partnering with technology, not competing against it. People need to interact effectively with customers and coworkers in order to have good jobs in the future, and businesses need people with those skills to reduce conflict and to drive performance and adaptation within the changing business landscape.

While there will be a great deal of positive impact from advances in technology, this shift is happening at an alarming rate. It is underway and accelerating. To be successful in this new world, we need robots and AI, but we also need people working at their full potential. Business agility and the reduction of conflict both depend heavily on the actions of people.

Eroding Employee Engagement

The fourth trend, disengagement, results in part from the first three. According to an Aon Hewitt report, *2017 Trends in Global Employee Engagement*, employee engagement is low, and slight improvements between 2012 and 2015 started reversing in 2016. In 2017, just 24% of all employees were characterized as highly engaged and another 39% as moderately engaged. That leaves 37% with little engagement and a downward trend overall.

There are many reasons for disengagement: lack of job security, unrewarded and unreciprocated loyalty, the threat of outsourcing, employment instability caused by the explosion of the so-called gig economy, and the changing nature of employment structures. For example, Uber drivers are not "employees" of Uber. They do not receive benefits of any kind, and Uber executives refer to them as freelance "entrepreneurs." Why should employees feel engaged and invested in their organizations when the organizations are less invested in their employees? Employee engagement and investment is a two-way street.

But why is employee engagement important? The Aon Hewitt report defines employee engagement as "the level of an employee's psychological investment in their organization." It is essentially the state of an employee's relationship with the company. Going into the Fourth Industrial Revolution, businesses will depend on their employees to drive and embrace the needed changes. However, the less engaged the employees, the less willing and interested they will be in that pursuit and in going the extra mile for their employers. And with trends like workplace conflict, human displacement, and change initiative failures, who can blame them? Our traditional approaches are only making this chronic problem worse.

The Collision of Trends

Each of these trends is unsettling, enough to keep business leaders and employees up at night. However, the problem gets far worse when we look at the collision between them. Taken together, these four trends—conflict, tremendous pressure to change our businesses and retool people in the Fourth Industrial Revolution, a poor ability to make those changes, and employees who need to help drive the change becoming increasingly disengaged—point to a large and widening gap between what we need and what we are able to do in our businesses. For example, at a time when we need people to focus more on interpersonal collaboration at work, conflict is pushing them in the opposite direction. This battle between conflict and interpersonal collaboration has to do with more than a skill gap. It also has to do with the *opportunity* and *motivation* to be collaborative. The structures and circumstances that exist in our businesses are detracting from and blocking collaborative behavior. In response, people may not see a strong "what's in it for me" and may actually feel that conflict is more advantageous than collaboration. Nevertheless, people pay a price in their performance, morale, and health when they work in an environment that is prone to conflict. This personal impact ultimately hurts the business as well. When conflict blocks collaboration, it perpetuates our poor ability to change and keeps us stuck. We are stuck in our conflict and traditional ways, which leaves us lacking in the ability to become agile, healthy organizations. In addition, this volatile and paralyzed status quo erodes employee engagement as people react to their environment with fear and frustration. In turn, this erosion further exacerbates the other three trends.

We can't ignore the essential role of people in business, now or in the future. AI is powerful, but it isn't going to run our companies or translate imagination into the next big business idea. It won't inspire people like other people can or ignite a co-creation that is far beyond the capability of any one individual. We are all being called upon to raise the bar on, well, being uniquely human. But this self-perpetuating vicious cycle is keeping us stuck.

The Time Is Now

As an executive-level manager and consultant to dozens of major corporations, I've seen the carnage from these trends up front. I can tell you that it is newly and uniquely heartbreaking to me each time. The costs are not just to financial performance and the bottom line but to real humans struggling in the face of pressure to perform optimally in a continually changing and challenging business environment, and doing so without the support they need or the proper tools to improve their own performance. They go home at night exhausted, not from the work but from the fear and emotional drain. Many worry about their jobs and are compelled to spend large amounts of time at work watching their backs. This is especially common for the more senior managers and executives. Reputations and careers are damaged and even ruined by high-profile, politically charged conflicts. Many workers suffer from almost daily conflict bred by unfortunate and poorly designed organizational structures and operational mechanisms. In the more severe cases, it's as if people are rats in a cage, and the food provided isn't enough to feed them all. People are essentially forced to fight for their survival, and they often get very ugly in the process. For the most part, people and businesses don't intentionally cause this carnage. In fact, they are largely unaware of how and why all of this is happening in the first place.

Time is now short and the pressures to solve these problems are mounting. What we have been doing *is not working*. If we keep doing things the same way, we will remain stuck. Many people will be out of work, and many businesses will simply be unable to keep pace with the changes or adapt to new opportunities and business circumstances. We would be wise to do something now, and not wait. And if all of this isn't enough, there is the bigger world picture to consider. Business has been, and will remain, a major factor in the world at a time when we face serious challenges on Planet Earth. Much needs to happen to help our people, strengthen the world community, and protect our planet. Collectively, the business community can play a leadership role, or it can make the problems worse.

These problems are happening now. It's time to do something. It's time for a new era in business.

How Business Could Be

These trends create a frightening scenario, but it doesn't have to be that way. Fortunately, there is a way through this mess—a new approach that can be used to address these trends head on.

A Vision for the Future of Business

Imagine business where conflict, the damaging kind that takes away and contributes nothing, is more the exception than the rule. We would certainly have more time to focus on doing our work and serving our customers. Because people are involved, however, we can never expect to fully eliminate conflict. But what if there was a way to significantly reduce it by eliminating things that spawn it and creating work environments and circumstances that are more about contributing than getting, more about sharing than grasping, more about collaboration than competition? There *is* a way.

Imagine an organizational ability to change that requires less effort, encounters fewer obstacles, and typically results in the achievement of sustainable change in a fraction of the time it has historically taken to either succeed or fail. Imagine a future full of creativity and innovation where people and technology form a powerful partnership. People understand that when they work together and help each other, powerful things happen through their co-creations. AI becomes very intelligent and supports this process while taking on many of the routine tasks at work. Imagine a new norm where our working environments feel safe. Collaboration is natural, effective, and rewarding. People help each other succeed. Office politics begin to fade out of fashion in favor of a more harmonious transparency. Teams are vibrant. Developing people is a privilege. Revenue and profits increase. More jobs are created.

We can transform the workplace, generate prosperity, and set a positive and responsible example for the rest of the world. This is all very possible. It can happen if we start to look at structures, norms, activities, and people from a new perspective; build our businesses with this bigger picture in mind; and advance the way we work. We can start now, and change our course.

The Language of Energy

How do we change course from our current self-destructive path toward the healthy, productive, and prosperous vision of how it can be? How can you do this in your business right now? The answer is: *We can achieve this vision by unlocking the* energy *of our businesses.* Yes, energy is something we all feel and know about but don't really talk about as we sit around our conference room tables. Our business culture generally views this topic as off limits. People are afraid to bring it up for fear they will look like metaphysical fools and find themselves at a desk in the basement. But now it's time to talk about energy; our future depends on it. Doing so will allow us to look at and understand more deeply how our businesses and people operate and to solve real problems, not symptoms.

Most leaders and managers focus on managing business outcomes, which, while important, are only about *what* got accomplished. The limited information at the surface of a business is just the tip of the iceberg. It tells us very little about *how* the work got accomplished. By managing the energy of your business and yourself, you will not only have a much deeper visibility into how work gets done, you will have tremendous insight into how you can make the business work substantially better.

You may be thinking "I already spend a lot of time working to make things better in my business." Yes, I suspect you do. But without the benefits of managing energy, you're probably working at best just below the surface of the water that surrounds your "iceberg." This book will take you much deeper. It will help you see things you have never seen, and you may well do things you have never done. It's a whole new view of the world of work.

As leaders, managers, and employees, we are charged with making things happen. Sometimes our efforts and solutions work, and sometimes they don't turn out as planned. When they don't, we try to figure out what happened, and usually we have plenty of opinions on the matter from those around us. But often we are left with a gnawing feeling that we really don't know what happened, not with any real clarity. But here is the interesting thing about this dilemma. Even when things do work, we don't know why—with any real clarity—for the same reason we don't know why things didn't work. We lack visibility and deeper understanding. So it all becomes one big crapshoot with us blindfolded and one hand tied behind our backs. And we keep rolling the dice.

Much of what happens along the path of work is invisible yet essential to the accomplishment of desired outcomes and organizational change. We need the ability to understand where things are working and where they aren't. We need a tangible paradigm that can be used to evaluate, affect, and optimize this hidden path.

I've spent years contemplating what that paradigm would be, striving to connect my direct experience in business with some sort of systematic and repeatable approach that I could share with others. Finally it dawned on me. The conduct of work has a currency, just as the conduct of commerce has a currency. As it happens, energy is the currency of work, just as money is the currency of commerce. All currency flows. At certain points in that flow it accumulates, and at others it is depleted. Sometimes the changes are explosive, and at other times they are quite subtle and slow. These fluctuations and variations are indicative of what is happening along the way. Wouldn't fluctuations and variations in the currency of work, then, tell us about what is happening in the flow of that work? In fact, they do.

Energy is the currency of every kind of work, no matter how simple or complex. To introduce this new paradigm, let's look at a sports example before we head back into the world of business.

When I was in college, I rowed on the crew team. I mostly rowed in eights, which meant there were eight oarsmen in the boat. I occupied the stroke position at the front of the oarsmen, but since we traveled backward in crew, I was the last to cross the finish line. This also meant that the puddles generated by the other seven oars in the water floated by after every stroke. Actually, we flowed past the puddles as the boat moved, but the point is they were always on display. With some practice, you can tell a lot about the stroke of an oar by the puddle it leaves. For example, a well-executed hard pull leaves a large, well-shaped puddle with a "hole" in the middle. A light pull leaves a smaller puddle with less of a hole. When an oarsman has trouble getting the oar out of the water, the puddle is distorted. So by watching the puddles from my position as the stroke oarsman, I could tell a lot about how hard and effectively each member of the crew was rowing. This was important because crew is about synchronized movement with everyone pulling their weight. If we got out of sync and I saw or felt the problem before the coxswain did, I would tell the coxswain, who sat right in front of me facing the crew, and he would shout out the feedback to the particular oarsman. As the oarsman responded, we usually got back in sync.

But it didn't stop at puddles. There were other indicators. For example, there is a physical phenomenon that strokes experience when the rowers behind them rush their slides. Rowers sit on a seat that slides backward as they take a stroke and forward as they then recover. To be in sync, everybody has to go back at the same speed and then go forward at the same speed. Sometimes less experienced crews have a tendency to go forward faster than they should, which is called rushing their slides. That means they are out of sync with the stroke, who sets the pace. The physical effect that slide rushing has on the boat makes it very difficult for the stroke to recover and move up his slide. It also slows down the boat. When this happened, at times I felt like I was expending as much energy recovering from my stroke as I did making it. Not good. And then there were the great moments in crew when everything and everybody was in sync. We called it swing. It was amazing. The boat would start to hydroplane on the water, and you could hear bubbles flowing under the hull. We were no longer eight oarsman and a coxswain. We were a single, harmonious unit.

What does this story have to do with energy as the currency of work? Rowing a boat is a form of work. The better that work flows, the faster the boat goes. Every oarsman contributes to the work by generating energy that helps move the boat forward. But we can also see that when the oarsmen were not in alignment, energy was created that actually slowed the boat down. This negative energy counteracted some of the positive energy, and the net effect was that the boat slowed down. This example illustrates that the "currency" of the work involved in rowing the boat, (i.e., the ultimate variable that determines how fast the boat goes from the starting line to the finish line) is energy. An equally important point from the story is the existence of the *indicators*—the puddles, the slides, and the bubbles. Each one provided important information about the energy in the boat. Some indicated problems that generated negative energy, and some indicated a glorious work effort.

All of these characteristics of energy translate to the world of business and organization management. The work and the indicators are different, of course, but the same principles apply. When we learn to identify and pay attention to the indicators of energy, we gain deep insights into work and how to optimize it. Since energy is invisible to most people, we need indicators to make the energy visible. Things like high performance, low performance, resistance to change, and chronic conflict are examples of the many indicators that manifest in organizations. But as in crew, in management we need a context to make sense of the indicators and understand what they are telling us. In the crew example, the context includes the work goal (moving the boat quickly), the work itself (rowing), and the involved assets (boat, oars, seats, and people). Understanding this context gives meaning to the indicators—puddles, rushing seats, and bubbles—and allows us to "see" the energy dynamics of the crew and take actions to optimize it. In business management, the context has similar characteristics to those in crew but different specifics. For example, there are work goals (e.g., a project goal), the work itself (e.g., the work of the project), and the involved assets. The assets involved in a particular context may include business elements, such as organizational structure, role definitions, business processes, systems, incentives, and the people involved in the project as team members, stakeholders, users, customers, and so on. Every work stream, from the smallest individual work effort to the largest business function, has its own context and set of involved assets. Within that context, the involved assets collectively affect the energy of the work stream, positively and/or negatively. In the work streams, what we are striving for is the business version of swing, where all the involved people and elements are aligned in their energies, which are aligned to the goal of the work. In diagnosing problems, we are looking for misalignments, because misalignments always create negative energy. In crew, these are things like a misalignment of effort among the oarsmen, misalignment in the speed with which oarsmen move up their slides, and misalignment in the timing of the oars as they enter the water for a stroke. All of these things create negative energy that slows the boat down. Once they are recognized, all of them can be corrected to optimize the performance of the crew and the speed of the boat. In business, misalignments occur at all levels. At the enterprise level, they are caused by flaws or insufficiencies in the design of enterprise elements (e.g., organizational structure, systems, business processes, departmental role definitions, incentive structures, etc.). They also occur within groups or teams due to differences in goals and agendas, variations in work effort and approach, differences in capability levels among involved people, among others. And they occur within individuals themselves in their performance of work due to misalignments of intellectual, emotional, and capability factors with what they are being asked to do and/or how they are being asked to do it. As in crew, all of these misalignments create negative energy that works against the positive energy of the work effort. By recognizing and addressing these misalignments, we maximize alignment among the players in the work stream and optimize the work outcome.

How do we go about building alignment among the players in a work stream? To begin with, we need to recognize that energy is a very real thing. In the world of physics, energy is defined as *the capacity of a physical system to perform work*. That definition carries easily into the world of business, where the "physical system" is a company, agency, or educational institution. Its level of energy, which is determined by the success of its collective work streams, determines its current capacity to perform work. During any given time period, the trick is to generate more energy than is used in the performance of the work. For any business, the greater the net gain in energy, the more successful it will be.

For the purposes of this book we recognize two kinds of energy:

1. **Positive energy** is the type of energy just discussed. It gives a business its capacity to perform work, which ultimately includes the production of products and the provision of services. Businesses receive money for their products and services, which injects positive energy back into the systems.
2. **Negative energy** opposes and/or wastes positive energy, which takes away from the ability of a business to perform work. Conflict is the most common manifestation of negative energy. It is extremely wasteful, and it produces its own collateral negative energy that affects the ability of people to perform work. It damages and erodes assets like products (quality and value) and people (health and engagement). Think of negative energy as positive energy that has gone to the dark side.

Every business creates both positive and negative energy. Creating positive energy and avoiding the creation of negative energy should be the primary goal. Companies are systems. At any given moment they are throwing off some amount of positive energy and some amount of negative energy. The net of those two energies is either positive or negative. Where the needle points at any given time is like a barometer of the current state of the business. The cumulative total of these energy readings over a period of time, say three months or a year, determines the overall health of the business. And yes, overall health determines top- and bottom-line performance.

Positive energy drives successful business. It translates into money and many other benefits and valuable outcomes for our customers, employees, stakeholders, and stockholders. The root of business is not about money. It's about positive energy. Money is a by-product. If you want financial success, manage the energy.

Both positive and negative energy affect people. In business, people make products and provide services. How well and how efficiently that happens has everything to do with the energy they generate and the energy around them. People's energy, influenced by the environment they work in, affects what people bring to the table every morning, how they work, and what they pay attention to. At the macro level, the collective energy of a business drives social norms, company culture, and the relationship between the business and the rest of the world. If we are to advance the way we work, we must manage the energy of our businesses. Only then will we finally have the clarity to understand how things work, what gets in the way, and what it takes to more consistently achieve good outcomes. This book delves into how energy is at work in our businesses and how we can optimize its positive impact while avoiding many of its damaging manifestations. In this book you will learn to recognize, "see," understand, and manage energy as effectively as you see and manage visible things (e.g., processes, financials, etc.). Energy is just as tangible and manageable as what you currently see. Through a host of real-world stories and examples, you will discover a new power and set of tools to transform your own business, how you work, and how you work with others.

Challenging Traditional Business Norms

Our traditional business norms don't incorporate the concept of managing energy. "Energy" is not on our radar screen. Instead, we focus on trying to manage things that we can see directly. As a result, we often unknowingly attempt to improve outcomes with what seem like obvious traditional solutions. Unfortunately, these business norms are frequently more akin to bandages or miss the boat entirely. Here is a common example I have seen in several companies.

A company experiencing significant internal conflict is becoming increasingly concerned about its ability to serve its customers and provide a good customer experience. Reports about employees handling customer interactions and relationships poorly are quite common, and customer satisfaction ratings are alarmingly low. Consequently, company leaders decide to put every customer-facing employee through customer service training. This traditional strategy is based on the notion that if leaders can change the part of the company that the customers see and "touch," they can create a positive customer experience.

That sounds logical! All of the conflict and negative energy generated within the company will be nicely hidden away by the bandage wrapped around the company. But the problem is that the bandage soon falls off, exposing, in this case, the ugly conflict and energy. There goes the positive customer experience. The training has little sustainable impact on customer focus because the factors causing internal conflict continue to impact people on the front lines, robbing their attention and energy, eroding cooperative efforts to serve customers, and pushing workers into a conflict mode. This is the irony of achieving customer focus. You must first look inward and get your house in order before you can effectively focus outward. But that irony is not obvious from a surface-level view and actually seems counterintuitive. When we don't look at problems through the lens of energy, we often don't understand them, and we certainly don't solve them.

The good news is that we don't have to stay stuck where we are. When we learn to look at our businesses as energy systems, we shift our focus and attention from symptoms to root causes. This helps us see business norms and "obvious solutions" for what they are—often temporary bandages—and instead focus on applying solutions that heal the real problems.

This book is about teaching people to apply this new approach and to leverage the internal workings of their businesses to achieve external success in the marketplace.

Understanding Business Through the Lens of Energy

To understand and manage energy in business we must first recognize what I call the *Energy Equation*. Fundamentally, this equation is like any other. An equation is a statement that asserts the equality of two expressions. The two expressions, of course, have an equals sign between them. In business, the left expression has to do with how the business, team, or person is expressing itself or will be expressing itself once we make improvements.

The right expression is the business outcome. So, looking forward, if we have a particular outcome in mind, we can affect the way the business/team/person is expressing itself to optimize the likelihood of achieving that desired outcome. Similarly, the Energy Equation helps us understand why things are the way they are (i.e., why we are getting the current outcome). Specifically, the current situation/outcome is a result of how the business and people are expressing themselves and the net effect that has on the energy within the context of the activity and goal. Understanding the equation gives us insight into how to help improve that expression (for existing activities and operations) or design it well (for new activities and operations). All of this optimizes our outcome.

To be clear, this book does not offer the perfect equation or methods to accurately measure and quantify every aspect of energy flowing through the business landscape. Perhaps that is somewhere in our future. Nevertheless, this book does offer the ability to more clearly understand the elements involved in a current "expression," the relationships between those elements, how all of that affects energy, and how that energy determines the outcome. Energy ties together and helps explain what we can see and hear. More important, however, energy gives life, direction, magnitude, and a deeper understanding to the patterns that emerge. These patterns provide a much deeper and more insightful view into the business.

Given this more informed view, the Energy Equation begins to look like the business version of the X-ray machine that could fundamentally change the way we operate in business. By identifying where energy is being wasted (e.g., through conflict or misalignment) or poorly used, we can unlock the "hidden" energy and apply it toward a positive outcome. As you will see in the chapters ahead, doing this has far-reaching implications for business and the people in it. Now let's dive in to how energy works in business.

Energy Only **Seems** *Hidden*

You may ask, "How do we look at and talk about energy when it seems hidden?" You would be right that it *has* largely been hidden from our collective awareness. As long as that is the case, we can't talk about it. I once heard some words from a wise man that seem to capture our circumstance while reminding us that there is more to this world than meets the eye:

There are more things in this world that are unseen and unknown than things that are seen and known. Things that are unseen and unknown remain unseen and unknown, until they become seen and known.

A goal of this book is to help make energy, as it pertains to business affairs, "seen" and known. While the energy itself will remain invisible for now, at least to most people, it can be seen and managed based on its direct effects on other things—like people, performance, and money. In that way, "seeing" energy is like discovering a new planet. Historically, scientists have detected the existence of new planets and their approximate size by observing the gravitational effects on other nearby planets. It wasn't until later that they actually saw the new planets. So, for now, we don't have to literally see energy to know it is there, to manage it, and to understand its power.

How We "See" Energy and Understand Its Messages

Now let's start our journey from the somewhat esoteric concept of managing energy to the very tangible ways in which it can be done. Along the way you will learn how energy works so that you can confidently incorporate strategies and methods for managing it in your business and work.

Seeing and managing the energy of a business often requires finding the triggers of negative energy and converting them to triggers of positive energy. A central theme is that people's negative *behaviors* are usually the *result* of triggered negative energy, but the *trigger* of that negative energy is usually a *misalignment*. Said another way, the people's negative behaviors are visible, just like distorted puddles in the crew example were visible. They are visible indicators of problems. But the triggers of those negative energies are misalignments, which we cannot see directly. That's why businesses so often make the mistake of treating behaviors instead of solving underlying problems (i.e., misalignments). These misalignments come in several forms. I will address one of the big and most pervasive forms first.

Early in my career, a very experienced organizational consultant shared with me a "consultant's secret." I listened eagerly as he spoke these words: "If you want to know how a business works, follow the money. If you want to know where and how a business is broken, find the places where control and responsibility are out of alignment."

Little did I know the powerful effect these words would have on me, my career, and the many businesses I have helped. These words have proven to be more than true. It turns out they provide a doorway into the management of energy in business.

Let's dissect these words a little bit to see why this is the case. The first part of the statement has to do with how things work. Things can work well, and things can work poorly. The phrase "how things work" does not imply one or the other; it simply means that money makes things happen. Money itself is a form of energy. It's like the blood that flows through our bodies bringing oxygen, water, and nutrients to the various organs and functions at work within us. Everywhere the blood flows, something is given the fuel (i.e., energy) it needs to "work." It may work well, or it may work poorly, but it "works." In a business, the flow of money can be healthy, and it can be dysfunctional. Since a business is never a perfect thing, most businesses have both healthy and dysfunctional aspects in their flow of money. The trick is to fuel the right things—positive, healthy business functions—and to make sure that unhealthy functions are remade to become healthy.

How do we know a positive, healthy business function when we see it? That takes us to the second part of the statement: "If you want to know where and how a business is broken, find the places where control and responsibility are out of alignment." It follows that when control and responsibility are *in* alignment, you have a healthy business function.

But why is this alignment so important? Because it is fundamental to the successful performance of work. Alignment facilitates the performance of work. Misalignment breeds conflict and opposes the performance of work. On a more personal level, people want to be successful in their work, but if they are given a job without sufficient control over the work or adequate resources to accomplish it, their chances of success are greatly compromised. People naturally react to this responsibility without control in many different ways, and none of them is good. Their concern is that they will "fail" and be held accountable, perhaps even be fired. And they get angry because the situation is so unfair!

The main point is that when people are exposed to situations where they have responsibility without sufficient control (i.e., misalignment), especially in social organizations like businesses, they have negative human reactions that produce negative energy, which hurts the business and the flow of work. By watching these negative human reactions, you can get a sense of the negative energy behind them. And by working backward toward the source of the problem, you can usually spot the misalignment that is triggering the reaction. After many years of following negative energy toward the source of the problem, I am still amazed at how well it works, and how most problems of this nature are caused by the misalignment of responsibility and control. What's more, this approach gives us an indirect yet powerful view of negative energy at work in our businesses.

Consider an example of a broken business function and how it relates to energy.

A Broken Business Function

A scientific instrument company, which we will call Alchemy Instruments, manufactures and sells high-end electronic equipment to business clients across North America. It recently reorganized its sales force into two groups. The Product Group is organized around the company's product lines, with subgroups for each line. Those assigned to a subgroup are required to have deep knowledge and expertise in their product lines. They are instructed to sell their products to any potential client in the United States. The Regional Group is divided by sales regions in North America. There are six regions, and each region has an assigned subgroup within the Regional Group. Those assigned to a subgroup are required to have at least a general understanding of all products and product lines. They are instructed to sell all of the company's products within their regions.

During the reorganization, the senior VP of sales at Alchemy Instruments verbally encouraged sales staff in each group to work cooperatively with staff from the other group, as both groups "have something different to offer." Staff members in the Product Group bring a deep knowledge of the products, while staff members in the Regional Group have deeper knowledge of, and relationships with, clients in their regions. Soon after the reorganization, problems in the field began to surface.

A member of the Product Group and a member of the Regional Group discovered that they were both calling on the same client. Since both were compensated with a commission for every sale they made, they both felt they should "own" the sale. Neither one of them backed down, and a nasty argument broke out. The potential client became aware of the argument and fired them both, deciding that it was just too difficult to do business with Alchemy Instruments. Other similar incidents like this followed.

A member of the Regional Group was trying to sell a product to a client in her region. Because the product was quite complex, she asked a peer from the Product Group for help with the sale and scheduled a time for the two of them to meet with the client. The day of the meeting came and the Product Group salesperson was a no-show. The meeting was canceled. When asked later why he didn't show up, the Product Group salesperson said that something else came up that could lead to his own sale, and since he wouldn't get a commission for helping his peer, he opted to pursue his own sale instead of helping her. This deeply angered the Regional Group salesperson, who ultimately lost the sale, and a good client. Furthermore, she and many others began to view the senior VP's words about cooperation as hollow.

The VPs of the Alchemy Instruments Product and Regional Sales Groups, who both had group sales quotas to achieve, began to view each other as competition. A sale made by the "other guy's team" was considered a lost sale. Neither VP was coming close to hitting sales numbers, which polarized the VPs and their groups. Before long there was a whole lot of daily chatter among the sales staff about how to outdo the other group, gain an advantage, and even sabotage the other group's success. Sales staff was spending less time on selling and spending more time on competitive tactics—with those in their own company.

There was a general recognition that the groups needed each other to sell well, but their increasingly competitive relationship became a barrier to cooperation. Each VP spent hours in the SVP's office complaining about the other group and making a case for being in charge of both groups. Soon there was a flurry of gossip and speculation across both groups about who would win the battle. To the SVP, it seemed clear that these two managers could not work together, and he would have to remove one of them. He did so, and the "winning manager" celebrated victory.

A few months later, though, the winning manager was far from celebrating. Although everyone was under his umbrella, the same problems were still occurring, and now they were all his problems. The SVP fired him for his failure to bring the two groups together and took direct control of both groups. Months later, the SVP's efforts had been no more successful, and his own job was on the line.

Now let's analyze how this sales function at Alchemy Instruments is broken. Where are control and responsibility out of alignment? The answer is that both the Product and Regional Groups, and their staffs, had *responsibility* for selling and were given quotas for how much they had to sell. However, neither group had *control* over all of the resources required to sell effectively. Client knowledge and relationships, as well as deep product knowledge, were all required to be effective. This misalignment of control and responsibility spawned layer after layer of conflict and negative energy—in the field, between the VPs and their groups, and with clients who were unhappy about their customer experiences with Alchemy Instruments. When you look at this common example from the lens of energy management, you realize just how much conflict and negative energy is being generated, on an ongoing basis, from this basic misalignment of control and responsibility.

As designed, the sales department is an ongoing drain on the "positive energy bank account" at Alchemy Instruments. This is an unhealthy business function that needs to be fixed. But the larger concern is that this type of problem rages on in many businesses.

How Companies Miss the Target

Faced with this unhealthy business function, which is quite common, companies often don't understand or fix the problem because they don't look at the negative energy and trace it back to its trigger—the misalignment of control and responsibility. In this example, the SVP made a very common error. He viewed the problem as one of leadership among his VPs and tried to solve it by making staffing changes. He fired one VP and consolidated the groups under the other VP. When that didn't work, he made another staffing change by firing the other VP and taking direct control. And that didn't solve the problem either. It's easy to see how leaders fall prey to the temptation to blame, fire, and be done with it. First, their solution seems to make logical sense, and, generally speaking, no one challenges them on it. Second, by making these abrupt staffing moves, they are seen as bold and decisive leaders. Third, this type of solution is relatively easy and painless for leaders. With such temptation, it's no wonder the blame and fire routine is common. Unfortunately for all, it doesn't solve anything. As the saying goes, it's like rearranging deck chairs on the *Titanic*. This is a classic example of treating the surface-level *symptoms*—people who are not getting along.

By tracing the human conflicts and the associated negative energy back to its source, the misalignment of control and responsibility, we can clearly see that control and responsibility must be in balance *during every sale*. To make that work, there must be processes, protocols, clearly defined roles, and appropriate incentives. The shift has to be from individuals selling products to teams selling products and solutions. The issue becomes more of an operational problem than a staffing one. To solve the operational problem, the involved operational elements will need to be redesigned and implemented, along with a few adjustments to departmental missions at the organizational level, personal and team incentives, and some training on how all of this is going to work. We'll get into the details later on in the book.

The business world is full of examples where people treat surface-level symptoms, yet their misinformed actions usually go unidentified and unchallenged. Their well-meaning solutions seem like good ideas at the time. However, left unaddressed, the conflict and the negative energy remain. And the so-called solutions that people assume are correct add another layer of destruction on top of an already difficult situation. There is some good news, however. Instead of just hating the conflict and negative energy, we can use them as fingers pointing to the real problems—and the real solutions.

Misalignment Can Be Everywhere

In any given business, where do those "fingers" point? Where in the business is there misalignment that triggers negative energy? The answer is that misalignment in our businesses can be found virtually everywhere, including organizational structures, operational processes and systems, role definitions and authorities, the way decisions are made, and, last but not least, the way people work and interact.

Wherever misalignment is found, it almost always results in conflict among people. It is the conflict among people that ultimately creates the negative energy in a business. Let's look deeper into that conflict.

Chapter 2

Unintentional Conflict

It's June 2016 and a leading healthcare IT company is experiencing a tremendous amount of conflict around its implementation projects. The Professional Services group, which is responsible for implementing the company's clinical software products at client hospitals and clinics, is in charge of the projects. Each time the company sells a system, a client project is created and assigned to a project manager, who is given overall responsibility for the success of the project. Each project requires a cross-functional team of experts in the various disciplines associated with the system—radiology, ambulatory, pharmacy, and others. To serve as a source for these resources, functional departments within the Professional Services group have been formed around each of the disciplines. These departments hire and train people in the various specialty areas.

Mary Martin, a project manager (PM), is assigned to manage a new project. To build her project team, Mary requests resources from the functional departments. She gets the resources she needs and knows it is because new projects have a lot of visibility with senior management. However, three months into her nine-month project, the staffing commitments began to change. The Radiology Department manager, who was facing staff shortages in his department, reassigned Mary's full-time radiology lead to a new project that was just starting up. He offered Mary a different resource for only ten hours per week. About the same time, the Pharmacy Department

manager told Mary that her pharmacy specialist was also being assigned to
two other projects and would have to split her time among the three projects. Mary strongly objected to both staffing changes, but since Functional
Department managers had unilateral control over where and when their
people got assigned, Mary could do nothing to reverse the decisions and
was forced to make do with the resources she still had on her project team.
Consequently, she took a hit on her project, missed a major deliverable
deadline, and had to face the heat from her manager and client.

Most of the other PMs were encountering similar staff shortages and
project impacts. The effects of this rippled out from there. Facing these unfair
circumstances, PMs felt inclined to compete with other PMs for resources
and employed all kinds of methods to get and keep their projects staffed,
which of course created more resource scarcity for the losing project teams.
Some of the PMs' "recruiting methods" involved politics, destructive influence, and even coercion. The PMs easily justified these methods because that
is what they had to do to be successful with their projects. Meanwhile, the
conflict between PMs, and between PMs and department managers, raged on.

This is a very common example of what I call unintentional conflict.
People didn't wake up one morning and say to themselves, "I think I'll
pick a fight with another manager." The conflict was caused by *circumstances*
in the Professional Services group. These circumstances included unilateral
staffing protocols, understaffed functional departments, and an inadequate
escalation path for PMs who were not receiving the resources they needed
for their projects. Unfortunately, most people viewed the situation from the
surface level and blamed the PMs, since their participation in the conflict
was most visible and their recruiting methods were over the top. Noting
these observations, and the eroding performance across projects, the head
of HR offered to get some training for the PMs. The head of Professional
Services agreed and said he would give the PMs a good talking to as well.
So much for our traditional wisdom.

Understanding Conflict

As with most things in business, there is more to conflict than meets the
eye. Conflict is not just something to be dealt with or eradicated. It is an
indicator that tells a story about a business and its people. In that sense it is a

gift. By following these telltale stories, we can understand the many sources of conflict and their triggers, and then we can deal with the conflict much more effectively. First, however, it is important to understand that not all conflict is created equal.

The Two Major Types of Conflict

There are two major types of conflict. The first is *intentional conflict*, which is the type we normally associate with the word "conflict." Intentional conflict is initiated with a decided intent to engage in conflict. The second, more elusive and pervasive type is *unintentional conflict*, which is initiated without such intent. Here is a definition:

> Unintentional conflict in business occurs when opposing forces, most often people, are inadvertently activated against one another, causing unfortunate circumstances that interfere with a business interaction, operation, or outcome.

The key point here is that with unintentional conflict, there are opposing forces that are never intended. Nobody plans them or even knows they will occur. Instead, the opposing forces are created by *circumstances*.

The ultimate and ugly business result of conflict is the same, whether its source is intentional or unintentional. However, unintentional conflict is more prone to prevention. Therefore, it is important to know the difference between these types of conflict. Before we dive further into these differences, we need some clarity around conflict in general.

There Is No Good Conflict

Based on their definition and concept of conflict, some people say that some conflict in business is good. They point to a business world full of circumstances where people have different ideas and opinions, where they need to find common ground and agree on solutions. They call this process "good conflict." Indeed, if you define conflict that way, the statement that it can be good and necessary is correct. However, in this book we draw the line differently because giving conflict both a negative and positive connotation is potentially confusing in our discussion of energy. To avoid such confusion, we offer a clarifying definition and suggest that there is no good conflict. Here is the definition.

> In business, interactions among people become conflict when their personal agendas overcome a mutual regard for the common, larger business goal and agenda.

Let's break this definition down to highlight the important points. First, we all come to the table with our personal opinions and agendas based on things that we would like to see happen. Just having these opinions and wish lists is not wrong or bad. However, whenever we come across situations in business where we must achieve common business goals with others, we are able to collaborate effectively only when we each maintain a primary regard for the common, larger goal and agenda. It is fine if we also consider our own opinions and agendas in the process, but we must hold them loosely, keep them secondary, and be willing to let them go if a reasonable, suitable, and sufficient group idea presents itself during the collaborative process.

The moment we let our personal opinions and wish lists become more important than the larger business goal and agenda, we are crossing the line from collaboration to conflict. We are no longer working with others to create a business solution; we are working against others to get what we want. The energy of this selfish behavior is negative. When one person in a collaborative process does this, and others see or suspect that someone else's personal agenda is now at the forefront, those others are tempted to do the same thing. Before you know it, the entire collaboration has turned into a competition where conflict runs amuck.

Based on this definition, there is no good conflict. There are only good collaborations. A collaboration turns into conflict when its primary orientation becomes *personal*. Because this type of conflict is premeditated, it is intentional.

Intentional versus Unintentional Conflict

With the understanding that there is no good conflict, we now take a deeper look at the difference between intentional conflict and unintentional conflict. As described above and outlined in Table 2.1, the root cause of intentional conflict is a personal agenda. A personal agenda includes a premeditated goal and an orientation toward getting something for personal gain. The root cause of unintentional conflict, in contrast, is not personal at all. It begins as a reaction to *circumstances* that present themselves. Nobody plans the conflict. Nobody intends it.

Because the origins of these two kinds of conflict are different, any measures that may prevent the conflicts from occurring are also much different. In general, because of the personal genesis of intentional conflict, measures to address it necessarily tend to be personal and aimed at the person who is initiating the conflict. In contrast, because the origin of unintentional conflict is not personal, measures to avoid it tend to be impersonal and systemic in nature. Why is this distinction important? Let's use two examples to answer that question.

Intentional Conflict Example

Jane manages the Legal Department of a mid-sized internet technology company specializing in software applications for contract development and management. Tanya manages the Product Development Department. There has been friction between the two managers in the past over decisions to

Table 2.1   Characteristics of Intentional versus Unintentional Conflict

Intentional Conflict	Unintentional Conflict
Root cause is a personal agenda	Root cause is not personal
Premeditated goal; orientation toward getting	Begins as a reaction to circumstances
Measures to avoid are personal	Measures to avoid tend to be systemic

build or not build certain new products. Jane feels that legal factors are not fully understood or considered, while Tanya views Jane as getting in the way of progress. Both Jane and Tanya are potentially in line for the president position in the company's succession plan. Jane is worried that Tanya is being viewed as more successful because her last product was a home run.

The president has called a meeting of the executive team for this Thursday to decide whether to go forward with the latest product concept from Tanya's department. Jane sees her opportunity to discredit Tanya at the meeting and shake the company's confidence in her. The stage is set.

At the meeting, Jane quickly goes on the offensive, stating that she has some grave concerns about the legal validity of the product and the liability it would place on the company. She asks to make a short presentation, preempting Tanya's scheduled presentation. The president agrees. Jane presents a list of legal issues and concerns with the product, implying that Tanya and her team were careless in their product design and due diligence. Tanya is completely surprised, since Jane had not raised these issues previously during the due diligence period. Jane responded that she had tried to discuss them with Tanya in multiple phone calls and that Tanya "just didn't want to hear it." Even though that wasn't true, it was Jane's word against Tanya's, and right now Tanya wasn't looking very credible.

The president ended the meeting before Tanya could even present, saying "We need to regroup on this whole matter." Then he met with Tanya, telling her frankly that his confidence in her was shaken. Tanya defended herself saying that Jane never raised these issues so she could have a chance to work them. "She blindsided me at the meeting to make herself look good at my expense," Tanya said. The president also met with Jane, who was adamant that she had tried to raise the issues. The president realized that there would be no proving this one way or the other.

The relationship between Jane and Tanya became increasingly adversarial. After many attempts to coach both managers and get them to work together, the conflict continued. The coaching conversations were always difficult and uncomfortable for the president as he needed to address the personal attitudes and behaviors of both managers. The president finally realized he had to make a staffing change, but was torn between two good managers. Whoever took the hit would take it as a big personal blow and a smudge on their career. Before the president could decide, an employee came forward with some printed emails that had been left in a conference room. They were exchanges between Jane and one of her friends, also a company employee. In them, Jane bragged and joked about how she had taken Tanya down with her maneuvers and how it wouldn't be the last time.

The president's decision was now clear. He terminated Jane with cause that day and she was escorted out of the building. He marveled at how close he had been to releasing Tanya, and at the damage caused by the ongoing conflict that Jane had initiated.

It should be clear from this example of intentional conflict that it was born from a personal agenda. Jane placed her personal agenda over the company's success. When the truth came out and the source of the conflict was revealed, the measure to stop the conflict was sudden, final . . . and very personal.

Unintentional Conflict Example

The chief operating officer (COO) of a mid-sized healthcare IT company was assigned by the board of directors to establish a way for the company to handle urgent, high-priority projects that could lead to game-changing products for the company. At the next board meeting, the COO presented his "Skunk Works" protocol to execute high-priority projects quickly using top talent in the company. The Skunk Works protocol would be executed any time the company identified what he called a "red-hot project." The protocol included the following provisions:

- Red-hot projects would be managed personally by senior directors in the company.
- The directors have the authority to hand pick their project staff and reassign them from other projects as necessary.
- Given the urgency of the projects, the directors would be strongly encouraged to staff their projects with ample resources working in parallel tracks.
- Red-hot projects had priority for conference rooms needed for team meetings and working sessions.
- The progress of red-hot projects would be reviewed personally by the COO on a monthly basis.

The board applauded the COO for his Skunk Works Protocol and immediately assigned him his first red-hot project.

Three months later, the first project had been completed and was considered by the board a "raging success." With the Skunk Works protocol now tested and proven, the board assigned the COO three new red-hot projects. The COO's stock had gone up considerably with the board.

Two months later the COO was notified that several client implementation projects were in trouble and that morale in the Professional Services Group was very low. HR reported a spike in resignations, noting that "some of our best talent just walked out the door." Managers of the client implementation projects reported substantial delays on their projects, and clients were now escalating their concerns up the chain. It had become well known in the company that the implementation project managers were at odds with each other over who would be on their teams. It was as if they were competing more with each other than with the real competition. This began to affect other members of the Professional Services Group, who seemed to be organizing in factions around the project managers.

The COO was furious. The red-hot projects were the talk of the company, and those guys over in Professional Services were dragging everything down! It was time to get to the bottom of this, he decided, and some heads might roll. He assigned his chief of staff to investigate the problems and report back on the problem areas and problem people. Meanwhile, the COO scheduled flights to several client sites to apologize for the delays and provide assurances that the problems would be fixed.

Two weeks later the chief of staff and COO sat down to discuss the problems. The COO reiterated that he just wanted to know the problem areas and problem people and that he didn't need to know all of the other details. With a somber look on his face, the chief of staff reluctantly told the COO that the root cause of all of this was the Skunk Works protocol. The COO reacted with disbelief and anger, prompting the chief of staff to explain:

- About six months ago, with the formation of the first red-hot project, the client implementation teams lost several key staff to the project. Because they were some of the company's best people, they occupied key positions on the client implementation projects and had frequent client contact. This put a dent in the staff of several client projects.

While the teams were generally able to recover and stay on schedule, they felt dumped on by the company. They felt that the company had sent a clear signal that their projects were not as important as red-hot projects and that they were not as important as people who worked on the red-hot projects.

- Three months ago the implementation project teams were looking forward to getting their people back. Problems had cropped up in their absence, and they were needed to help put out some fires. Instead, the company launched the three new red-hot projects. The teams went crazy as they were "robbed" of even more good people.

- With holes in their project staffing, the implementation project managers started to feel the heat of missed deadlines and deliverable issues and began poaching staff from other teams. As the teams poached each other, the anger level grew, fingers were pointed, political maneuvering rose, and battle lines were drawn. "It appears that we have created a new set of silos and a great deal of conflict," the chief of staff commented.

The COO could object no more. He realized that, more than anybody else, he himself had caused the problems. It would have been easy enough to fire the VP Professional Services as a scapegoat and move beyond this, but the COO had integrity. He went back to the board, explained the problem, and told them the company would have to slow down on the red-hot projects while it fixed the problems with the implementation projects, staffing, and the Skunk Works protocol.

This example is, unfortunately, very typical of unintentional conflict. Notice that, in contrast to the example of intentional conflict, the root cause of the unintentional conflict was not personal. The COO and board did not set about trying to create conflict in the Professional Services Group. They thought, as we usually do, that they were doing the right thing. Who knew otherwise?

The conflict, initially between project managers and then among other Professional Service staff, grew out of the *circumstances* created by resource shortfalls and having project staff cherry-picked. These circumstances centered on a key misalignment. Implementation project managers who were being held accountable for the success of their projects did not have control over staff commensurate with their responsibilities. In response, they did what they could do to keep their projects staffed and on track. As resources tightened further, they became more desperate and resorted to even more desperate means to staff their projects. If you asked them, they were just trying to do their jobs. The whole thing generated a tremendous amount of negative energy.

As is typical with unintentional conflicts, the solution was a systemic one. The COO would fix the broken Skunk Works protocol and resolve the resource shortfalls. These kinds of changes tend to be well understood and applauded by people in companies.

One thing that is interesting about this story, and virtually every story of unintentional conflict, is that this problem and conflict could have been avoided in the first place. What happened after the board's original request and the subsequent development of a flawed protocol bred the conflict. It's interesting that the protocol seemed so brilliant at the time. We must learn to look deeper and consider a new set of criteria for evaluating effectiveness and sufficiency when designing business changes.

Traditional Conflict Management

Much has been written on the topic of conflict and conflict management. The underlying premise of most books and articles is that conflict is going to happen, and we need ways to work through it, contain it, and resolve it. Who would argue with that? We live in a world where conflict abounds. A common unspoken assumption is that we are limited in our ability to prevent conflict from happening so we should focus on dealing with it when it does happen. All of this seems to make sense. However, the lens of energy gives us a different perspective. Let's take a closer look.

Too Little, Too Late

The methods and approaches suggested by this traditional body of work on conflict and conflict resolution, while quite important and impactful, are generally too little and too late to resolve our pervasive conflict problem. Once conflict is raging, stopping conflict can be like trying to stop a runaway freight train traveling 100 miles per hour. It would be better if we could have just fixed the brakes in the first place. Traditional efforts to measure the cost of conflict have focused largely on the final "chronic" stages of the "disorder," essentially ignoring the energetic damage and cost incurred up to that point. For the most part, we have been addressing and measuring only the tip of the iceberg.

Current Research Indicators

In spite of these limitations, it is useful to review current research, even if to simply get a sense of how big the tip of the iceberg is. Here are some examples:

- An overwhelming majority of employees (85%) have to deal with conflict to some degree and 29% do so "always" or "frequently" (CPP Global Human Capital Report 2008, 3).
- Some researchers believe that unresolved conflict represents the largest reducible cost in many businesses (Dana 2005, chapter 3; Slaikeu and Hasson 1998, xii).
- The typical manager spends 25% to 40% of his or her time dealing with workplace conflicts (one to two days of every workweek) (Kabcenell Wayne 2005).
- A representative study of 446 closed claims reported by small- to medium-sized enterprises with fewer than 500 employees showed that 19% of employment charges resulted in defense and settlement costs averaging a total of $125,000. On average, those matters took 275 days to resolve (Hiscox 2015, 6).
- It is not unusual for conflicts to escalate rather than being swiftly resolved. In fact,

> Nine out of ten employees (89%) have experienced a workplace conflict that escalated.... as many as one in six (16%) report that a recent conflict remains unresolved, having lasted longer than expected and/or becoming increasingly intense....
>
> The destructive emotions experienced by those involved in a conflict at work don't simply vanish. Over half of employees (57%) have left a conflict situation with negative feelings, most commonly de-motivation, anger and frustration. (CPP Global Human Capital Report 2008, 5–6)

- Regarding the health effects from stress caused by sources such a workplace conflict:

  - Forty-three percent of all adults suffer adverse health effects from stress.
  - Seventy-five percent to 90% of all doctor's office visits are for stress-related ailments and complaints.
  - Stress can play a part in problems such as headaches, high blood pressure, heart problems, diabetes, skin conditions, asthma, arthritis, depression and anxiety.
  - The Occupational Safety and Health Administration declared stress a hazard of the workplace. Stress costs American industry more than $300 billion annually.
  - The lifetime prevalence of an emotional disorder is more than 50%, often due to chronic, untreated stress reactions. (WebMD 2005–2019)

Needless to say, even the tip of the iceberg has some very large costs associated with it.

An Uphill Battle

The difficulty in dealing with conflict after it is in play is that it has already gained emotional momentum. Battle lines are drawn. Tensions are high. There are important things, or at least things that seem important, at risk. What is worse is that these conflicts are often self-sustaining. There is a ready supply of emotional powder to fill the keg, and any little spark will set it off—again and again.

Most HR managers will tell you that managing conflict in the workplace is a time-consuming process that is seldom fully successful, if at all. But why is that? Why does it consume so much time and effort, often with only marginal success?

Kenneth W. Thomas and Ralph H. Kilmann (2009–2019) have created the Thomas-Kilmann Conflict Instrument, an assessment that determines how people tend to respond to conflict. According to the instrument, there are five key styles for managing conflict:

1. **Forcing.** Using your formal authority or power to satisfy your concerns without regard to the other party's concerns

2. **Accommodating.** Allowing the other party to satisfy their concerns while neglecting your own
3. **Avoiding.** Not paying attention to the conflict and not taking any action to resolve it
4. **Compromising.** Attempting to resolve the conflict by identifying a solution that is partially satisfactory to both parties but completely satisfactory to neither
5. **Collaborating.** Cooperating with the other party to understand their concerns in an effort to find a mutually satisfying solution

From an HR perspective, Forcing may be appropriate occasionally, perhaps in a crisis situation, but will likely be only a temporary solution. Accommodating didn't happen or it wouldn't have become an HR matter in the first place. Avoiding, which may be appropriate for minor conflicts, didn't happen either. That leaves Compromising and Collaborating as the logical goals. Collaborating is generally the optimal solution, but Compromising can be satisfactory. The rub is that both of these outcomes require open, usually mediated, conversations and a willingness among the involved parties to find a resolution. This process is generally a messy, time-consuming affair since emotions, attitudes, and beliefs are at the table too.

Wouldn't it be easier if those involved found a way to collaborate from the beginning? Yes! Wouldn't there be a better chance of success if the process of identifying how to collaborate could occur before conflict arose and before emotional levels—things like anger, fear, and hate—spiked upward? Yes again!

This is why traditional conflict management is too little, too late. While it is necessary, it is not at all sufficient. Fortunately, there is another way.

Forms of Unintentional Conflict

As mentioned earlier, it is easier to prevent unintentional conflict than intentional conflict. Therefore, finding the sources and working to prevent unintentional conflict in its germination stage holds major promise in our effort to reduce conflict. In this section, we look at the origins of unintentional conflict as a first step toward the prevention of conflict at its source.

Why Unintentional Conflict Has Been Unseen

It's easy to see conflict when people are locked and loaded in preparation for battle or firing away at their adversaries. But what is not obvious, in most cases, is how those involved came to draw arms in the first place. Recognizing unintentional conflict means understanding its origin, and its origins are circumstances that are largely unseen from a surface-level vantage point. Our businesses create these circumstances unknowingly, and we don't automatically associate them with conflict.

As people, we tend to frame problems in terms of the things that are directly impacting us and causing us pain, discomfort, and/or difficulty. For example, to use a playful metaphor, if we were to get run over by a buffalo, we might blame the buffalo when, in fact, the problem was the renegade cowboy who started a buffalo stampede at the edge of town. Nonetheless, the buffalo that ran over us was highly memorable and certainly had an impact—in more ways than one. So we tend to focus on the buffalo, the thing that directly impacted us. Next thing you know, there is a warrant out for the buffalo's arrest or, worse yet, the local restaurant is running a special on buffalo burgers. Unfortunately for the buffalo, we solved the wrong problem.

This is what happens with unintentional conflict, and it is why people often think the problem is the buffalo (i.e., the conflict). In reality, the problem is what caused the conflict in the first place. Because the real problem is usually a step or two back, it often goes unnoticed. When that happens, unintentional conflict remains unseen. How, then, do we flush out these hidden origins? Where and how should we look for unintentional conflict?

Unintentional Conflict Can Be Anywhere

No part of a business enterprise is immune from unconditional conflict. While it tends to show itself in interactions among people, the contributing factors from even a single conflict can be many and varied. Given that, and to facilitate the identification, evaluation, and resolution of unintentional conflict, it is useful to apply a model that divides a business into discrete parts, with clear definitions of each part. Doing this provides a common language and a framework for evaluation. In the remainder of this section we present such a model and use it to provide examples of unintentional conflict in various parts of the business enterprise.

The Enterprise Elements Model

The Enterprise Elements Model divides a business into discrete, tangible elements. These elements are major components of the "system" that constitutes the business. We introduce the model here as a framework for identifying and understanding unintentional conflict. Specifically, each enterprise element can be considered and evaluated as a potential contributor to unintentional conflict. Once the sources of the conflict are understood, the model is also a useful framework for redesigning or modifying the business to resolve sources of conflict and improve the function and performance of the affected areas. Thus, we use this core model throughout the book as a framework and a language for managing the energy of business.

The Enterprise Elements Model divides the business enterprise into three levels: organizational, operational, and individual (people). In turn, each level is divided into its primary elements. Tables 2.2, 2.3, and 2.4 list the major elements at each level along with brief descriptions.

Table 2.2   Major Elements in the Organizational Level

Organizational Element	Description
Culture	The cultural elements and/or styles for thinking and working (e.g., collaborative, forward thinking, traditional, hierarchical, political, etc.)
Leadership	The leadership elements and characteristics of the leadership team, and the individual leaders, in terms of their ability to lead, inspire, and achieve the desired vision
Structure	The characteristics of the organizational structure, including department roles, responsibilities, and reporting relationships (e.g., traditional hierarchical, project-oriented, matrix, hybrid structure, etc.)
Communications	The formal and informal communication in the organization, particularly around important company developments and change initiatives as they relate to the people
Organizational Expertise	The organization's expertise conducting the business of the enterprise within its defined industries

Table 2.3   Major Elements in the Operational Level

Operational Element	Description
Program Delivery	Processes, templates, and protocols in support of program/project planning and management; level of program managers' control over program resources and associated accountability, and overall program delivery performance levels
Program Portfolio Management	Operational mechanisms in place for deciding what programs (e.g., product development, systems development, organizational change, revenue producing) will be implemented, how programs will be funded, how the portfolio of programs will be tracked/managed, and how program visibility will be provided to program stakeholders and executives
Operational Governance	Defined and recognized authorities, rules, and protocols for making decisions regarding operational matters, including operational direction, utilization of money and resources, priorities, review and acceptance of deliverables or work products, and any other operational matter where decisions are required
Operational Planning and Budgeting	How the organization performs annual operational planning (e.g., program identification, departmental goal setting, technology infrastructure targets, product planning) and budgeting, (e.g., incremental based on previous year, zero based, etc.)
Essential Producing Processes	Definition and implementation of the primary overarching processes for the business to provide for adequate work consistency, clear role definitions and accountabilities, a basis for program planning and estimation, and a foundation for continuous process improvement
Functional Capability and Capacity	The levels of capability (detailed functional processes and tools) and capacity (qualified staff trained in the functional processes and tools) that are in place in the enterprise functional areas/departments

Table 2.3 (*Continued*)

Operational Element	Description
Technology/ Systems	The state of the organization's technology and systems regarding their ability to support the organization's infrastructure (e.g., phones, networks, computers), functional areas (e.g., payroll system, finance system), customer-facing processes (e.g., help desk), and products
Knowledge Management	How the organization manages and provides access to information (e.g., intranet, databases, etc.), analyzes and converts information and experience into knowledge (relevant and personalized information), and leverages knowledge in daily operations to improve performance.

As shown in Table 2.2, the organizational level includes five major elements: culture, leadership, structure, communications and organizational expertise. These elements each have a broad footprint that touches everyone in the business. Therefore, they have significant potential impact, both positive and negative.

Table 2.3 shows the major elements present at the operational level. These eight critical elements cover the operational drivers related to conducting work, making decisions, applying technology, allocating resources, building capability and capacity, and managing enterprise knowledge. Like railroad tracks for the enterprise, they guide people in where to go, what to do, and how to do it.

Table 2.4 defines the six major elements at the individual level. Each of these elements affects the actions, abilities, and motivations of the *people* in the business enterprise. People can be the last line of defense against unintentional conflict, or they can be agents that act out the conflict. Therefore, the elements at the individual level always have a big impact on the performance of the business.

While the Enterprise Elements Model is relatively comprehensive, some businesses may have elements unique to them. To accommodate that, the model may be amended with additional elements as needed. This ensures the applicability of the model to virtually any business.

Now that the enterprise elements have been introduced, the question is: How does unintentional conflict arise within these elements at each of the three enterprise levels? To answer that question, the following examples

Table 2.4   Major Elements in the Individual Level

Individual Element	Description
Roles	The way roles are defined in the organization in job descriptions, team assignments, and general responsibilities; relationships between roles (e.g., overlapping, complementary), and the general degree of empowerment versus the responsibilities of each role
Attitude/ Motivation	In general, the attitudes and levels of motivation among people in the organization toward their work and the business
Foundation/ Performance Skills	The types and levels of nontechnical skills in the organization that enable the people to conduct the business of the enterprise, including interpersonal business and communication skills
Technical Knowledge/ Expertise	The types and levels of hard technical skills in the organization (e.g., HR, finance, IT, functional areas, professional services, etc.)
Performance Expectations	The performance expectations (e.g., billable time, sales quotas, production targets, etc.) among people in the enterprise
Incentives	How people are incented to perform and the level of impact it has on motivation

briefly characterize the origin of unintentional conflict within each element. Stories and case studies in subsequent chapters provide additional examples and illustrate how most significant problems (and solutions) involve the interaction of multiple enterprise elements.

Conflict in Organizations

Unintentional conflicts that are created, at least in part, by elements at the organizational level tend to impact everyone in the business in one way or the other. At the top of the impact list is the *organizational structure*. More than any other element, the organizational structure organizes the business. It defines roles, responsibilities, and reporting relationships at the senior (macro) level. A well-designed structure supports and aligns with the mission and operations of the business. One complements the other. Conversely, structures with less thoughtful designs breed confusion and uncertainty in roles and responsibilities at the departmental level. Overlapping roles and responsibilities often lead to turf wars, while responsibility gaps can lead to finger pointing and accountability issues.

Another common problem arises when companies try to do too much with their structures instead of recognizing that some boundaries are better defined by operational policies, procedures, and protocols. For example, companies may slice the pie in too many ways, attempting to recognize in the structure everything from functional areas to regions to product lines. Too many subdivisions tends to enhance the silo effect, which creates an us/them mentality ripe for conflict.

Unclear roles and responsibilities at the department level, often coupled with unhealthy competition, often lead to issues in the *leadership* element. These issues tend to polarize executives and senior business leaders, making agreement on important business decisions difficult. And as much as leaders may try to keep their executive team dynamics private, employees often know when their leaders don't agree with one another. This dissonance can lead to the formation of factions around the various leaders, which multiplies the potential for conflict many times over. The formation of factions injects a cloudy bias into *communications*. Miscommunication becomes more frequent, fear and anger levels rise, and aligning people to accomplish important projects is much more difficult. Consequently, substantial change initiatives are much more challenging and the potential for conflict rises dramatically.

Company culture, which is essentially long-term collective energy and norms, can become dysfunctional or even outdated. There will always be those who want to change things and those who want to protect the culture and status quo just the way it is. Any imbalance between what a culture is and what it ought to be is an opportunity for potential conflict. In a rapidly changing world, a business that holds onto outdated cultural beliefs, attitudes, and norms is enabling the erosion of its *organizational expertise*. In such environments, we often find that some people do things one way and others do them another. The stage is then set for conflict around how things are done. The dilemma is both intellectual and emotional.

Needless to say, the level of negative energy created by unintentional conflict spawned at the organizational level can be quite high, primarily because the breadth of its impact is so large. Virtually everyone in the company is affected on an ongoing basis.

Conflict in Operations

At the top of the impact list on the operational level are the overarching *essential producing processes*. In most cases, their contribution to the creation of conflict has less to do with what is there and more to do with what is *not* there. What needs to be in place is a high-level definition of processes associated with the major things a business does for its customers and for itself. Things like service delivery, product development, system development, and internal change initiatives are among essential producing processes. These broad and important activities typically involve many parts of the business, so clear definitions of roles and responsibilities within the processes, usually at the functional department level, are extremely important. Unfortunately, such clarity is often not present in businesses, and the various departments are left to figure things out themselves. When that happens, let the games begin! Watch out for confusion, power struggles, and massive finger pointing.

Well-defined essential producing processes with embedded departmental responsibilities provide an excellent starting point for documenting the missions and responsibilities of the various departments. With this clarity, each department can focus on developing and maintaining its *functional capability and capacity*. Building capability (detailed functional processes and tools) and capacity (qualified staff in sufficient quantities trained in the functional processes and tools) is absolutely critical to the performance of the business. Unfortunately, however, most businesses underemphasize and underincentivize these capability and capacity activities in favor of execution. Execution is often regarded as more interesting, exciting, and rewarding.

The problem is that effective execution is not possible without adequate capability and capacity. The other problem is that shortfalls in capability and capacity are fertile ground for conflicts. The work delays, errors, and waste that occur when people are under pressure to perform without adequate resources provide perfect reasons to argue, blame, and throw each other under the bus.

This resource problem is exacerbated in team-oriented companies with weak or underdeveloped *program delivery* mechanisms. These weak mechanisms fail to adequately knit together people from the various departments into high-performing cross-functional teams. As businesses begin to recognize their need to support teams by moving into well-designed matrix structures, many fall short, at least initially, on their program delivery functions. This breeds conflict within teams and between departments, primarily because people tend to bring their departmental identities and silo mentalities into projects.

As discussed earlier in the book, the way money flows in a business is very important. This flow generally starts with the *operational planning and budgeting* process. Many government agencies, school districts, and companies approach planning and budgeting as they did the year before, and the year before that, and the year before that. The major problem is that the annual plan often lacks important details, and the connection between the work to be done and the budget is underdeveloped. A department gets the same budget as it did the year before with a 3% increase. Never mind how much work workers have to do this year. As a result, the business may have relatively vague expectations around what the department will accomplish that are not aligned with the department's budget. Cue the conflict.

Budget battles get worse throughout the year when leaders have to decide what projects and programs to fund and which ones to stop funding. Without good *program portfolio management*, these decisions become highly political, bullies get the upper hand, and influence becomes destructive as opposed to constructive. People suffer, projects suffer, and the business suffers. This conflict and dysfunction is also seen on a broader scale when *operational governance* is inadequately defined. Few things trigger conflict more readily than ambiguity around who makes what decisions and how those decisions are made. Virtually any operational matter, including decisions around operational direction, how money is spent and how resources are utilized, how priorities are set, and even how deliverables and work products are reviewed and accepted can trigger fierce conflict if operational governance authorities and protocols are not established up front.

Another good way to start a series of barnyard brawls is to implement new *technology/systems* without careful planning, preparation, and involvement of end users. The list of potential conflicts seems endless—everything from how a function will work, to who has access to what, to when, and how it will be implemented. Similarly, *knowledge management* is becoming both more important and more of a lightning rod for conflict. Some people share knowledge and insights easily, while others hold onto knowledge as a form of job security. As the saying goes, knowledge is power. But trapped knowledge is bad for business. The stage is set for a host of conflicts.

Each of these elements at the operational level is related to how things work. There are a lot of moving parts and a lot of people moving them. Operations can be a well-oiled machine or a poorly designed one with friction among the parts. Unfortunately, many businesses have significant friction, which leads to an unhealthy dose of ongoing unintentional conflict.

Conflict Among People

As stated earlier, unintentional conflict, whatever its origin, almost always shows itself in the form of behaviors and attitudes among people. But while people are generally the recipients of unintentional conflict, they can also be the origin. At the individual level, unintentional conflict is created by the interactions of people and their reactions to one another. We address this at the individual level later in the book when we delve into positive collaborative behaviors and some of the more common negative behaviors. Here we address people as a collective and discuss the various elements of that collective.

Topping our list of individual enterprise elements is *roles*. Similar to poorly defined department roles at the organizational level, poorly defined and overlapping positional roles and assignments often lead to confusion, turf wars, blaming, and ongoing feuds. There is nothing like unclear roles and responsibilities to turn what could be a cooperative effort into a fight. "He has no business doing that. That's my job!" "I should have been the one going to that meeting!" "She is doing a power grab!" Once these situations start, there is plenty of fuel to keep the conflict going.

Foundation/performance skills, the interpersonal business and communication skills that enable people to conduct business, collaborate, and interact effectively, can go a long way toward helping people avoid creating circumstances that invite conflict. Conversely, when these skills are not present or are underdeveloped, people tend to create conflict inadvertently. Such people often lack adequate awareness and empathy. Typically, they know not what they do. Their behaviors can look annoying, challenging, uncaring, insensitive, stubborn, and self-centered—and all of that is unintentional! Nevertheless, these behaviors spawn reactions from others that often constitute the first volley of a conflict exchange. The skills that help people collaborate and provide interpersonal services effectively are addressed in detail later in the book. What is important here is the level of these skills across the collective group of people in the business or in a targeted portion of the business (e.g., a department).

Inadequate *technical knowledge and expertise,* the "hard" skills of the business and a person's job, can also lead to unintentional conflict. People depend on the ability of others in the business to do their jobs. When others lack the skills or knowledge to do their jobs properly, others are negatively impacted. This often leads to anger, frustration, and blaming. Similarly, if someone has a bad *attitude* or lacks *motivation,* they usually deliver a subpar performance, and, again, others are negatively impacted. At the group level, poor attitudes and motivation due to difficult circumstances in the business are like unspoken agreements to behave in dysfunctional ways. For example, people may tacitly agree that they are all entitled to come in late, leave early, and spend lots of time gossiping with coworkers. Meanwhile, the business suffers, problems become worse, and the resulting pressure, mistakes, and anger make the workplace ripe for conflict.

Difficult, unrealistic, or undefined *performance expectations* can also lead to unintentional conflict. For example, consulting companies and professional service groups often require their consultants to work a high number of billable hours each week. This puts tremendous pressure on the consultants and can eventually move some to feel desperate. People who feel unfairly pressured and desperate tend to rationalize harmful behaviors like open competition for work, political moves to hurt others and give themselves an advantage, and targeted hostility.

These "justified" negative behaviors are also common when *incentives* are either inadequate or applied to conflicting goals. It is bad enough when people feel tremendous pressure to perform, but when they are poorly incentivized, they tend to throw up their arms and eventually give up. Worse yet, if they find themselves working at cross-purposes with others due to conflicting incentives, arguments and battles will almost always occur.

By now it should be clear that unintentional conflict can and does originate in virtually every corner of the business enterprise. This is not to say that all businesses are created equal. Some are worse off than others. Nevertheless, unintentional conflict is having a major negative impact on our businesses. In the next section we explore the huge price associated with this conflict.

The Cost of Unintentional Conflict

In this chapter we have described how and why the negative energy caused by unintentional conflict, as well as the mechanism of unintentional conflict itself, are largely unseen. To help the unseen and unknown become seen and known, we've provided examples of how unintentional conflict arises at the individual, operational, and organizational levels to reveal its nature and pervasiveness throughout the business enterprise. And examples of broken business functions and the destructive path of unintentional conflict have illustrated just how serious this hidden cancer can be. Now we address the cost associated with all of this unintentional conflict.

Calculating the Price Tag

What is it worth to you and your company, agency, or school to do something about unintentional conflict? How much money is unintentional conflict costing your business, and how much could be saved by avoiding it?

Naturally, the answers to these questions will vary from business to business. To help inform you about your own business, the remainder of this chapter provides a methodology that you can use to assess the cost of your own energy and financial drain. The model is called the **Universal Model for Estimating**

the Cost of Unintentional Conflict. After presenting the model and its development, we apply it to an example company (a real company renamed to protect confidentiality) to provide a general idea about how big the unintentional conflict problem is in business. If you are not a numbers person, the methodology and calculations in this material may be a bit tedious for your tastes. If that is the case, you may want to skip to the end of this chapter to see the bottom–line estimate and read about its implications. If you have an appetite for numbers, read on!

A Universal Model for Estimating the Cost of Unintentional Conflict

There are three steps involved in estimating the cost of unintentional conflict:

1. **Apply the cost estimation framework.** The process begins with the enterprise levels and their elements, as defined by the Enterprise Elements Model introduced earlier in this chapter. This model serves as an overall framework for cost estimation.
2. **Establish cost buckets.** Through analysis of several instances of unintentional conflict, we recognized that within each enterprise level, there are three basic types of costs: inefficiency, realized risk, and lost opportunity. Bracketing these three cost types within each of the three enterprise levels creates nine "cost buckets." Ultimately, we will create a cost estimate for each cost bucket.
3. **Estimate the cost.** We estimate the costs for a particular business by forming a basis of estimate and then using that to guide and inform the generation of the cost estimates. Specifically, we do four things:
   a. We consider *examples* of unintentional conflict for each of the nine cost buckets to characterize the nature of cost impacts and their drivers in each cost bucket.
   b. We utilize conflict *research* cited earlier in the book to help calibrate the estimates.
   c. We utilize an *estimation methodology*, which provides structure when generating the actual estimates for each cost bucket.
   d. We generate cost estimates for the business.

The remainder of this section provides details on each of the cost estimation steps and shows how to apply the model to your specific business.

Apply the Cost Estimation Framework

We have already utilized the three enterprise levels—organizational, operational, and individual (people)—and their associated elements in this book to provide examples of unintentional conflict. The Enterprise Elements Model is an excellent framework for cost estimation because it is relatively comprehensive and easily understood. Therefore, we adopt it here as our cost estimation framework.

Establish Cost Buckets

Every instance of unintentional conflict has a cost impact. We analyzed many examples to determine the nature of their impacts. The analysis revealed a pattern wherein the three primary cost areas—inefficiency, realized risk, and lost opportunity—emerged as applicable at each of the enterprise levels. The rationales behind these three cost areas are described below:

- **Cost of inefficiency.** In reviewing examples of unintentional conflict, it is clear that most lead to inefficiency. Naturally, when we are in conflict, we are not working together. When we are not working together, we are not aligned. We are inefficient—often grossly inefficient. There are plenty of examples in business where conflict consumes people, leaving them little time and energy to work productively for the business. Based on its common occurrence, inefficiency is the first obvious consequential cost of unintentional conflict. We measure inefficiency in terms of *lost operational dollars*.
- **Cost of realized risk.** A second area of cost, which is less obvious but still significant, stems from the risks to the business caused by unintentional conflict. For example, a delay in a project caused by unintentional conflict may expose the company to risk that would have been mitigated by completing the project on time. Such risks take many forms: legal, regulatory, competitive, employee health, and others. And when a risk is realized—that is, when what we were afraid could happen actually does happen—often a boatload of money is required to deal with it.

This is the cost of realized risk. Because realized risks, like inefficiency, impact our operational budgets, we also measure the cost of realized risk in terms of *lost operational dollars*.

It should be noted that asset depletion, both human and material, often occur as a result of unintentional conflict. However, to simplify our model, we equate asset depletion with lost operational dollars, given the fact that operational dollars are typically utilized to replace the depleted assets.

- **Cost of lost opportunity.** This cost area may be the most obscure and is perhaps the most deadly to a business. For example, when unintentional conflict slows the pace of operations and erodes the quality and value of products and/or services, customers may move to other competitors, which creates a loss of revenue and market share for the company. We measure lost opportunity in terms of *unrealized revenue dollars*.

    Situations that lead to lost opportunity can ultimately lead to a loss of *relevance* in the marketplace, which can be the kiss of death for a business. In most businesses there is a tipping point after which sufficient relevance is lost. While our model does not capture this phenomenon, it should be considered when reviewing the impacts of unintentional conflict in any business.

Estimate the Cost

The three enterprise levels, *Organizational, Operational,* and *Individual,* and the three cost areas within each, *Inefficiency, Realized Risk,* and *Lost Opportunity,* create nine buckets of cost to estimate. For each bucket, we have also identified the unit of measurement, or *type of cost,* based on the cost area involved. Specifically, inefficiency and realized risk are measured in operational dollars. Inefficiency eats away at a company's operational budget, as does recovering from realized risk. Lost opportunity, in contrast, is measured in revenue dollars. These are sales left on the table due to factors stemming from unintentional conflict. Now that we know what we are estimating, we turn our attention toward establishing a strong basis of estimate.

Consider conflict examples in each bucket. While our goal is to generate rough order of magnitude estimates, we still want to establish a clear and concrete basis of estimate. To help with that, Table 2.5 provides examples of unintentional conflict in each of the nine cost buckets. Note

Table 2.5   Examples of Unintentional Conflict by Enterprise Level and Cost Area

Enterprise Level	Cost Area	Examples of Unintentional Conflict
Organizational	Inefficiency	■ Poorly designed organizational structure with overlapping responsibilities leads to confusion, power struggles, and factions and consumes time and energy. ■ Poor or absent formal communication mechanisms lead to rumors, gossip, and ultimately conflict that consumes resources.
	Realized Risk	■ Ready, fire, aim culture increases carelessness, leading to mistakes that are exacerbated by conflict and lead to realized legal or regulatory risks.
	Lost Opportunity	■ Leadership shortfalls lead to confusion about company direction and path, causing conflict about what to do/not do, which leads to missed opportunities. ■ Poorly designed flow of money underfunds key areas causing resource competition and quality issues, leading to poor customer satisfaction and lost opportunities.
Operational	Inefficiency	Weak process for operational planning and budgeting leads to suboptimal distribution of money, leading to weak key capabilities, shortages, internal competition, blaming, and throwing people under the bus, which all eat away at valuable resources. Absence of clearly defined high-level essential producing processes and a well-developed program management capability lead to silos that breed conflict and cause major inefficiencies.

Table 2.5 *(Continued)*

Enterprise Level	Cost Area	Examples of Unintentional Conflict
		Poorly defined decision-making authorities and protocols lead to conflict, which drains time and resources.
	Realized Risk	Poorly defined or underperforming systems lead to unauthorized work-arounds that cause product defects and delays, leading to internal conflict and blame, angry customers, and lawsuits.
	Lost Opportunity	Poorly designed or missing governance/decision-making mechanisms lead to political infighting, underfunded products, errors and product delays, customer dissatisfaction, and missed opportunities.
		Underdeveloped and understaffed functional areas cause capability and capacity shortfalls that lead to blaming and resource competition, which impact customer service levels and satisfaction, resulting in lost clients and opportunities.
Individual	Inefficiency	Underdeveloped interpersonal business and communication skills lead to misunderstandings and conflict, which cause project delays, resistance to change, and infighting.
		Poorly defined and overlapping roles lead to infighting and turf wars, which cloud accountability, impact performance, and result in inefficient and ineffective performance.

Table 2.5 *(Continued)*

Enterprise Level	Cost Area	Examples of Unintentional Conflict
	Realized Risk	Insufficient technical knowledge among staff members causes company blind spots, which lead to uninformed arguments over direction/resolution, causing poor decisions and actions that lead to lawsuits, financial issues, employee health issues/missed work, and regulatory liabilities.
	Lost Opportunity	Poor attitudes and low motivation lead to conflict among staff members and eroding customer service and satisfaction levels, and cause lost customers, lost opportunities, and negative reputation.
		Service delivery staff members are not incented to work with sales staff on upsells, causing conflict between the departments, which leads to lost sales opportunities.

that each example starts with some deficiency in one or more elements at the particular enterprise level and describes how that deficiency leads to unintentional conflict and its resulting cost.

Consider conflict research. The examples in Table 2.5 address the genesis of unintentional conflict in our nine cost buckets. To augment these examples, we also consider the research on conflict cited earlier in this chapter. This research is not about the origin of the conflict but about where the conflict ends up (i.e., its ultimate impact). From that research we know that conflict overall is a huge problem. As we mentioned, some researchers believe that unresolved conflict represents the largest reducible cost in many businesses, a cost that manifests itself in many ways, including employee health issues, turnover, lawsuits, low morale, employee distraction, and much more. Therefore, when generating a rough order-of-magnitude estimate of the cost of unintentional conflict, significant research indicates that the numbers are quite large. This consistent finding helps us calibrate the general magnitude of our estimates.

Establish a cost estimation methodology. In estimating of the cost of unintentional conflict, the examples and research are supporting actors. The star of the show is the Cost Estimation Methodology, which provides an approach for systematically estimating costs. The approach involves the following factors at play within each of the nine cost buckets:

- **Trigger volume.** For a given cost bucket, how often do events that trigger unintentional conflict occur?
- **Number of affected people.** When unintentional conflict is triggered by an event, how many people tend to be affected?
- **Magnitude.** What is the magnitude of a given event and its resulting conflict and impact?

These factors are multiplicative. That is, if you multiply trigger volume by number of people affected by a given incident times the magnitude of a given incident, you get a systematic and logical basis of estimate for any given cost bucket. Importantly, it turns out that the nine cost buckets differ in their "profiles" across the three factors. Ratings of individual factors vary from low, to moderate, to high, to very high, and the combination of ratings across the three factors creates a unique estimation profile. Table 2.6 provides the estimation profiles for each cost bucket.

- Triggers of unintentional conflict leading to *inefficiency* are quite common across all three enterprise levels. This makes sense because there are so many ways and opportunities to trigger conflict that results in inefficiency, whether it is a poor organizational structure that breeds conflict every day or people with underdeveloped interaction skills who frequently "miss" in their communications and end up in conflict.
- The number of people affected by conflict originating from organizational and operational factors is generally high because structures, processes, and systems touch many people. Conversely, the number of people affected by conflict originating from individual/people factors tends to be small for any given interaction; often such conflict involves only two individuals.

Table 2.6   Estimation Rationale for Unintentional Conflict

Enterprise Level	Cost Area	Trigger Volume	Number of Affected People	Magnitude
Organizational	Inefficiency	High	High	Low to Moderate
	Realized Risk	Low	Moderate	Low to Moderate
	Lost Opportunity	Moderate	High	Moderate to High
Operational	Inefficiency	Very High	Moderate	Moderate to High
	Realized Risk	Low	Moderate	Moderate to High
	Lost Opportunity	Moderate	Moderate	Moderate to High
Individual	Inefficiency	Very High	Low to Moderate	Moderate
	Realized Risk	Moderate	Low	Moderate
	Lost Opportunity	Moderate	Moderate	Moderate

- Triggers of unintentional conflict that lead to realized risk are relatively infrequent. However, when they do occur, the cost impact can range from low to high, depending mainly on the nature of the realized risk.
- The cost impact of lost opportunities triggered at the organizational and operational levels can be severe. We see this, for example, in companies with systemic issues that block customer focus and lead to a spiral down effect in the marketplace.

Ultimately, we will use the model to estimate operational dollars and lost revenue dollars. But we need the model to be universally applicable across businesses with different size operational budgets and potential revenue. To provide for this, we create a *cost profile* using *percentages* as our units of measurement. For example, we estimate the cost of inefficiency at the organizational level as a percentage of the operational budget. In applying the model to a specific business, the percentage estimates for the nine cost buckets become weighting factors against the company's operational budget and revenue.

Specifically, our units of estimation for the *inefficiency* and *realized risk* buckets will be *percentage of lost operational budget* (where operational budget = cost of goods sold + expenses). And our unit of estimation for *lost opportunity* will be *percentage of unrealized revenue* (the percentage increase in actual revenue that remains unrealized).

Table 2.7 provides a worksheet for creating an unintentional conflict cost profile for any business. Use the right-hand Estimate column to capture the percentage estimates for each of the nine cost buckets.

Generate cost estimates. After explaining the model, including the framework, cost buckets, and basis of estimates, we are ready to estimate numbers. In estimating numbers, you must have a particular business in mind. To provide an example here, we used a real company that is typical in many ways. The name of that company cannot be revealed due to confidentiality agreements. For our purposes we will call the company Anybiz. Anybiz is a billion dollar company.

You can apply the model to any company. Doing so is a fairly simple matter. Simply think of your own business when generating cost estimates. Your percentage estimates will form your *custom cost profile*, which you can then translate into the estimated dollars that unintentional conflict is costing your business.

Table 2.8 shows the completed Anybiz cost profile with our percentage estimates for each cost bucket. For example, for the first cost bucket, inefficiency at the organizational level, we estimate that 5% of the operational budget is wasted by inefficiency caused by unintentional conflict. While this may seem like a big number, consider the information provided in Table 2.6. For this cost bucket, both trigger volume and the number of affected people are high. Even though the magnitude from any given event is low to moderate, the high number of events and affected people gives this bucket substantial cost impact. In addition, Anybiz has a fair amount of unintentional

Table 2.7   Cost Profile Worksheet for Unintentional Conflict

Enterprise Level	Cost Area	Type of Cost	Unit of Estimation	Estimate
Organizational	Inefficiency	Operational $	% Operations Budget	%
	Realized Risk	Operational $	% Operations Budget	%
	Lost Opportunity	Revenue $	% Potential Revenue	%
Operational	Inefficiency	Operational $	% Operations Budget	%
	Realized Risk	Operational $	% Operations Budget	%
	Lost Opportunity	Revenue $	% Potential Revenue	%
Individual	Inefficiency	Operational $	% Operations Budget	%
	Realized Risk	Operational $	% Operations Budget	%
	Lost Opportunity	Revenue $	% Potential Revenue	%
Total % Operations Budget				%
Total % Potential (Lost) Revenue				%

conflict at the organizational level primarily because the role of sales and professional services in the sales process are not well defined, and the matrix structure within the professional services group has not been formalized. Thus, an estimate of 5% of operational budget is actually conservative.

The estimated percentages across the nine buckets range from 2% to 7%. While there is clearly variability across businesses in their makeup and in their cost profiles for unintentional conflict, this example provides a profile

Table 2.8   Example Cost Profile for Unintentional Conflict

Enterprise Level	Cost Area	Type of Cost	Unit of Estimation	Estimate
Organizational	Inefficiency	Operational $	% Operations Budget	5%
	Realized Risk	Operational $	% Operations Budget	2%
	Lost Opportunity	Revenue $	% Potential Revenue	7%
Operational	Inefficiency	Operational $	% Operations Budget	7%
	Realized Risk	Operational $	% Operations Budget	3%
	Lost Opportunity	Revenue $	% Potential Revenue	5%
Individual	Inefficiency	Operational $	% Operations Budget	6%
	Realized Risk	Operational $	% Operations Budget	2%
	Lost Opportunity	Revenue $	% Potential Revenue	4%
Total % Operations Budget				25%
Total % Potential (Lost) Revenue				16%

that we can use to estimate the cost of unintentional conflict for a company that is typical in many ways.

When we add up the percentages in the table, we find that the total cost of unintentional conflict to Anybiz is 25% of its operational budget and 16% of its potential revenue. When we consider the prevalence of unintentional conflict in our businesses at all levels, these numbers are quite plausible.

Now that the cost profile for Anybiz is complete, it is a fairly simple matter to translate the profile percentages into dollars. To do that, we need to know the basic financials found in a standard income statement:

- Revenue
- Cost of goods sold (COGS)
- Expenses
- Net profit

With this information in hand, the remaining steps are a sequence of straightforward calculations, which are shown next for Anybiz.

1. Starting with the figures from the income statement, Anybiz had the following financials (approximate figures):
   - Revenue: $1 billion
   - COGS: $580 million
   - Expenses: $320 million
   - Net profit: $100 million (10% net profit margin)
2. Based on the financials, the total operational budget for Anybiz is:
   - Operational Budget = COGS + Expenses = $580 million + $320 million = $900 million
3. The cost profile indicates that unintentional conflict had the following cost impact:
   - Operational budget: 25%
   - Potential (lost) revenue: 16%
4. Now we calculate the cost of unintentional conflict in dollars.
   - Operational cost = Operational budget × Percentage impact = $900 million × 25% = $225 million
   - Lost opportunity = Revenue × Percentage impact = $1 billion × 16% = $160 million
   - Total cost = Operational cost ($225 million) + Lost opportunity ($160 million) = *$385 million*

This means that Anybiz, our $1 billion company, loses $385 million *each year.* This is a stunning figure. You may wonder what the company's financials would look like if it didn't have the burden of $385 million of unintentional conflict.

We know that the revenue would be the original $1 billion plus the $160 million in lost revenue for a total of $1.16 billion. For operating costs, a 25% reduction in operational budget would put the operational budget percent (in relation to the new revenue) at 67.5%. That is, 90% (original figure) × 75% (a 25% reduction) = 67.5%. Revenue × 67.5% = Operating costs. Therefore:

Revenue = $1.16 billion
Operating costs = $783 million
Potential profit = *$377 million*

This analysis suggests that eliminating unintentional conflict in Anybiz could increase revenue by 16% and nearly quadruple net profit. That prospect is amazing, especially when you consider that the savings would occur every year.

But one more set of calculations is needed to bring these numbers into what we might call an approachable business scenario. Because it is impossible to *completely* eliminate unintentional conflict, we should not assume that will happen. Instead, we will set a very conservative goal of a 20% reduction in unintentional conflict and rerun the numbers using the same company financials.

The 20% targeted reduction in unintentional conflict has the following effect on the Anybiz cost profile in Table 2.8:

- Operational budget: 25% (original value) × 20% (reduction) = 5%
- Potential (lost) revenue: 16% (original value) × 20% (reduction) = 3.2%

The cost of unintentional conflict in dollars is:

- Operational cost = Operational budget × Percentage impact = $900 million × 5% = $45 million
- Lost opportunity = Revenue × Percentage impact = $1 billion × 3.2% = $32 million
- Total cost = Operational cost ($45 million) + Lost opportunity ($32 million) = *$77 million*

To calculate the potential increase in profit by avoiding 20% of the unintentional conflict, we first generate the potential revenue by adding the original revenue to the lost opportunity for a total of $1.032 billion. For operating costs, a 5% reduction in operational budget would put the operational budget percentage (in relation to revenue) at 85.5%. That is, 90% original × 95% = 85.5%. Therefore:

- Revenue = $1.032 billion
- Operating costs = $882 million
- Potential profit = *$150 million*

So, with a conservative 20% reduction in unintentional conflict, these numbers suggest we can increase net profit by 50%, year in and year out.

But what about government agencies, schools, and nonprofit organizations that don't make a profit? While they clearly use different financial models, the same general cost estimation methodology is applicable, except that the benefits accrue in different ways. For example, schools and government agencies experience increased revenue in the form of better performance against their missions and more satisfied "customers." The significant reduction in operational costs would allow budget reductions, increased spending on new programs and improvement initiatives, salary increases, or a combination of these things. Nonprofit companies, like for-profit companies, will enjoy the benefits of revenue growth. On the cost side, nonprofits will experience cost reductions in ways similar to schools and government agencies.

Implications of the Cost Estimate

Is there a more noble cause than reducing unintentional conflict? Is there a better way to improve the health and financial performance of our businesses? Who would have imagined that a growing cancer that has been largely unseen and unknown was so huge and pervasive? And what will the world be like when we begin to manage the energy of business and reduce unintentional conflict? We could pay off the U.S. debt, put everyone back to work, and have cash to invest in the kinds of things we need to keep our businesses, planet, and people healthy.

But let's start with you and your business. If you want to build organizational power and resources, make your workplace a more pleasant and productive place to work, or clear out the cobwebs that get in the way of serving your clients and making a difference in the world, manage the energy and take action to reduce unintentional conflict.

Next we look at a set of pragmatic steps for doing this in your business by creating shared space.

Chapter 3

Shared Space

A few years ago I challenged myself and my team at Advance Consulting with a question. What do we call that thing we help clients achieve that everybody senses and appreciates but no one has a name for? I threw out some examples to get our creative juices flowing.

- A team that is firing on all cylinders, seems steeped in creativity and innovative ideas, and has a graceful productivity that comes from everyone working in concert
- A conversation between two people to understand and solve a common business problem, who are clear on their shared goal, build on each other's thoughts and ideas, and achieve a common understanding and vision in a way that leaves them feeling energized and even joyful
- A business process that just works, where people who have the required expertise each perform their jobs well, are available at the right times, and execute with skill and camaraderie, unencumbered by negative outside influences

The conversation with my team went on for weeks as we struggled to find a name that captured the essence of "the thing." Then one day one of my colleagues mentioned the phrase "shared space." That was it. The name stuck. In this chapter we explore shared space, including methods for designing and implementing it, along with strategies for creating it.

The Power of Shared Space

I describe shared space as a positive energy field where effective work, creativity, and innovation can happen. Shared space gives those involved in any work effort substantial power to move forward—usually in a very successful manner. Much of this advantage has to do with a heightened ability to understand problems, formulate solutions, and either overcome or avoid obstacles. As I further developed the concept of shared space within the context of energy, it struck me that creating shared space was the antidote for unintentional conflict. Let's look at how that works.

The Antidote for Unintentional Conflict

From the lens of energy, conflict is two or more opposing forces. It follows that the antidote for unintentional conflict is to change the *circumstances* that create conflict into circumstances that promote an alignment of energy. The concept of shared space emerged as the antidote of unintentional conflict in recognition of this fact. How we create shared space and avoid creating unintentional conflict is the focus of this chapter.

In a shared space, people can collaborate, align, and work together effectively. In shared space, there is very little cause or opportunity for the seeds of unintentional conflict to be sown. No seeds, no triggers around which conflict can grow. Eureka!

Creating shared space as a solution for unintentional conflict involves the redesign or adjustment of the factors causing such conflict to be the current expression of the business. At the enterprise level, which we discuss in this chapter, these are the elements in the Enterprise Elements Model. At the individual level, they also include the personal "ingredients" that we bring to the table in our interactions. We discuss those in detail in chapters 4 and 5. All of these factors are fair game for adjustment and/or redesign. We have discussed how organizational and operational misalignments lead to unintentional conflict. We have also discussed how, as people, we often miss each other in interactions, which often leads to unintentional conflict. We can turn around all of these circumstances by making the adjustments needed to change the flow of energy from opposition to alignment.

Perhaps the most important adjustment of all is to the people in a business. Just as conflict usually shows itself in the form of behaviors among people, shared space requires that people have the motivations, attitudes, and skills to help promote that shared space. In other words, through their behaviors, people help create the circumstances surrounding shared space.

> *Sharing space with an individual or group is about focusing on the bigger picture and the common good we can create together, not on our own agendas.*

But let's be clear about agendas. Creating shared space does not require that we strip ourselves of all personal agendas. That wouldn't be a practical expectation. However, it does require that we hold our personal agendas loosely and keep them secondary to the larger agenda and the common good. This is an important distinction because people will always have personal agendas. It is human nature.

The creation of shared space is a universal concept that applies equally to the way we organize our businesses, define processes and systems, make decisions, and interact with each other. In other words, it applies to the *entire* business enterprise. Creating shared space is an approach for avoiding unintentional conflict throughout the enterprise. Even better, the shared space is where people can work together and collaborate effectively with a focus on serving customers. It is a space where positive energy is created. It is, and can be, what drives important outcomes like customer satisfaction, innovation, and business growth.

Shared space is not a guarantee that unintentional conflict will be avoided completely. But it is a powerful way to avoid a lot of such conflict. Given the size and pervasiveness of unintentional conflict, this has huge implications.

Fixing a Broken Business Function with Shared Space

Remember our broken business function in chapter 1? We will use that case study to show how we fix such business problems through the creation of shared space. As a quick refresher, here is a summary of the original problem.

A scientific instrument company, Alchemy Instruments, manufactures and sells high-end electronic equipment to business clients across North America. It recently reorganized its sales force into two groups.

- The Product Group is organized around the company's product lines, with subgroups for each line. Sales staff members in the group are instructed to sell their products to any potential client in the United States and Canada.
- The Regional Group is divided into six sales regions in North America. Those assigned to a region within the group are instructed to sell all of the company's products within their regions.

Although the senior VP of sales encouraged sales staff in each group to work cooperatively with staff in the other group, problems began to surface in the field soon after the reorganization was completed. Members from both groups were calling on the same clients, cooperation and cross-group support was at best a low priority, and the VPs of the two groups were at odds. The two groups became polarized and competitive. Less time was being spent on selling and more time was being spent competing with those in their own company.

Each VP spent hours in the SVP's office complaining about the other group and stating why that they should be in charge of both groups. To the SVP, it seemed clear that the two managers could not work together, and he would have to remove one of them. He did so, and the "winning manager" celebrated victory.

Although everyone was now under the winning manager's umbrella, in a few months he faced the same problems, and now they were all his problems. The SVP fired him for his failure to bring the two groups together and took direct control of both groups. Months later, the SVP's efforts had been no more successful, and his own job was on the line.

We know from the previous discussion that the SVP's method of solving this set of problems was "obvious" but ineffective. Let's take a different path. We will approach this broken business function in three basic steps: analyze the problem, design shared space, and implement the changes.

Analyze the Problem

The Presenting Problem

Our analysis begins with the presenting problems. Sales are down and certainly not meeting expectations. The two sales groups are competitive, uncooperative, and even antagonistic. Efforts to make them get along seem only to drive the behaviors underground. Alchemy is losing customers and market share. And all of the goals that drove the reorganization, like a desired blending of customer relationships and product expertise within the sales process, remain unmet.

How Things Work

You will recall that if you want to know how things work, map the flow of money. Annual planning and budgeting at Alchemy created a budget for sales and, within that, separate budgets for the product and regional groups. Therefore, those who work in the two groups received their salaries, commissions, and expense reimbursements from their groups. These people know where their bread is buttered and therefore feel a strong loyalty to their groups. Given the absence of other mechanisms promoting cooperative behaviors, group loyalty, reinforced by the flow of money, is the name of the game.

The Unintentional Conflict Among Those Involved

We described the conflict behaviors in the presenting problem, but what are the (nonpersonal) circumstances that give rise to the conflict? The answer in this case is that there is a misalignment, and at least one other factor supports and exacerbates the misalignment.

The Misalignment

The misalignment is between control and accountability at both the group and individual staff levels. As mentioned earlier, both the product and regional groups, and the staffs within those groups, had *responsibility* for selling and were given quotas for how much they had to sell. However, neither group had *control* over all of the resources required to sell effectively. Client knowledge and relationships, as well as deep product knowledge, all had to be present for effective selling. Exacerbating this misalignment is the incentive structure. The group VPs and sales staff were all incented to sell. They were not incented to sell cooperatively. Their incentive structure offered nothing to lead them to support or cooperate with the other group. Nor did the flow of money incentivize them; it simply kept them loyal to their siloed group.

The Root Cause Problem

The primary root cause problem at Alchemy was that the sales paradigm no longer fit the sales reality. The old paradigm that worked when Alchemy's products were less complicated and seldom bundled with services was that an individual salesperson could, without support, take the sale all the way through the sales funnel (process). As the complexity of Alchemy's products increased and bundled services became more common, the knowledge needed at the table to support a sale grew substantially, and no one person could be expected to know it all while building and maintaining customer relationships. While Alchemy created two groups to house the needed resources for this complex world, the company did nothing to change the sales paradigm. Alchemy needed a team selling paradigm, but it stayed with the individual sales paradigm and expected that to work. This set up the circumstances for a great deal of unintentional conflict, as we have seen.

Notice in this analysis the difference between the presenting problem and the root cause problem. The presenting problem was based purely on what was seen—the behaviors of salespeople and the resulting sales shortfalls. In contrast, the root cause problem is a thoughtful description of where the problem is coming from within the context of the changing Alchemy business environment. It gets to the circumstances that are the source of the unintentional conflict and negative energy. In order to fix this broken business function, we must solve the root cause problem. You can easily see from this example why it is so easy and common for businesses to attack the presenting problem and ignore the real one.

Design Shared Space

With a clear understanding of the root cause problem, we can set about designing a shared space that will encourage the behaviors, collaboration, and knowledge sharing that Alchemy is looking for. We start by identifying the new operating concept.

Identify the New Operating Concept

To change the sales paradigm, Alchemy has to make team selling work. That means the company has to go from misalignment to alignment at both the group and the individual levels. At the individual level, every sale will have one, and only one, salesperson in the lead. This is because there has to be a lead for any group activity, and having more than one leader is a setup for conflict. The lead person will "own" the sale, and the others need to be willing and motivated to support the sale.

Now we must decide which group will take the lead on sales. It makes sense for salespeople from the regional group to be in the lead because for any sale, there is one *primary* client relationship, but the possibility of many involved technologies and products. Putting the product side in the lead, therefore, would cause confusion about who is in the lead when multiple technologies are involved in a sale. For this reason, the regional group and its staff will have the lead role.

We need to have staffing protocols for individual opportunities whereby the lead salesperson identifies the products likely to be sold and requests the assignment of representative sales staff from the product group. And perhaps most important, the incentive structures for all sales staff and the VPs need to motivate individuals to play their roles effectively as part of a team. This is particularly true for people in the product group, who may feel a loss from not being in charge of the sales process or the teams. People must clearly see and believe that if they play their role well, they will sell more and receive higher compensation than they did before.

This operating concept will keep control and responsibility in balance during every sale. The sales leads will have overall responsibility for the sales and will have control of the product people needed to support the sales. The product staff will have responsibility to support the sales in their product areas and will have the knowledge and control needed to execute in their roles. This balance will also apply at the group level, where the VPs will clearly understand that they, and their groups, depend on each other for their success. They will both be incented on total company sales.

Identify Needed Changes and Design New Elements

Using the Enterprise Elements Model as a guide, we can now identify the desired state for all *involved* elements within the organizational, operational, and individual parts of the enterprise. Table 3.1 shows the desired states for each involved enterprise element.

Several points are important as we go through the process of designing shared space.

- *Starting with a clear operational concept is essential.* It forces the discipline of defining how things will work in the future before getting into the details of what has to be done to build it. From a clear operational concept, we can identify the involved enterprise elements and design what we need in each one.

- *This approach results in a comprehensive shared space design.* Like most large changes, this design involves several enterprise elements at all levels. The design process led us to the understanding that, unlike the foiled staffing adjustment described in the story, this solution is more focused on operational and individual elements. It is interesting that this solution emphasis wasn't obvious at the beginning of the story. That is because we are designing shared space to manage energy, which is not directly visible. If we want to fix the entire iceberg, we have to address the larger part below the surface.

- *This is an integrated design, as opposed to a set of disconnected point solutions.* That is, the function of each element supports the functions of the others. There is an internal consistency among the elements that collectively achieves the vision in the operational concept. We have designed each enterprise element to be in alignment with the others.

- *There are no obvious misalignments in the shared space design.* As it is designed, this shared space will not generate unintentional conflict.

- *This comprehensive solution requires more work to design, develop, and implement than surface-level solutions often seen in business.* You may ask,

Table 3.1   Desired State of Involved Enterprise Elements for Alchemy Instruments

Organizational Element	Desired State
Structure	The group roles and responsibilities will reflect a matrix structure within Sales as described in the operational concept. Both groups will report into the Sales SVP. At the individual level, people will report into their groups for administrative matters (e.g., training, payroll, annual reviews, etc.). However, when they are occupied as members of sales teams, people in the Product Group will report to leads in the Regional Group during all sales activities. These sales teams will come and go as sales opportunities arise and conclude.
Communications	Communication protocols for how sales staff will communicate with each other and the customers will reinforce the various roles within the sales process. For example, the sales lead will actually make the deal with the customer; others will support the conversation with information, solution ideas, etc.
Essential Producing Processes	The end-to-end sales process, often called the sales funnel, will be redesigned to embody team selling. For example, new sales leads (i.e., opportunities) can come from anyone and anywhere, but once they are identified, they are assigned to a salesperson in the Regional Group who has proximity to the customer. That salesperson "owns" the lead and is responsible for moving it through the sales funnel toward the ultimate sale. The salesperson's initial communications with the customer qualify the lead, provide general information about the products and services, and identify customer need and interest areas. When the client expresses interest in a deeper conversation and a custom solution,

(Continued)

Table 3.1 *(Continued)*

Organizational Element	Desired State
	the sales leader requests resources from the applicable product groups as needed. The sales team then educates the client with product information, formulates a custom solution, prices it, and presents it. The sales lead follows up with any needed negotiation and closes the deal.

Operational Element	Desired State
Functional Capability and Capacity	With individual roles defined within the sales process, roles and responsibilities are aggregated at the group level for the Product and Regional Groups. Capabilities in the Product Group will focus on hiring and training sales staff with deep product knowledge, solution development abilities, and strong presentation skills. Capabilities in the Regional Group will focus on hiring and training sales staff with broad product knowledge; business acumen; and relationship, negotiation, and team leadership skills. The needed capacities (number of people) for both groups will be estimated based on their roles in the sales process and the number of sales attempts per year.
Operational Planning and Budgeting	The annual budgets of the two groups will be adjusted to accommodate their needed capacities and the activities required to build and maintain the needed capabilities.

Individual Element	Desired State
Roles	Job descriptions for the salespeople and VPs in the two groups will be reworked to capture the new responsibilities for each role and delete old responsibilities that are no longer applicable.

Table 3.1 *(Continued)*

Individual Element	Desired State
	Defined decision-making authorities for each position will help ensure that all have adequate control to do their jobs.
Technical Knowledge/ Expertise	Provide training, exposure, and coaching in the technical areas listed in functional capability and capacity and in the overarching sales process.
Performance Expectations	Establish sales quotas for the two groups and the sales staff. Those in the Regional Group will have the most responsibility and time invested in a given sale, so the expectation is that Regional Group staff will be involved in fewer sales than the Product Group staff. In addition, Regional Group staff will be expected to build and nurture customer relationships in their regions. Product Group staff will be expected to maintain their product expertise and communicate it eloquently in support of sales. All are expected to work as a team.
Incentives	Incentives will be aligned to performance expectations and desired behaviors. Those in the Regional Group will receive the highest commission per sale, given their high level of involvement. Those in the Product Group will receive less commission per sale but will be involved in more sales, giving them equal commission opportunity as those in the Regional Group. The two Group VPs will both be incented on total sales, which will promote a cooperative effort.

(Continued)

Table 3.1 *(Continued)*

Individual Element	Desired State
Attitude/ Motivation	While all of the listed factors will have an influence on attitudes and motivation among the sales staff and VPs, the required shift is substantial and expected to take some time before, during, and after implementation of the changes. The desired destination is clear. We want positive attitudes around work and coworkers and staff highly motivated toward team selling and behaviors.

"Why should we go to the effort and expense of this comprehensive solution when we could probably cut some corners and do OK?" The answer is that you can always cut corners, but there is a price to pay. At best, you will leak energy. At worst, your partial solution won't work at all. Either way, you can do it now, or do it later. You may as well do it right the first time and let the benefits start accruing as soon as possible.

Implement the Changes

Once the changes that will create shared space are designed and developed, they must be implemented. Implementing any significant change is potentially difficult. Several change management models can be utilized to guide the implementation, and we make no attempt here to judge, prioritize, or rewrite those popular models. Any one probably could work. However, regardless of the model you use, it is important to have an implementation/change management *strategy* that is based on an understanding of energy.

Of all the enterprise elements, often it is hardest to shift people's attitudes and motivations. We address that in detail later on in the book. Change would be a lot easier if we didn't have to deal with people! However, to optimize our chances of success in working with the affected people, we recommend *implementing all elements together at the same time.* Collectively, the elements will frame and encourage the desired behaviors while helping to prevent people from engaging in what we might call mischief. Examples of mischief include overt and covert resistance to change, doing things the old way instead of the new way, gossiping, and spreading rumors. We prevent a lot of mischief by taking away opportunities to exercise these dysfunctional behaviors. Parallel implementation of all involved elements, if achievable, is almost always the optimum path. Right off the bat, this moves the implementation needle pretty far to the right. As we discuss in the next section, implementing in a more serial fashion causes energy leakage along the way that often chokes the life out of the change initiative. Lengthy serial implementation is one of the top ten *real* reasons why transformations and change initiatives fail.

Similar to the issues that spring from drawn-out serial implementations are the issues that arise when we give people too many options that ultimately have to be discussed and debated. Too many choices make it extremely difficult to achieve a necessary level of agreement and alignment among the people, which threatens the entire change initiative. People should be appropriately involved in change, but it can't be a democracy. Leadership, guidance, and visible leaders who are walking the talk are essential, especially during the early stages of change. And when we want people to change how they work, we need to give them very prescriptive guidance and direction. Again, the newly designed enterprise elements, implemented together, provide much of the needed guidance and direction.

Once we have created this sort of gated community of change, with roads, signposts, and rules of engagement, we can then focus on driving the adoption of the desired attitudes and motivations. Roads, signposts, and rules are all well and good, but we must still get people to follow them and want to follow them. It is best that people not have too many work options while they are going through this internal transformation.

Let's walk through how the implementation of shared space, utilizing our parallel implementation strategy, would look.

Develop the Plan

The plan covers how, when, and by whom each redesigned enterprise element will be implemented. Overarching activities such as communication, training, and measurement are included. And a risk management plan identifies risks, mitigations, and avoidance strategies.

Establish Commitment, Communications, and Readiness

Before we begin to implement, we establish an adequate state of readiness for change among those who will be affected by the change. In this case, members of the product group and the regional group receive multiple communications with consistent messaging through various channels to explain why the change is being made, how they will be involved and affected, what is expected of them, why it is good for the company, and what's in it for them. Interviews, focus groups, and town hall sessions give people the opportunity to vent and ask questions. In addition, to uncover silent resistance that may not surface in a public forum, leaders hold one-on-one meetings with some of those involved and put out an anonymous survey to gather additional feedback. All of these initiatives are designed to bring down the level of anger and animosity between the groups and pave the way for a cooperative effort. Implementation begins when the people are ready and open to the change.

Implement, Monitor, and Drive Adoption

A full-day offsite meeting is scheduled to kick off the implementation. All staff members from both groups are invited; attendance is mandatory. The day is filled with a series of presentations, starting with the VPs, and continues with activities designed to educate staff on how things will work going forward. These topics include the new structure and sales process, group and individual roles, additional training they will receive, and performance expectations and incentive structures. Staff members are told where they can go with questions and issues going forward. The day ends with a mix of excitement and doubt about whether this change will work.

As implementation begins, there are early adopters, resisters, and everything in between. Vocal resisters are given air time with leaders who hear them out and help them sift through which concerns are real and which are perceived. Some converts are then harnessed to provide change leadership among doubters. Covert resisters are more difficult to deal with or even identify. They seem to form an invisible coalition of people who were still holding onto their anger and animosity toward the other group and harboring resentment about their new roles and how the company wants things to work.

Fortunately, the newly designed processes and other associated elements strongly encourage staff to start selling as teams. Collectively these processes address the number-one issue: motivation. As the weeks go by, more and more staff members are having success with the new paradigm, and their success stories are shared and celebrated. As the successes mount, intrinsic motivation propels the sales staff forward in the change.

Because the new process requires specific and visible behaviors, and because sales performance is tracked on an individual basis, the covert resisters become increasingly exposed. Although their numbers were dwindling, they still have significant influence within the groups and are blocking full adoption of the new behaviors. The attention of leadership begins to focus on who among the resisters can be salvaged and who has to be terminated. The three most influential resisters are terminated, which sends a clear message to the other resisters that they either have to get on board with the new way of doing things, or get off the train. At this point it is clear to the resisters that they can't win this battle, and their behaviors and sales performance soon show visible improvement.

Sales are a bit slow the first month but quickly pick up after that as more people experience success within the new team selling paradigm. By the end of the first quarter, sales are ahead of the previous quarter and still climbing. By the end of the first year, the new paradigm has become, for most, the way we do things around here. Sales are up over 25% from the previous year, and people are celebrating.

Observed conflicts between the two groups drop by about 50% when the implementation begins and continue to taper off from there over the next few months. At that point any remaining conflict is most often about resistance to change, not the unintentional conflict that prompted the change in the first place. Fortunately, the sales leaders are astute and can see the difference.

Refine

As the adoption progresses, lessons are learned that lead to some refinement of the enterprise elements. The process is modified to be more explicit about roles, the regional team leads receive additional training on supervision and project management, and incentives are adjusted to reflect the refinement of roles in the process. These refinements are well received by the two groups.

Overall, the change is extremely successful. The investment that Alchemy made in changing the sales groups is recouped in the form of higher sales during the first four months of implementation. And the incentives keep rolling in at a faster pace thereafter. The creation of shared space in the sales department at Alchemy is regarded almost universally as a huge success. Through the steps outlined here, the company changed the expression of the business in the energy equation to create the outcome it was looking for—an ongoing, systemic shared space where team selling thrives.

Now that you have seen an example of how to resolve a broken business function with the creation of shared space, we will give you some tools and approaches for doing this in your own business.

Models for Creating Shared Space in the Enterprise

The goal of this section is to provide you with tools that will guide you in clearly understanding problem areas in your business, designing your shared space solutions, implementing the changes, and driving their adoption. As you will see, with some relatively minor tweaks, this process also works for new enterprise designs where new goals and capabilities, as opposed to problems, drive the changes. These models provide a general roadmap and are not intended to be exhaustive. Yet the detail is sufficient to put you on a path of creating shared space in your business.

Model for Diagnosing Problems and Conflict

We begin with the first part of the roadmap, which is to diagnose the problems and conflict. This process starts with what we see and observe and digs through the layers of understanding down to the root cause level. It is at the

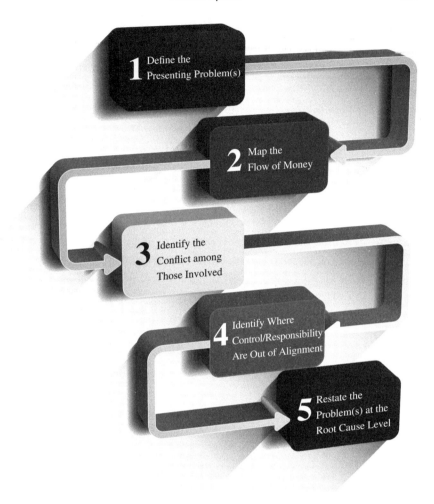

Figure 3.1   Diagnosing Problems and Conflict

root level where we truly understand the problems. Figure 3.1 illustrates the process for diagnosing problems and conflict.

The process begins with *defining the presenting problem(s)*. Presenting problems are the things we can see and observe. There is no analysis in this step, only clear observation. How are the affected people behaving, in general? What are the current states of performance, productivity, and so on? What are your observations about morale, attitudes, and anger levels? What things are not working? Whatever it is, just state the observations.

Next, *map the flow of money* through the problem area and supporting areas to understand how the function currently works. How does the flow of money reinforce current behaviors and contribute to the problems? Does the flow of money empower or disempower those involved? Do support functions like IT and HR have budget and resources pointed toward activities that contribute to the dysfunction or toward activities that support a balanced operation? There is energy in money that can work for or against the business. Keep in mind that changing the way money flows is potentially a part of your solution.

Now *identify the conflict among those involved* in the problem area using available information and your own insights. You don't need to recount every negative encounter that has occurred. Boil it down to what is most important. What are the behavioral patterns? Do certain types of conflict occur regularly? What do they point to? How is energy being drained? If possible and practical, quantify the level of conflict as a baseline so you can show concrete progress as you implement your solution.

Your analysis up to this point should have prepared you to *identify where control and responsibility are out of alignment.* Usually it is most effective to approach this step first at the organizational level, then operational, and then at the individual level. This is because organizational factors inform operational factors, and organizational and operational factors inform people factors.

Look at the organizational structure, department role definitions, and decision-making authorities. Then look at leadership and culture to see how they contribute to the problem. At the operational level, start by looking at expectations and resources. These things often point the way to misalignments. Then, at the individual level, start with people skills, positional role definitions, and decision-making authorities. If you have exhausted everything else, look at individual people who may themselves be causing significant problems. There is usually one overarching misalignment of control and responsibility in any major problem, and everything else is a supporting actor. Find that one misalignment and clearly state it.

Once understood, *restate the problem(s) at the root cause level.* This step requires your analysis and insight. Remember in the Alchemy example that the misalignment affected every salesperson and both groups. Every salesperson was expected to sell, but no one had control over all of the needed resources. The analysis of that circumstance required the mental leap to the root cause problem, which was the need to make team selling work and, at the same time, eliminate the misalignment. In this step, you naturally have to eliminate the misalignment, but *how* you do that is the creative, insightful part. The answer may be obvious, or it may require a deeper contemplation. Look for the new model or paradigm in this step.

Model for Designing Shared Space

Armed with a clear understanding of the root cause problem, you are ready to design the shared space that will resolve it. Without this clear under-standing, you will almost certainly fail to solve the real problem. Figure 3.2 shows the process for designing shared space to solve the real problem.

The first step in designing shared space is to clearly and succinctly *describe the new operating concept*. This is a creative endeavor requiring you to visualize how business will be conducted in the new paradigm. In the Alchemy example, this step required thinking through how sales teams would work, how many leaders each would have, which group the leaders would come from, how team staffing would work, and how sales staff from both groups would be incented and motivated to work together.

Designing your operating concept may be an iterative process. You put something out there and then test it to see if it hangs together. You test it by asking questions like these: Will the people be motivated to work this way?, What problems do I foresee cropping up?, and Am I providing enough specificity and guidance about how people need to work? As you test, find problems, and refine, your operating concept will come into focus. You can be pretty sure your operating concept is solid when you are no longer able to find potential problems.

With a clear operating concept, you can move to step 2, *identify needed changes* in the enterprise that will create the shared space and enable the new operating concept. You accomplish this by building a table like Table 3.1. In this step, you start your table by identifying the *involved* elements within the organizational, operational, and individual parts of the enterprise (i.e., the left column of the table). In doing this work, you must strike a balance. If you needlessly involve a particular enterprise element or multiple elements, you

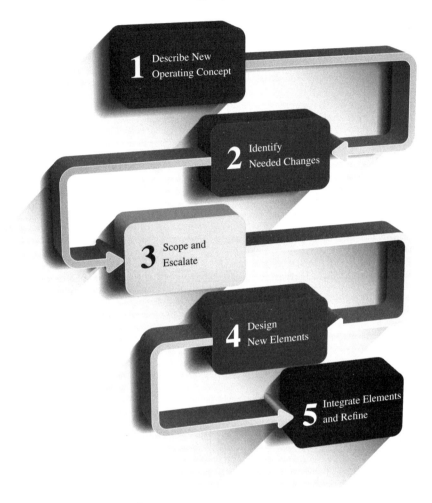

Figure 3.2   Designing Shared Space

will be wasting time and money. If you leave out elements needed to support the operating concept and eliminate the misalignment, however, you may compromise the entire solution. At best you will leak energy like a cracked dam leaks water. Unfortunately, the tendency in business today is to cut corners, so the omission of critical elements is by far the more likely scenario. Just know that at some point, you may be better off doing nothing than cutting corners.

The third step, *scope and escalate*, comes next precisely because of the problem of cutting corners. Often change leaders cut corners not because they want to but because their authority, control, and/or budget do not allow them to make changes in some of the higher-level enterprise elements (e.g., structure, major processes, and incentives). In this case, if you are that change leader, the best you can do is identify which elements you can do something about and which need to be escalated for recommended action.

If the change you can make will not adequately implement your new operating concept and solve the misalignment, now is the time to go up the chain with that information. Perhaps you can hand your leaders copies of this book as you explain the consequences of not doing what is needed. I encourage all leaders to recognize the importance of complete solutions and do what they can to make necessary changes to higher-level enterprise elements. The return on investment alone should make it more than worth your time and resources. If you are limited in resources, consider having fewer initiatives but doing them thoroughly. Your higher success rate should soon pay for itself.

The fourth step is to *design the new elements.* You now build out the table you started in step 2 to describe the desired state for all involved enterprise elements. Collectively, these elements must now include the mechanisms and adjustments that will achieve the desired operational concept. As you design each element, ask questions: What does this element need to be and accomplish?, How will this element work with and fortify the other elements?, and What specific mechanisms must this element include? As with your analysis, it is usually best to approach this design in the sequence of organizational, operational, and individual elements.

The fifth, final step in this model is to *integrate, test, and refine* your shared space design. Put it all together and test it by mapping the new flow of money and checking for any remaining misalignment of control and responsibility at the people, project, and department levels and within operational systems and processes. Check for internal consistency and to make sure each element will work in concert with the others to create the desired operational concept. Adjust as needed until you achieve a tight integration, at least on paper.

Model for Designing New Enterprises and Functions

If you are designing a new enterprise or new major functions within an enterprise, your path will probably be less difficult than it is for those changing existing enterprises, particularly in the implementation step.

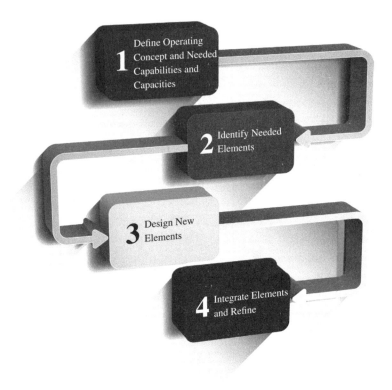

Figure 3.3   Designing New Enterprises and Functions

As discussed earlier, moving people through change is often the most difficult step. If what you are designing is brand new, the people who will participate in it have nothing to lose or compare it to. Not having to give something up paves the way for a much faster and easier adoption.

The Model for Designing New Enterprises and Functions is similar to the Model for Designing Shared Space. The primary difference is that instead of designing shared space to fix a problem, you are designing shared space to optimize work in a new enterprise or business function. Figure 3.3 illustrates this modified flow.

The process begins with *defining the operating concept and needed capabilities and capacities*. Defining the operating concept is essentially the same process as before. However, defining needed capabilities (what you can do) and capacities (how much you can do) is a new detail that applies both to the enterprise as a whole and to individual (major) functions within it. At the enterprise level, capability and capacity are essentially about what the enterprise needs to be able to accomplish to achieve its business and/or strategic plan. Address this level with fairly broad brush strokes. At the major function level (e.g., a department), summarize the capabilities and capacities of the particular function. As reference, see the description of functional capability and capacity in the Enterprise Elements Model discussed in chapter 2.

The next step is to *identify the needed enterprise elements*. Again, begin building a table like Table 3.1 listing the involved enterprise elements. If you are designing a new enterprise, you can expect to list all of the elements. For new functions, start with the full list and eliminate any that are definitely not needed. When in doubt, leave the element on the list and remove it later if you confirm it is not needed. (Note: We omit the scope and escalate step here on the assumption that whoever is designing a new enterprise or function is empowered to do so, and no escalation is required.)

Now complete your design table by *designing the new enterprise elements*. Bear in mind that although you are designing from scratch, the goal is still to create shared space in all aspects of the enterprise or function. The same thinking and discipline applies.

Finally, *integrate the elements and refine* your design as before to achieve a fully integrated set of enterprise elements. In addition, perform testing to make sure the integrated design is sufficient to provide the needed capabilities and capacities.

Model for Implementing and Managing Change

Regardless of your careful analysis and thoughtful design, implementing and managing change is always a tricky affair. As Obi-Wan Kenobi said in *Star Wars*, "We must be cautious." The way to be cautious in implementing and managing change is to anticipate and avoid as many problems as possible so that when problems do occur, you have the horsepower (energy) to keep your initiative on track. Managing change is about managing energy. Know in advance how much energy you will need, and don't run out before you get to the end. Look for opportunities to fill your energy tank whenever you can. Initiatives that fail do so most often because they run out of energy before they reach the point of sustainable change.

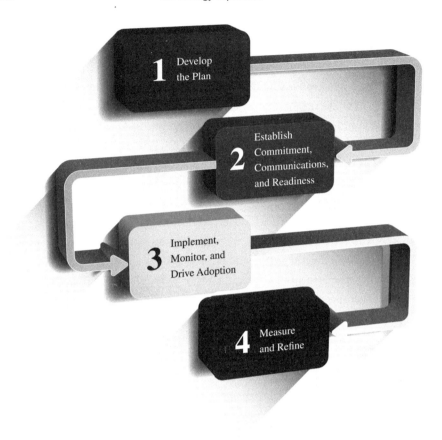

Figure 3.4   Implementing and Managing Change

Figure 3.4 illustrates the four primary steps involved in implementing and managing change. Let's walk through the steps.

The first step is to *develop the plan* to thoroughly address development and implementation of all involved enterprise elements. The plan should specify how, when, and by whom each redesigned enterprise element will be developed and implemented. Remember, a parallel implementation strategy is usually optimal, so make sure your plan includes enough people with appropriate expertise to tackle each of the elements. Now is the time to build a case for resources. The plan should include any activities necessary to establish an adequate level of readiness among those involved. Also include overarching activities, such as communication, training, and measurement. Finally, a risk management plan identifying risks, mitigations and avoidance strategies is an essential ingredient of being cautious.

The next step is to *establish commitment, communications, and readiness.* You don't want to leave the gate, look around, and find yourself all alone in your change initiative. A strong start is extremely important because you need to quickly build momentum, which is energy. Commitment, communications, and readiness will help you do that. In the second half of the book we discuss in detail the things within people that ultimately need to be aligned with the change initiative for it to be successful. While readiness for change does not assume full alignment, it does assume enough alignment and engagement so that people are at least motivated to start down the path of change.

Although it is important to achieve that initial level of commitment among the people involved, it is equally important to get a major commitment among involved leaders and managers to support and take appropriate responsibility for the change. At the leadership level, one bad apple can spoil the bunch, so do what you can to build management commitment. Communicate with all affected people in different ways to inform them about the change, why it is being made, how they will be involved and affected, what is expected of them, why it is good for the company, and what's in it for them. Mix broadcast messages with two-way communication (e.g., interviews, focus groups, and town hall sessions) to give people the opportunity to express their views. They may have misconceptions, which you can correct, and you will undoubtedly pick up some valuable information. It is essential that all of the messages delivered through these various means are consistent. Mixed messages have a way of fueling speculation, distrust, and rumors that work against establishing an adequate state of readiness.

Once you have achieved an adequate state of readiness, it's time to *implement, monitor, and drive adoption.* Depending on the size of the change, you may want to create a kick-off event to create positive buzz and momentum. Such events are usually part educational and part motivational. However you do it, you want to build energy. As you move through your implementation steps, you are doing three important things. First, you are monitoring the progress of the implementation work itself, solving problems, and making course corrections as needed. Second, you are monitoring people's reactions to the changes. As change happens, emotions are stirred, and people react in a host of "creative" ways that may get ugly. People may resort to overt or covert resistance, coalition building, lying, and diverting attention away from their mischief to avoid detection or responsibility. All of this is negative energy pushing back against your initiative. Therefore, it is very important to stay on top of these negative reactions and neutralize them whenever possible. If you utilize a parallel implementation approach, as discussed earlier, you will stifle much of the mischief before it begins and protect your energy reserves.

The third thing you are doing is driving adoption of desired skills, behaviors, and attitudes among those affected by the change. As discussed later in the book, you are not finished with your change until you have reached a sustained level of adoption. The best way to do that is to help people see and experience, as quickly as possible, how the new way of doing things will be good for them and the business. Continue to monitor the indicators of adoption, and influence people in ways that will move them along the change curve.

No implementation plan is perfect, and you can't anticipate everything that will happen. As adoption progresses, your initiative may run into problems or obstacles that require you to modify or further *refine* your enterprise elements. For example, in the Alchemy story, the regional team leads received additional training on supervision and project management, as these were new areas of responsibility and their initial performance as team leaders suggested that additional training was needed. In addition, incentives were refined to reflect a more detailed definition and understanding of roles in the sales process. Such refinements plug cracks in the dam to keep them from leaking energy. Let your compass always be the creation of shared space. That means being attentive to building alignment, reducing conflict, and mitigating obstacles.

Strategies for Creating Shared Space in the Enterprise

In this section we look at *general strategies* for creating shared space in a business enterprise. These strategies are broadly applicable to business transformation and change initiatives of any kind, and are things to consider and keep in mind regardless of the specific goals of your initiative.

Start with How People Need to Work

Helping people work and collaborate more effectively is usually our end goal. While it is profoundly important to recognize the power and influence that enterprise elements have on people doing work, it is not a good idea to start there. It is far more effective to start with how you want people to work, see what keeps them from working in that way, and design solutions to promote that way of work. For example, in the analysis and design phases of the Alchemy example, we recognized that we wanted people to sell in teams, not as individuals. This became the basis for the entire design. Although this may sound like a no-brainer, it isn't. People often miss or skip this step and, as a result, fail to effectively promote the way people need to work.

In chapters 4 and 5 we dive into the energy of work and the true nature of collaboration. These chapters provide considerable insight into and clarification of how people need to work so we can design the enterprise to support it.

Follow the Money

Earlier in the book we discussed the strategy of following the flow of money to find out how things work in a business. Money is energy, and money is power. The flow of money can detract from the way things should work, or it can promote it. The flow of money can breed conflict or promote shared space. Therefore, it is essential to map the flow of money to see how things currently work and then change the flow of money as needed to support the new design. But as I said before, we must be cautious. When you start messing with things like departmental budgets, you will get pushback, to put it mildly. Managers derive power and status from their budgets, and they often take any reduction as a personal threat.

The problem is that if we are really going to make a difference in our businesses, if we are truly serious about building shared space and business excellence, we sometimes have to slaughter sacred cows. One of the most common sacred cows is the budgeting process and the flow of money into division/departmental budgets. For example, companies with traditional hierarchical structures usually have difficulty making their teams work effectively because the flow of money is backward. It flows directly to the departments instead of the teams. The teams, which are responsible for executing projects and programs, have to beg and borrow resources (people) from the departments. Consequently, program managers don't really control the resources on the projects; departments control them. To fix this problem, to create alignment and promote high-performing teams, money should flow directly into the program budgets, and programs should buy (or rent, if you prefer) resources from the departments to staff their programs. The departments are likely to resist initially, protecting their sacred cow, but making this shift in the control of money is the necessary thing to do.

Another aspect of managing the flow of money is using money as a lever to choke off dysfunctional behavior in businesses. For example, I worked with a company that was facing significant pressure to keep costs down. We discovered that some organization managers launched pet projects to do new things without the knowledge and consent of senior company leaders. They were able to do so because the budgeting process was sloppy and left them with more money than they needed to perform their particular function in the company. To make matters worse, we discovered that several of these projects were being duplicated with competing pet projects in other departments. The company could ill afford this inappropriate and wasteful use of money. In response, we launched a zero-based budgeting process that effectively choked off funding for unauthorized projects. A lot of money was saved. The point of the story is that sometimes we can eliminate dysfunctional behaviors in businesses by choking off the money that feeds them. The flow of money can be a powerful lever of change that creates alignment of control and responsibility and a healthy flow of energy.

Target Conflict and Energy Leaks

As we have seen, unintentional conflict takes a huge toll on our businesses by wasting and draining energy. One strategy to improve performance and derive bottom-line benefits is to go after the conflict, see what it is telling us about the business, find the root cause misalignments, and adjust the enterprise to correct them. Whether you mount an organizational campaign to reduce conflict or do it within initiatives targeted at specific business goals, you would do well to adopt a systematic strategy for reducing conflict in your organization.

Similarly, as you implement change, you will want to be on the lookout for the many forms of energy leaks that may occur. Resistance, rumors, miscommunications, and unfettered personal agendas all cause energy leaks that can sabotage your change initiative. Covert resistance is the most difficult leak to deal with and potentially the most damaging. Watch for the indicators of this negative energy (e.g., attitude shifts, propaganda, alliance formation, etc.), and be ready to neutralize it whenever possible. Try appealing to the best parts of people first, but be prepared to deal with their ugly parts if you must.

Recognize the Whole Organization Chart

Whether businesses recognize it or not, when they start forming cross-functional teams to perform complex work, they have automatically become matrix organizations. The problem occurring at many companies is that they don't give much attention to designing and developing their matrix organizations, where people are hired into functional departments but do most of their work as members of cross-functional teams. One aspect of that problem is that they do not recognize the whole organization chart. Typically, their focus is on the functional side of the matrix, which looks very much like a traditional organization chart. People overlook that there is a project/program side to the chart that identifies who reports into what projects. Often those reporting relationships are not even recognized, even when people spend 80% or more of their time working on projects. This blind eye toward program reporting relationships disempowers teams and contributes to a major misalignment of control and responsibility, which of course promotes conflict. Even though the project/program side of the organization chart is dynamic as projects come and go and teams re-form, it is a good strategy to maintain the project side of the organization chart and give it adequate recognition and visibility. After all, in many businesses, the bulk of the work is accomplished by teams. *Where* the work is being done in a business should be a major area of focus as we align business energies to support the conduct of work.

Define Both Reporting and Customer Relationships

Businesses are generally adept at defining reporting relationships among their people. They typically do this with lines connecting boxes in their organization charts. However, another type of relationship often goes unidentified and unacknowledged in companies, in spite of its relative importance. It is the internal customer relationship. An obvious example of internal customer relationships occurs in businesses with shared service groups (e.g., IT, HR, finance, legal). Staff members in the shared service groups must recognize that those whom they support within the business are their internal customers, who should be treated no differently from external customers. This doesn't mean that staff members report to those internal customers; it means they *serve* those customers.

This distinction between reporting and serving is quite important as these are two very different kinds of relationships. Most people seem to automatically understand direct reporting relationships: "You are the boss. I work for you. You can tell me what to do. You can promote me or fire me." Although many managers work to downplay it, there is an authoritative element at the core of reporting relationships. This authority is not present in internal customer relationships. Customer relationships are, at their core, about service. People seem to easily understand this service relationship with external customers, yet they often have difficulty when their customers are internal. This difficulty usually boils down to the authority factor, or lack thereof. For example, "Why should I serve you when you have no authority over me? Why should I serve you when I occupy a higher position in the company than you do?" When people lack the understanding that authority has no place in a customer relationship, they tend to bring authority into the equation and find reasons not to acknowledge or honor internal customer relationships. When that happens, they aren't motivated to serve their internal customers.

This problem can be a very serious. In many larger businesses, for example, the value chains, which constitute major pipelines of energy, involve literally dozens of internal customer relationships. Every time an internal customer relationship is not honored and subpar service is provided, energy in the value chain is eroded. Multiply that by a couple of dozen internal customer relationships, and we have a major problem. That's why it is so important for businesses to define and incentivize internal customer relationships and for the people in the businesses to acknowledge and embrace them.

Embracing internal customer relationships is doubly important because making and keeping these relationships healthy is a major tool in creating shared space. A good example is related to the shift toward solution selling occurring at many product companies that bundle services with products to create custom business solutions. A common problem with solution selling is friction between the sales team, which sells the complex solutions, and the professional service group, which implements them. The professional service staff typically complain that "Sales sold us down the river" with a price that squeezes their budget and with customer expectations that they can't meet. Sales staff complain that the professional service staff don't help them enough with these complex sales. "After all," they reason, "the professional service staff are the experts in our products and services."

This is not a new problem. It's just getting worse and more visible as solution selling becomes more prevalent. Companies have tried all sorts of things over the years to solve this problem, usually with only marginal success. For me, following the energy on this problem led me to an insight that actually solved it. The key breakthrough was the definition of an internal customer relationship.

The solution requires a paradigm shift where a professional services design and planning team is assembled when a major sales prospect becomes an opportunity (e.g., when the customer wants a proposal). Whereas sales historically created the custom solutions and priced them at this point in the sales process, the planning team is now charged with designing, estimating costs, and planning the solution. That way, if the company wins the business, the professional services group owns the plan and is willing to be accountable for its implementation. The sales lead develops pricing (informed by the planning team's cost estimates) and bundles it with the solution and plan in the form of a proposal and/or presentation to the customer—with support as needed from the planning team. With this approach, professional services designs and plans, sales sells, and solution selling becomes a team sport. However, to make this work, we have to make sure everyone involved is motivated to do his or her part.

In this new sales paradigm, sales gives up control of the solution design, cost estimation, and planning. However, in exchange, the sales lead is recognized as an *internal customer* of the planning team. That means the planning team must ultimately please the sales lead as one aims to please any customer. The beauty of this customer relationship is that it allows planning team members to apply their detailed knowledge in creating the design and plan (who better?) while giving the sales lead an appropriate level of control and influence as a customer. To reinforce this customer relationship, the design and planning teams are given modest commissions on won business. Doing this helps to ensure that all are aligned to the

common cause, which, in this case, is making sales. When I first implemented this new sales paradigm in a business, revenue doubled in three
years. Profits also increased as the implementation projects, which were
now better planned and estimated, performed much better. The paradigm
has never failed.

This is but one example of where a defined internal customer relationship can have a major positive impact on the value chain. As you create
shared space in your enterprise, pay attention to the value chain and the
relationships of people along the chain. You will find that customer relationships often define their optimum dynamic. The trick then is to get everyone
to recognize and support those relationships with appropriate incentives,
expectations, training, and communications.

Align Control and Responsibility in Everything

We talked earlier about aligning control and responsibility to fix misalignments that breed conflict and drain the energy of the business. Because this
alignment is central to everything we do, the strategy here is to look for
misalignments *everywhere* and fix them when detected. Although it is unrealistic to expect perfect alignment in everything, it is appropriate to strive
toward that goal and use it to drive our understanding and solutions. In my
experience, finding and fixing misalignments never fails. Use this approach
as a compass and come back to it whenever you need direction.

Build Capability and Capacity

Many leaders and managers show little interest in building capability (what
we are able to do) and capacity (how much of it we can do). For most,
building capability and capacity is not as sexy as the execution side of the
business. Therefore, it is often given minimal attention, which, ironically,
cripples the ability of people and teams to execute. Furthermore, insufficient
capability and capacity is the root cause of a huge amount of inefficiency,
dysfunction, and conflict in business. It follows that building adequate capability and capacity is an essential ingredient for building shared space. An
investment of time and energy here will almost always pay off in a big way.

Make Operational Governance and Decision Making Explicit

We are used to the term "governance" being used at the board level. However, there is another huge area of governance that applies to decision making within the operations of the business. I call this operational governance. At the top of the food chain, governance relates to decisions about what products, capabilities, and major systems a business is going to invest in. At the working level, governance relates to decisions and decision-making authorities associated with even minor business processes. Add it up, and if governance isn't working well, conflict at all levels of the organization will grow. The key is to proactively render decision making explicit, to decide how each decision type will be made, and by whom, before the decisions actually need to be made. Targeting operational governance is a strong strategy that can lead to major benefits with a modest investment.

Drive Interpersonal and Collaborative Capability

The previous strategies relate mostly to improving the organization and operations of the business. However, we cannot ignore the impact of the people. Specifically, if we want them to be more collaborative and adept at delivering interpersonal services, we need to equip them with the necessary skills and drive the associated behaviors. Don't expect this to happen by putting people in front of online training modules. Developing collaborative skills and behaviors goes much deeper than knowledge into the realm of the interpersonal, where there is no one right answer. In chapter 5 we discuss in detail the type of interpersonal skills needed to enable effective interpersonal services, productive business interactions, and collaboration.

Chapter 4

Work and the Dimensions of Energy

Some years back I sat down with the CEO of a mid-sized technology company that had engaged my company to help with its stalled turn-around and its transition toward becoming a large company in a fast-growing sector. I was directly involved in the engagement, playing the roles of executive coach and organizational advisor. My interviews with a number of company staff and executives provided the fodder for my analysis of the company's situation and problems. I was now with the CEO, whom I will call Mark, to give him my preliminary report and advice. He was particularly interested in what was stalling his turnaround progress so I focused on that.

"Mark," I said, your company has been around for about 15 years and among your staff you have about 70 veteran employees who have been with the company most of that time. They know your products like no others and much of this knowledge exists only in their heads. Documentation is still pretty sparse, so they hold the keys to the kingdom. As I looked for areas of resistance to your turnaround efforts, I discovered that they informally formed a gang over the years that amassed tremendous power and exercised bully tactics when necessary to get what they wanted. This self-serving strategy revolved around their own job security, compensation, and comfort. They've been operating covertly and effectively, protecting the status quo. They want you to fail so they can keep things the way they are, and your highly visible reputation for firing people every time something goes wrong is not helping. They're afraid and are circling the wagons."

I named the gang the Underground Railroad and told Mark their attitude was that "CEOs come and go, but we stay. We are the real power in the company." I advised him to cool his habit of making employee terminations public events and solve the root cause problems, which I outlined for him, without overly threatening the veterans. "Get your products documented, take your power back, and then rock that boat if you still need to." Unfortunately, Mark didn't heed my advice, preferring his usual tactics over my suggestions. In response, the veterans dug in and the turnaround remained largely stalled. About six months later things caught up with Mark. The board removed him from his position and sold the company to a rival. It's never a good idea to underestimate people or to fail to adequately take them into account. In order to optimize any business, function, or change initiative, we must understand the energy that people bring to their work and strive to align it around common business goals.

The Dimensions of Energy in Work

Up to this point in this book, we have focused on the profound effect that enterprise elements can and do have on the way people interact in a business. They can promote effective interactions or they can promote conflict. Now we shift our focus to the work itself within the business. The enterprise elements that surround people are only part of the picture. As we discuss in this chapter, we, as people, bring things with us to our work that interact with the surrounding environment to determine the outcome of our work. This blending is the intersection of, and interaction between, the enterprise and the individual.

This blending of energies has an infinite number of possible recipes and outcomes. Throughout a business there are multiple people at any moment in time conducting or participating in work streams. Each work stream has an energetic makeup and outcome that contributes to the collective energy of the business. Ideally, we would like every single work stream to go well and contribute the maximum possible amount of positive energy to the enterprise. That being the case, first we need to understand the things that make up work so we can go about optimizing the work stream.

The Dimensions of Energy and Their Ingredients

The Dimensions of Energy in Work model identifies and organizes the various factors that are involved in, and influence the outcome of, work. The model is based on careful observation of people at work and the things that influence them along the way. As shown in Table 4.1, there are four dimensions of energy in work. The first one, the Environmental dimension, is what surrounds and externally impacts the work. Its ingredients are the enterprise elements that have been the focus of this book so far. (Although it is true that what happens outside the walls of a business affects the work within it, it does so through the four dimensions described here, so we address the energy of those outside factors within this framework.) The other three dimensions, Intellectual, Personal and Directional, are things about the person doing the work. The ingredients of these dimensions are personal attributes. Taken together, the four dimensions of energy determine the work accomplished in any given work stream. The energy of work flows through these dimensions and, as we will see, the nature of the dimensions determines the nature of the work outcome and the energy associated with it. The four dimensions of energy, their ingredients, and their contributions to work are defined next.

Environmental Dimension

The Environmental dimension is what surrounds the person doing the work, and *frames* the work effort. It is composed of the *business environment*, which is made up of the organizational, operational, and individual

Table 4.1   The Dimensions of Energy in Work

Work Dimension	Ingredients	Work Contribution
Environmental	Business Environment (i.e., the enterprise elements)	Framing
Intellectual	Clarity and Knowledge	Understanding
Personal	Intent, Attention, Engagement, Effort	Conducting
Directional	Skills and Behaviors	Navigating

enterprise elements. Together, these elements provide the field of play for doing work while also constraining it, sometimes appropriately (e.g., a well-designed business process) and sometimes inappropriately (e.g., a poorly designed system). The environmental dimension can and does have a profound effect on how people work.

Intellectual Dimension

The Intellectual dimension relates to what the person knows and *understands* about the work. Its two ingredients are clarity and knowledge. *Clarity* is the degree of understanding around what the business/unit wants and what the person is being asked to do to support it. *Knowledge* is the person's intellectual capability and understanding associated with the work to be done.

Personal Dimension

The Personal dimension is about the character, attitude, and effort that people bring with them to *conduct* the work. It drives their personal experience with the work, which can be anything from joyful immersion to disgust and avoidance. It has four ingredients. *Intent* is what the people intend to do and not do regarding the work, which encompasses their goals and agendas, personal beliefs and attitudes, and personal positions regarding the work. *Attention* is how much attention the people give the particular work versus other things, and has a lot to do with how much they value and prioritize the work. *Engagement* is people's interaction and relationship with organizational elements, operational elements, and people who are needed to and/or are involved in doing the work. And *effort* is their degree of action and intensity in accomplishing the work. As the name implies, the personal dimension is about our own characteristics, motivations, and attitudes. That makes it powerful and worthy of self-reflection as we do our individual work. Its partly hidden nature also makes the personal dimension more difficult to see and influence in other people.

Directional Dimension

Whereas the Environmental dimension is akin to the field of play, the Directional dimension relates to how the person doing the work *navigates* the field. The quality and impact of the navigation, and the choices made along the way, are driven by the *skills and behaviors* of the people doing the work. In particular, these are the skills and behaviors for doing the work and interacting with people and systems involved in the work.

The Big Picture

Figure 4.1 provides a big-picture view of the flow of energy in work. It shows how the four dimensions of energy are involved in any work stream. The ingredients that make up these work streams cluster into two major parts: the enterprise elements, which surround us and frame our work, and the more personal work elements, which we bring with us. The figure also illustrates how work becomes multidimensional when others

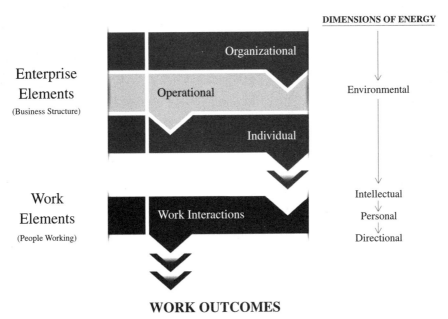

Figure 4.1 The Flow of Energy in Work

are involved. This complexity gives rise to the need for effective interactions and collaboration, which, of course, also affect work outcomes. (See chapter 5.) Overall, the figure illustrates the primary things and energies involved in work as a basis for both understanding and improving the conduct of work.

Next, we dive deeper into the dimensions of energy and some of their more important implications.

Implications of the Dimensions of Energy

The four dimensions of energy and their ingredients have a number of significant implications regarding work performance and management, talent management, change initiatives, enterprise design, performance improvement, and a host of other endeavors. We explore some of these implications here, starting with some general observations.

A Lot Going On

Taking the four dimensions of energy and their ingredients together, there is much more going on with work than meets the eye. When we recognize that every ingredient is constantly in play while a person is working, we begin to get a sense of the great swirl of energy that blends together to ultimately create the work outcome. No wonder managing ourselves and others can be difficult with all of that going on.

Good In, Good Out

The better the ingredients in the work stream, the better the outcome. Therefore, if we want to improve outcomes, we have to improve and align the work ingredients. We discussed the need for alignment among enterprise elements in the first three chapters. Now we extend that concept and need into the more personal elements of work. This concept becomes the basis for important performance improvement strategies for individuals, groups, and entire businesses.

Bad In, Bad Out

Deficiencies (misalignments) in any one or any combination of the ingredients in the work path will impede work progress and/or quality and/or speed. As is the case with enterprise elements, misalignment among personal work ingredients can lead to conflict, both internal and external. If we want to maximize work progress, quality, and speed, we need to be paying special attention to the ingredients with identified deficiencies that are not well aligned with the desired outcomes.

Overcoming Deficiencies and Obstacles

It is actually quite common for people in work streams to face deficiencies and misalignments in quite a few work ingredients while still producing an acceptable, albeit compromised, outcome. We learned this over the years teaching consulting skills to people in businesses. For example, we often observed significant dysfunction in the Environmental dimension that created pervasive conflict and made virtually any work much more difficult. In those organizations, the most valuable application of consulting skills was to help people get work done within their own dysfunctional companies and agencies. In other words, the new consulting skills and behaviors augmented the Directional dimension and gave people greater ability to navigate their work in a difficult environment.

Time and again these people overcame enterprise deficiencies to produce acceptable and, in many cases, very good work outcomes. Unfortunately, it took a great deal of energy to overcome the deficiencies, which made the businesses inefficient at best. The point is, overcoming obstacles and deficiencies is very common, very costly, and yet possible. The resilience of people at work can be quite impressive, but it comes with a price to them and the business.

Showstoppers

At the other end of the spectrum are the showstoppers, negative work ingredients that can stop a work stream or render it completely ineffective. Only one or a small handful of these ingredients can seriously impair work. This is true even if all of the other work ingredients are stellar and well aligned. For example, if a manager is part of a work effort that she does not agree with, she may simply never give it her attention. She may just let the effort die on the vine.

Showstoppers are often the stuff of personal agendas and office politics. However, they also occur more innocently. For example, someone simply may not have sufficient knowledge and understanding to complete the work. However they occur, showstoppers tend to be extremely wasteful. And in a political organization with a lot of conflict, they become weapons.

People who use showstoppers for their personal and political gain know intuitively that it takes a whole lot less energy to stop a show than it does to move it forward. This gives them considerable power and influence with relatively little investment of time and energy. Meanwhile, all of the energy that was invested in the work up until it was stopped is wasted; it produces nothing for the business.

Our Traditional Wisdom Isn't

As managers practicing surface-level management, our typical inclination when we see work that isn't going well is to attribute the problem to the person or people doing the work. Unfortunately, we typically don't go much deeper than that. In truth, sometimes the people are the problem, and sometimes they aren't. When we understand that the problem can lie in any one or a combination of work dimensions, we see how limited we are by our traditional "wisdom" and antiquated management techniques.

Often our best people bring more to the table than others in the Directional, Intellectual, and Personal dimensions. They are better able to overcome obstacles, especially organizational dysfunction and politics, to produce acceptable work outcomes. Others run into trouble where the star performers overcome, and we judge them as if they are wrong for not being stars. That is not to say that we shouldn't move out chronically poor performers, but it suggests that there are often better ways to solve the real problems. For example, if we redesigned some dysfunctional organizational and operational elements, we could eliminate some major obstacles so that people don't have to be such star performers to get their work done, nor would they have to invest so much energy to overcome obstacles.

Training

When people have problems with their work, businesses often respond with training. Training can help the Directional dimension (interpersonal skills and behaviors) and the Intellectual dimension (hard/technical skills). Training can have a major impact on improving work, especially when the primary deficiencies are in the Directional and Intellectual dimensions. However, when other deficiencies are present and involved, they erode the impact of the training if they are not addressed. Unfortunately, this is often the case. Worse yet, when the primary deficiencies are outside of the Directional and Intellectual dimensions (i.e., when they are in the Environmental and/or Personal dimensions), training provides, at best, a coping mechanism.

Performance Improvement

Performance improvement is most often associated with improving the efficiency of a business process, which is a type of work stream. Usually the process itself is modified to improve the outcome. This is effective when the process, which lies in the Environmental dimension, is the primary deficiency. However, when there are other deficiencies and they are left unattended, a lean process may not help much. The positive impact of the process improvement is eroded. Perhaps there is a knowledge deficiency in the Intellectual dimension, or a resource shortfall in the Environmental dimension. Or perhaps there is a pervasive attitude problem in the Personal dimension that impedes the work. In any event, performance improvement needs to be approached in a holistic fashion that considers all work dimensions.

Change Management

There are countless books and articles on change management, but there is no model that always works. Furthermore, when we look at the fact that a large majority of change initiatives fail or significantly underperform, we see that, on average, change management models contribute to failure more often than to success. What are we missing?

The answer lies in the dimensions of work and the many involved ingredients. One of the biggest reasons change initiatives fail is that most address only a portion of the ingredients involved and leave the rest unattended. Anything that requires people to significantly change the way they work challenges their personal ecosystem, and addressing only part of the ingredients without recognizing the overall system often makes people feel like the business just doesn't get it and doesn't really care about its people. Therefore, managing change is, by nature, multifaceted.

Unfortunately, many companies hang their hats on good communication to drive change. They invest a lot of time and effort communicating with people to ensure that they have a good understanding of what will happen, what is expected of them, and how they will be affected. The degree of their understanding affects (to some extent) their performance in changing the way they work. However, there is more to work than the Intellectual dimension. While it is not practical to crawl into people's heads to affect every aspect of their work, the insights we gain through the lens of energy do suggest that we look under the hood of work and rethink our paradigms for managing change. We address this further in chapters 6 and 7.

In General

Many more implications derive from the dimensions of energy and their ingredients. We covered some general ones here. One common characteristic among all of the examples is that the model provides significant new insights into how and why things happen, and don't happen, in business. Work is a complex blend of many ingredients. Each ingredient has an effect on the work stream. If we are to improve work streams, we must improve and align the work ingredients. But there is another factor we must consider when analyzing and choosing the best way to improve work streams. That factor, which we cover in the next section, has to do with the *interactions* between work ingredients.

One Thing Affects Another

In our discussion of work so far, we have characterized individual work ingredients much like one might characterize ingredients of a cake. Each has a standalone impact when mixed with the other ingredients. For example, if you add more sugar, you will have a sweeter cake. The separate ingredients largely determine the taste of the cake overall. This is all true for work as well. However, for both work and cakes, it is also true, and quite important, that the ingredients interact and affect one another, similar to chemical reactions. While this does complicate things to some degree, it can also help guide us in our approach to improving work streams.

It Rolls Downhill

To introduce this concept, we will go back to the Alchemy Instruments example, both before and after the problems got fixed, and look at it from our new perspective of work. Specifically, we will focus on how ingredients in the environmental dimension affect those in the Personal dimension.

Again, here is a summary of the original problem.

Alchemy Instruments is a scientific instrument company that manufactures and sells high-end electronic equipment to business clients across North America. It recently reorganized its sales force into two groups, the Product Group and the Regional Group. The Product Group is organized around the company's product lines, with subgroups for each line. Sales staff members in the group are instructed to sell their products to any potential client in the United States and Canada. The Regional Group is divided into six sales regions in North America. Those assigned to a region within the group are instructed to sell all of the company's products within their regions.

Although sales staff in each group were encouraged to work cooperatively with staff in the other group, problems began to surface in the field soon after the reorganization was completed. Members from both groups were calling on the same clients, cooperation and cross-group support was at best a low priority, and the VPs of the two groups were at odds. The two groups became polarized and competitive. Less time was being spent on selling and more time was being spent competing with those in their own company.

The root cause problem turned out to be the wrong sales paradigm (individual selling), which was created by a host of ingredients in the environmental dimension, from the organizational structure to business processes to incentives. Instead, a new (team selling) paradigm was needed. The old paradigm caused a great deal of unintentional conflict between the Product Group and Regional Group and the people within the groups.

Now, with that background, how did all of these dysfunctional Environmental ingredients affect the Personal ingredients of an individual in one of the groups? The short answer is that they had a major impact on the personal ingredients. The longer answer lies in an analysis of the four ingredients in the Personal dimension: intent, attention, engagement, and effort. While there is certainly variance among people in the groups, this analysis focuses on the pervasive characteristics across the groups.

Intent

The SVP of Sales, who engineered the reorganization, wanted people from the Product Group and Regional Group to work together. He encouraged it. However, given the environmental circumstances, that was the last thing they wanted to do. They were incented to sell individually, not cooperatively. Furthermore, as the divide between the two groups widened and competition heated up, there was a disincentive to working with "those other guys." The intent for the individuals in the groups was to do as much individual selling as possible and "may the best people and group win."

Attention

People tend to put their attention on what is most important to them. In accordance with their intent, the salespeople put most of their attention on individual selling. Conversely, they paid little or no attention on doing things that would promote cooperative selling. They were not interested in building relationships with the other group, teaming up on sales calls, or doing much of anything that would take them away from their individual selling.

Engagement

Again, the SVP wanted people from the two groups to engage each other and work together to engage the clients. While there were some attempts to do this early on, people who tried it met with disappointing results. Remember the Product salesperson who stood up a Regional salesperson in a client meeting? The Product salesperson had "better" things to do (i.e., individual selling). A barrier formed between the groups and their people, and any attempts to engage the other group fell by the wayside. The only engagement that mattered was engagement with external clients.

Effort

Given the state of the other three Personal ingredients, you can imagine where people did and did not apply effort. They did apply effort to individual selling. Except for a short time following the reorganization, people did not apply effort to cooperative selling.

Now, given the state of the Personal ingredients among the salespeople involved, what were the chances that cooperative selling was going to work? It simply wasn't going to happen. The Environmental ingredients drove the behavior of the salespeople toward individual selling and created a breeding ground for conflict.

From this story, you can see that the ingredients in the Personal dimension were profoundly affected by those in the Environmental dimension. Personal ingredients that live within people contain receptors, sensing devices that are influenced by environmental conditions. While the environmental conditions provide the triggers for unintentional conflict, people ultimately choose how to react to those conditions. The more inclined people's Personal ingredients are toward conflict, the more difficult it is for them not to engage in conflict when triggered. In this story, we essentially rolled out the red carpet to conflict. The only chance to avoid it was for a person to mitigate this trigger/receptor relationship between the Environmental and Personal dimensions with a strong set of skills and behaviors in the Directional dimension—plus a lot of fortitude. Only then, with a great deal of effort, could someone navigate the sea of potential conflict.

A Success Story

Now we fast forward our story to its happy ending, when the real problems were fixed and cooperative selling was working. We will examine how the newly designed set of involved enterprise elements (Environmental ingredients) had a much different effect on the Personal ingredients.

The team selling paradigm had been fully implemented. This paradigm affected the same Environmental ingredients that were previously involved in the old paradigm. Now they were redesigned around the new operational concept, implemented with a coordinated plan, and adopted by the sales staff. Sales were up, and the mood was very upbeat. Let's look at how the four Personal ingredients were transformed due to the new influence from the redesigned Environmental ingredients.

Intent

The salespeople were now incented to work cooperatively in a team selling paradigm. They could no longer derive compensation from individual selling. Furthermore, they could see that team selling was working. Their intent now was to make team selling work better and better. They wanted relationships with those in the other group to be strong, as they could see how this helped them work better in teams. They wanted their own individual reputations to reflect that they were team players who could be counted on to do their part well as members of sales teams. They were still keenly interested in having strong client relationships, but they understood that no longer meant trying to do everything needed to make a sale and being the only point of contact in the company. They shared ideas and success stories with each other and set their sights on continuing to improve team selling performance.

Attention

Attention followed intent and was squarely on team selling.

Engagement

The salespeople engaged each other and the clients in new ways. Because relationships with those in the other groups (and their own) were important to them, they reached out frequently to initiate cooperation and engaged each other with mutual respect. They worked as teammates on the sales teams. They engaged clients now within the context of their individual roles on those teams.

Effort

Instead of spending time fighting and competing with those in the other group while protecting their individual selling turfs, salespeople focused their efforts on team selling and collaborative work. These efforts were rewarded with success and higher compensation.

What a difference in the work streams of the salespeople. This scenario illustrates how people change. In the business world where change is constant, it is essential to understand the inner workings of people and how they are affected by what is around them in the business. *This story shows us that our change initiatives are not complete and sustainable until the four ingredients in the Personal dimension come into alignment with Environmental ingredients designed to bring about that change.* The change is not complete until we have adequately changed the work streams of the individuals involved.

We need to use this understanding—that some work dimensions and ingredients affect others—to design our business transformation strategies, sequencing, and plans. It's all about energy and about how one thing affects another.

In the next section we look at how this new perspective can help us understand work stream issues at a deeper level so we can improve them through sustainable change.

Optimizing Work Streams

In order to optimize a work stream, we must first diagnose it to understand the work ingredients and their deficiencies/misalignments. We can then take action to minimize or eliminate deficiencies while aligning the involved work ingredients overall. However, not all work streams are created equal. There are three types of work streams. Each type has its own level, purpose, and optimization approach. The three work stream types are:

1. **Individual work stream.** This is the work of an individual person. Improving an individual work stream is about improving the performance of a person in the business.
2. **Common work stream.** A common work stream is one where multiple people do the same work. This is often a repeatable business process for individual work. Improving a common work stream is about improving the combined performance of everyone involved in a particular kind of work.
3. **Collective work stream.** A collective work stream is a combination of different people performing different work streams in support of a larger common goal. Teams, in their many forms, are usually associated with collective work streams. A collective work stream is often summarized by a schedule with various tasks and timeframes. Improving a collective work stream is about improving the work of a team.

In this section we look at examples of each type of work stream and discuss strategies for diagnosing and optimizing them.

Individual Work Streams

Improving individual work streams is a common goal for us as individuals doing work as well as for managers with people whose work streams could use some improvement. Both target individuals and their performance. Either way the impact will be on a single person's work. While the impact of this improved energy within the overall enterprise may be relatively small, we must remember that every single person in the business can have a positive impact, and all of that energy adds up quickly. Even though individuals can't fix everything on their own due to the fact that they are surrounded by enterprise elements outside of their control, they can do a lot. Essentially they have control over the Directional, Intellectual, and Personal dimensions.

Improving your own work stream is somewhat easier than improving someone else's work stream. First, you are obviously privy to your Personal ingredients. With a degree of introspection, you can evaluate your intent and what drives it: goals/agendas, personal beliefs/attitudes, and personal positions about the work. You have direct access to that information. You are also aware of how much attention you give to the work stream, your tendencies toward engaging other people and things related to the work, and how much effort you put into it. In addition, you are largely in control of what you know (Intellectual dimension) and where you go (Directional dimension).

When we, as managers, embark on improving another person's work stream, we don't have that level of control, nor do we have a front-row seat into the person's thoughts. We must use the *indicators* of the energy flowing through people and their work streams (i.e., their work characteristics and quality, behaviors, patterns, attitudes, verbal and written messages, body language, etc.). It is easier to be unbiased and objective when helping others improve their work streams. When considering our own work, our well-honed defense mechanisms can kick in at any time and give us blind spots that don't help us improve. With this in mind, pairing a motivated individual with a manager or coach to develop their work streams is usually most effective.

Improving a work stream starts with diagnosing the problem(s). At one end of the spectrum, individual work stream diagnosis and improvement can be simple and fast; at the other end, it can be quite complex. We begin with some simple examples and then move toward complex ones.

Here are some simple examples of work streams gone awry that are quickly diagnosable:

- At the last executive team meeting, the president asked team members to create a one-page report on the top five problems they are challenged with and to bring it to the next meeting to discuss. At the next meeting, everyone had their report except the Marketing SVP. When the president asked the SVP about it after the meeting, the SVP remarked that she had a lot of meetings last week and couldn't get to it. When the president asked the SVP what she thought of the assignment, the SVP said it was fine but she didn't see how it would help anything in her case. What was the problem ingredient on the work stream? A lack of *Intent*. The SVP probably never intended to complete the assignment in the first place due to her negative opinion of the work.

- A high school principal asked teachers to access some of the school's new online courses to get a feel for how they worked and to share any problems or issues at the next faculty meeting. The principal told the teachers that the person who led the implementation of the courses was available to show them how to navigate the system and encouraged them to meet with him before they reviewed individual courses to avoid getting lost. At the next meeting, the principal was surprised that only about half of the teachers had reviewed the courses. After discussing the matter, it turned out that almost every teacher who had completed the assignment sought out the help of the system implementer, while the teachers who didn't complete it neglected to seek help. A few tried to access the system on their own but gave up. What ingredient in the work stream was the problem? It was a lack of adequate *Engagement*. Both the implementer and the system needed to be engaged before a course review could occur.

■ A skilled and experienced program manager known to have a high level of motivation has been assigned to manage five programs. Two of her programs were experiencing delays. When asked about it, the PM said that those two programs seemed less important than the other three, so she spent less time working on them. Where is the problem in the work streams for those two programs? *Attention* or, in this case, lack thereof. But there was no attitude problem that would suggest the PM didn't care or had some issue with the work. In this case, we must look a little deeper at the root cause of inadequate attention to the two programs. Clearly the PM didn't have enough time to go around. She was over-assigned. This wasn't her problem to solve. It is a resource issue in the Environmental dimension. This story reminds us that we are not necessarily finished with our diagnosis when we identify the problems in the Personal dimension. To be thorough and accurate, always look deeper for interactions and the real cause and effect.

From these examples, you can see that by applying the Dimensions of Work model to a particular circumstance, we gain clarity on the what, why, and how that gives us a laser focus into understanding and solving the problem. The model is a framework for understanding the flow of energy in a work stream. We can see where energy is obstructed (e.g., lack of intent or adequate engagement) and when it is insufficient for the work to be done (e.g., resource shortages). And we can see that the energy in work dimensions (e.g., Environmental dimension) affects those in others (e.g., Personal dimension).

Even given the relative simplicity of these examples, it is amazing how often we misdiagnose problems. Faced with problems, managers often react with a general frustration that "these people are not doing what I want them to do." Quite often their interventions are to repeat their orders, tell the person to fix the problem, or assign it to someone else. You can see from these examples that such general, uninformed interventions miss the mark. By looking at work streams through the lens of energy, we can avoid such mistakes and solve the real problems optimally.

Table 4.2 **Work Stream Analysis Tool**

Work Dimension	Ingredients and Root Cause Deficiencies	Planned Improvements and Recommendations
Environmental	Involved Organizational Elements	
	Involved Operational Elements	
	Involved Individual Elements	
Intellectual	Clarity of Work Assignment	
	Knowledge/Understanding of Work	
Personal	Intent (goals/agendas, personal beliefs/attitudes, and personal positions)	
	Attention	
	Engagement (with others and things related to the work)	
	Effort	
Directional	Technical Skills and Behaviors	
	Interpersonal Skills and Behaviors	

Individual work streams can and do become more complicated than the examples given for two reasons. First, when the work itself is complex, a work stream naturally becomes more complicated. Second, the work stream of even a simple task can become complicated when there are deficiencies and misalignments in several work ingredients. Either way, when things are complex, it helps to use the Work Stream Analysis Tool to diagnose the problems and plan the solutions. As shown in Table 4.2, the tool essentially lists the four dimensions of energy and their ingredients and provides space to list root cause deficiencies associated with specific ingredients as well as planned improvements and recommendations for each. To illustrate how to use this tool, we use the story of what initially seems like a simple work stream but is ultimately complex.

John Brown took a position as the VP of Operations for a midsize information services company. His position was responsible for all of the company's programs, of which there were four types: revenue producing (contracts), product development, system development, and internal change initiatives. To provide visibility up the chain, John's boss, the president, asked John to provide a monthly report with status on all of the active programs. The work stream we address in this story is the generation of the monthly report.

John pulled his directors together in a meeting to find out what systems and processes were in place to provide the information he needed for the report. The directors described a process where program managers provided their reports to their director and the directors compiled the information to generate reports for the VP. The VP then compiled those reports into the monthly operations report. That all sounded good and logical to John. He then asked the directors what information was provided in the reports. They said that each program report contained a description of activities/accomplishments/issues that occurred over the past month, planned activities for the upcoming month, and three status stoplights, which provided overall status for the program schedule, deliverables, and cost. Green meant everything was going as planned, or better. Yellow meant there were potential or emerging problems. And red meant there were significant issues (e.g., deliverable error, behind schedule, cost overrun).

John decided to go with that process to get information to develop his next monthly report. He asked his directors to send him their reports one week before his report was due. They agreed. However, the first time around, the reports dribbled in. John had to send out multiple reminders and was forced to start on his report before he had received even half of the needed information. The final reports came in one day before John's report was due, giving him little time to digest the information. He also noticed that every director used a different style and format for their reports; there was even more variance among program managers' reporting styles. Many described the details of their programs in great detail, and the directors didn't seem to be doing much to summarize or standardize the information. As a result, John ended up with over 100 pages of input.

John shuddered at the thought of delivering a 100-page monthly report but didn't have much choice, at least for this first report. Although he was quickly coming up to speed on the business, he had much to learn. He didn't yet know enough about the business to differentiate important from less important program details. For now, he had to leave it all in. The stoplights were the only thing that provided an overall status summary, so he decided to emphasize those in the executive summary of his report.

John finished his report two days late and sent it to the president, who read the entire report. In a subsequent conversation, the president thanked John for the report and kindly mentioned that it was "full of information." John said that he wanted to look at his process for creating the monthly report over the next few months to shorten it and make sure both he and the president were getting the information they needed while not having to wade through unnecessary details.

As John analyzed his work stream over the next few months and experienced life among the programs, he discovered a disturbing trend. Long-term programs that had consistently reported green stoplights were suddenly reporting red in one or more categories as they neared the end of their program periods. Cost overruns were threatening John's profit goal, and schedule delays were causing problems with clients. John dug into the problem and analyzed the programs. He discovered that program managers did not have enough granular visibility into the status of their programs and realized that the problem began with how the typically year-long programs were planned.

In the program plans, a big chunk of money (the program budget) was associated with a big chunk of work (all of the work to be done on the program). Consequently, program managers would color their cost stoplights green as long as they had money left in their budgets. When they neared the end of their programs and the money ran out before the work was done, they switched the stoplights to red. When this was reported in the monthly reports, managers were surprised all the way up the chain. John had little confidence that his monthly report was providing an accurate picture of project status, much less an early warning system. Furthermore, nobody could tell what parts of the program work were causing the cost overrun. The problems and resulting overruns could have occurred almost a year ago and only now were their impacts being revealed.

John knew that to solve the problem and give his program managers adequate visibility into status, the programs had to be planned in a more granular fashion. The planning process had to divide the work into smaller component pieces, with each piece being associated with the budget needed to do that work. That way, problems impacting budget could be identified early and dealt with then, when a difference could be made. John used the Work Stream Analysis Tool to document the deficiencies in the four dimensions of energy and identify planned improvements for each. Table 4.3 shows his analysis.

After completing his analysis, John marveled at the situation. The relatively simple monthly reporting work stream had uncovered a can of worms due primarily to the several dependencies his work stream had on Environmental ingredients. But John was grateful for the information and perspective his analysis provided. He knew that without making these changes, he could never be confident in his monthly report, much less in his ability to do his job effectively.

This work stream is a good example of why things that seem like they should be relatively easy, like a monthly report, can be difficult and frustrating. A surface-level manager may react to this situation and his expectation of easy by putting pressure on the directors to stop the surprises or else. The directors would then roll that pressure and fear down to the program managers. The program managers' monthly reports might get even longer as they try to document anything that could go south so that, if it does, they can say it wasn't a surprise. There would be a lot more yellow in the stoplights, a cover-your-ass maneuver to be able to say "I warned you." But none of this would really solve the problem. It would, however, cause a huge amount of conflict and blame.

The work stream in this story, which started out looking like a relatively simple individual one, is actually dependent on the other two types of work streams: common and collective. The individual work stream itself is relatively simple. Looking at John's analysis in Table 4.3, the individual work stream is focused on the VP refining the monthly operations report process and content while continuing to learn the business. The other ingredients in the analysis are related to the common and collective work streams that support the creation of the report. These additional work streams cannot be ignored because, as they say, garbage in, garbage out. That reality applies to energy and monthly reports. The VP has little choice but to lead the

Table 4.3 Monthly Reporting Work Stream Analysis

Work Dimension	Ingredients and Deficiencies	Planned Improvements and Recommendations
Environmental	**Involved Organizational Elements** ■ **Culture:** The culture among the program managers and directors is one of passive, reactive management. **Involved Operational Elements** ■ **Program Delivery:** The programs are not being planned with enough granularity to enable proactive program management. ■ **Essential Producing Processes:** The various functional processes involved within the programs are poorly designed and documented and are prone to inconsistencies. ■ **Functional Capability and Capacity:** The program planning and management processes are cursory and insufficient to meet the needs going forward. The monthly reporting process is in a similar state. ■ **Technology/Systems:** The new way of planning will exceed the capabilities of spreadsheets for scheduling and tracking.	■ In concert with implementing the improvements below, conduct a communications campaign, first among program managers and directors, and then among all staff, to announce, define, and reinforce new, proactive program planning and management expectations and procedures. ■ Correct this overarching problem by executing the improvements listed below. ■ To enable consistent, granular planning, more clarification is needed in the functional processes to create repeatable building blocks for program schedules. ■ The program planning and management processes will be reworked to provide guidance for the new way of planning and managing programs. A new monthly reporting process will be designed and implemented. ■ A program scheduling tool will be acquired and implemented to support the new planning process.

(Continued)

Table 4.3 *(Continued)*

Work Dimension	Ingredients and Deficiencies	Planned Improvements and Recommendations
Environmental, Cont.	**Involved Individual Elements** ■ **Technical Knowledge/Expertise:** Program managers and directors lack the specific knowledge and expertise on the new program planning and management processes. ■ **Performance Expectations:** Current performance expectations are vague and allow for last-minute surprises and reactive management.	■ Develop custom in-house training on how to plan and manage programs using the new processes and tools. Train the program managers and directors and all new-hires. ■ Develop written performance expectations for program managers and directors that embody proactive management and implementation of the above measures.
Intellectual	**Clarity of Work Assignment** ■ N/A **Knowledge/Understanding of Work** ■ VP is learning the business but still lacks sufficient knowledge of the work and programs to differentiate important and unimportant program details and to identify appropriate content for the monthly operations report.	■ VP will continue to learn the business through discussions with directors, program managers, clients, and peers.

Personal	**Intent (goals/agendas, personal beliefs/attitudes, personal positions)**	
	■ N/A	
	Attention	
	■ N/A	
	Engagement (with others and things related to the work)	
	■ Following current culture, the initial level of engagement between the VP and directors is transactional and not sufficient to change behavior.	■ VP will set up quarterly program review sessions with directors and program managers and weekly one-on-one meetings with directors to promote the change.
	Effort	
	■ N/A	
Directional	**Technical Skills and Behaviors**	
	■ N/A	
	Interpersonal Skills and Behaviors	
	■ The VP is still learning about the norms and expected behaviors in the company and does not yet understand how those affected will receive the change.	■ VP will meet with the other VPs and the president periodically to learn about norms and expected behaviors from them and seek their help and cooperation on managing changes.

necessary changes in the common and collective work streams. Let's look at those in more detail.

Common Work Streams

Common work streams are usually business processes, whether they are well designed and documented or just evolve naturally over time in the course of work. They involve multiple people doing the same thing. Usually the quality of the process design and its level of documentation determine how closely people follow a common process versus everybody doing it their own way. Sometimes the problem in a common work stream really is the process. But other times it is more than the process, or the problem may not even involve the process. That is why it is always important to evaluate all of the dimensions of energy in a work stream.

Our story includes three common work streams that provide inputs into the monthly operations report work stream: program planning, program management and oversight, and the program manager and director portions of the monthly reporting process. In each case there is a need and a goal for the people to *do things the same way.* That doesn't mean we want people to become nonthinking robots. It means we need a level of consistency in how people do these things in order to make the larger system work. Taken together, these three common work streams make up the bulk of what program managers and their directors do. Therefore, adjusting these processes is a big change for the group. It is, in fact, a culture change, which is why a culture shift is indicated in the analysis in Table 4.3. It also includes changing and bringing consistency to the way programs are planned, managed, and reported on; developing new capability and capacity among the program managers and directors, acquiring and implementing new scheduling technology, and developing new technical knowledge and expertise in the area of program management. To help promote the change, new (higher) performance expectations will be developed and communicated, and the VP will develop a deeper level of engagement with his staff.

What the table does not mention are the involved ingredients in the Intellectual, Personal, and Directional dimensions of the directors and program managers. There are two reasons for that. First, this book is not intended to be an exhaustive cookbook, and we don't want to bog down in details here. Second, the analysis is a good representation of a first pass done from the perspective of John, the VP in this story. John was understandably focused on his own Intellectual, Personal, and Directional dimensions.

What would ideally happen next, now that the existence of multiple common work streams has come to light, is that the Work Stream Analysis Tool would be applied separately to each common work stream, with ample attention to the more personal dimensions of energy in the work streams. These analyses would, of course, focus on the people who execute those work streams—the directors and program managers. This step becomes even more essential when a change of this magnitude is contemplated. Remember, we are not finished with our change until these personal ingredients are aligned with the Environmental ingredients and our desired work outcomes. Left unattended or partially addressed, the more personal dimensions of energy have a way of pulling things back to the way they were. Addressing these dimensions is often the difference between temporary and sustainable change.

Collective Work Streams

Collective work streams are becoming more and more common as businesses continue their shift toward the use of teams, especially cross-functional teams, to accomplish complex business endeavors. The basic strategy is to build teams with talent representing the various functional disciplines needed to complete the project or program. The functional team members, either formally or informally, bring with them the business processes needed to do their work on the program. When these processes are well defined and documented, usually by functional departments or centers of excellence that own the disciplines, it is much easier to plan the work of a program, and the planning can be done in a much more granular fashion. Conversely, when the functional processes are undefined or poorly defined and documented, functional work on the program can become a mystery to the program manager, who is probably not an expert in each functional area. Under these circumstances, program plans tend to be high level and vague. That brings us back to our story.

Our VP, John Brown, recognized that the programs themselves were collective work streams. They were composed of cross-functional experts performing a variety of work within the scope of the programs. The program plans were, unfortunately, vague. The program managers did the best they could, but the functional processes were not well defined or documented, so the work of the functional experts was largely a mystery. Furthermore, the work seemed to vary from person to person. Everybody had their own way of doing things. In short, the functional work streams that made up the programs were poorly defined, had a lot of variance, and were not sufficient to support the level of planning needed.

John flagged this problem in the essential producing processes section of his analysis. His discussions with the functional leaders further revealed that getting the processes better defined would be challenging. He knew that when the Personal dimension of energy among the functional experts was mapped out, it would reveal significant issues in the area of intent. Many of the leaders enjoyed the power of having the functional knowledge in their heads. From their perspective, it gave them value to the organization, which protected their jobs. Making that knowledge explicit for all to see would take that power away and make them feel vulnerable. Another obstacle was that people liked having the ability to do things their own way and perceived a consistent process as overly restrictive.

In spite of these obstacles, John knew that life would actually be better for the functional experts once his changes were implemented. Their work would be more effective, the teams would operate together much better, rework would drop, and errors would be avoided. Their new sense of value would come from the excellence of their work instead of the control of knowledge. The program managers would have the information they needed to create granular plans with better estimates and staff allocation. In executing those plans, the program managers would know when schedule, cost, or quality was threatened so they could take action immediately to resolve the problems. And, finally, John would have confidence that his monthly operations report was giving him and others visibility into the proactive program management that would make the programs highly successful. At last, John's individual work stream would be all it needed to be.

Although John knew that the effort to work with the functional departments to better document their processes would be substantial, he also knew it would pay big dividends. And, for the company this story is modeled after, it did.

Optimizing the Dimensions of Energy

In this chapter we took a deep dive into the nature of work. We viewed work as a flow through the four dimensions of energy—Environmental, Intellectual, Personal, and Directional—and defined the ingredients in each dimension. We saw that each dimension contributes importantly to the work but can also block or starve the overall flow of energy. We also explored how profoundly the energy of the Environmental dimension, which surrounds the people doing the work, can affect the Personal dimension in those people, both positively and negatively. And we parsed out the three types of work streams—individual, common, and collective—and used a story and a tool to illustrate how to approach optimizing each type.

Within all of this discussion, some significant insights emerged:

- **The need to understand how work works.** We took a deep dive into work because good work is what we want people to do in business. That sounds simple enough, but what is amazing is how limited our view of work has been. Now the moving parts in work have been revealed, giving us powerful new visibility, insight, and tools to optimize it.
- **The contribution of people.** While the role and impact of the Environmental dimension in work is huge, the role and impact of people is also huge. In the business of optimizing work, we should never look at one without looking at the other. In the end, people are needed to do the work. They need to be understood, managed well, and taken care of.
- **The nature of change.** The world is full of change initiatives and business transformations that don't stick. In the end, they create little sustainable change. Many have studied and written about this problem and have no doubt contributed wisdom to the matter. Most offer a list of reasons why initiatives fail. Unfortunately, however, the success needle hasn't moved much at all. One thing we've been missing is the fact that change is not complete or sustainable until the dimensions of energy and their ingredients are adequately aligned. We explore this idea further in chapters 6 and 7.

■ **Avoiding surface-level management.** Most leaders and managers learned surface-level management in business school or on the job. It has been the norm in business for many years. As we explore the energy of business, we see just how limiting that has been. At the surface, where the view is limited, we misdiagnose problems, take actions that don't resolve the real problems, and hurt people and business performance in the process. And, until now, no one was the wiser. Now that the lens of energy has given us new wisdom and insight, we have an opportunity to move away from surface-level management toward managing the energy of business.

In the next chapter we explore the final aspect of work, the interactions among people.

Chapter 5

Collaboration and Interpersonal Services

One of the most memorable collaboration experiences I have had occurred in 1999 when I was invited to participate in a knowledge management training session hosted by Kent Greenes, SAIC's newly minted chief knowledge officer. There were about 15 of us in attendance, all open and eager to taste the cutting edge of knowledge management. The environment was ideal for learning and collaboration, and the group had bonded during our morning activities. In the afternoon Kent divided us into three teams of five people each and explained the rules of our next activity. Each team would be given a box of small wooden blocks, some wooden skewers, rubber bands, and a small stuffed toy rabbit. A cute story that went along with all of this escapes me, but overall the object of the game was to use the materials to raise the rabbit as high off of the table as possible. As a test of strength, the structures were required to withstand an earthquake, which was to be simulated by dropping a phone book on the table next to the structures. There would be three rounds of play, and the team with the highest rabbit at the end of each won the round.

Kent assigned the teams to private rooms with no windows and started the clock on round one. My team struggled a bit in the beginning but then seemed to find its collaborative groove. We built a platform out of the blocks, fastened the skewers to the top of the platform using the rubber bands, and then mounted the rabbit on the tip of the highest skewer.

It was our masterpiece. Kent called time and then he and another judge visited each room, simulating the earthquakes and measuring the heights of the rabbits. We came in second place, and were determined to improve in the next round. Kent brought the teams together into a neutral room and encouraged each team to ask the other teams questions about how they approached the activity. This gave my team some valuable insights, as the other two teams had thought of strategies and approaches that we hadn't. Armed with that new information, we jumped right in to round two, hitting our stride immediately. We again came in second place but, more important, all of the rabbits were substantially higher than they were in round one. What was strikingly clear was that the internal collaboration within each team, augmented with the cross-group Q&A collaboration, was a powerful recipe for learning and innovation.

In preparation for the final round, Kent had the entire group visit each of the rooms to see each team's creation and ask questions about it. I found the ingenuity of all three teams to be quite impressive, each in its own way. After this show-and-tell, Kent sent us back to our rooms and started round three. Armed with the innovation secrets from the other two teams, my team went to work to put our rabbit into the stratosphere. Every aspect of our contraption had a purpose and strategy that emerged from all we had learned and experienced during the activity. In the end, our rabbit was over twice as high as it had been in the first round, and all three rabbits were inches from the ceiling. It was absolutely obvious and undeniable that the collaboration had produced something much greater than the sum of the parts. Granted, we were collaborative people in an ideal collaborative environment, but the activity showed us all what is possible when agendas and energies are aligned and people are unencumbered in their expressions of creativity. Although it is unrealistic to expect a home run from every business collaboration, our collective challenges suggest a relatively urgent need to move in that direction.

The Importance of Collaboration

We started this book by highlighting a growing need in the Fourth Industrial Revolution for people to become more effective at collaboration and interpersonal services. Based on our definition of collaboration in this chapter, all interpersonal services are a form of collaboration. In collaboration, people with common and aligned goals have a series of *interactions* that ideally lead them to the achievement of those goals. That's also the case with interpersonal services, the essence of which is mutually beneficial collaboration. For example, a sales interaction is a form of interpersonal services. The salesperson has a goal of selling something, making money, and pleasing customers. Customers have a goal of figuring out what product or service they need and buying it for a fair price. Thus, the salesperson's and the customer's goals are aligned. The collaborative interaction is about exploring options, identifying the best one, and then negotiating the price and terms of the deal that leaves both parties satisfied. The whole experience is a mutually beneficial collaboration. Therefore, improving our ability to collaborate also improves our abilities to provide interpersonal services.

We also discussed a variety of ways that organizational, operational, and individual elements, the Environmental dimension of energy, can and do affect the way people in business interact with one another. It is clear that if we want people in business to have productive interactions and to optimize the management of energy in the business, we must consider all of the enterprise elements and do what we can to optimize them. Nevertheless, at the end of the day, interactions are among people, and no matter how well or poorly the enterprise elements are designed, people have the power to make or break business interactions. Their positive interactions can grow shared space, and their negative interactions can erode it. Therefore, we turn our attention now toward these interactions and their relationship to collaboration.

Collaboration continues to be a big topic in business, and people generally understand the need for it. This is true probably because when collaboration doesn't exist, it's usually quite obvious. People are at odds, not on the same page, angry and frustrated, and not making much progress in the work at hand. Most observers would say, "We need more collaboration here!," and they would be correct. Unfortunately, the way to accomplish collaboration can be elusive. This chapter shines some light on why that's the case and what we can do about it.

The Types of Collaboration

Research, literature, articles, and sales pitches on collaboration define and approach the topic in very different ways. Although there is some general agreement on the positive effects of collaboration that we are all looking for, there is certainly no agreement on what it is and how to accomplish it. Therefore, we start here with a short discussion on the different types of collaboration and some definitions to clarify our area of focus.

This truncated definition of collaboration from BusinessDictionary (2019) does a good job of summing up the many definitions out there:

Collaboration is a cooperative arrangement in which two or more people work jointly towards a common goal.

What we find, however, is that there are different methods and forums for working jointly. Specifically there are three primary types of collaboration: institutional, asynchronous, and dynamic.

Institutional collaboration is when the entities collaborating are businesses, educational institutions, and/or government agencies. While individuals are obviously involved, the key distinction here is that the interactions are primarily about group-to-group conversations and relationships.

The interactions associated with *asynchronous collaborations* do not occur at the same time, thus the term "asynchronous." For example, people making contributions to a Google Doc may do so hours, days, weeks, or even months apart. Software developers may upload and download software modules to and from a common managed software repository throughout the project's life cycle. The primary characteristic of asynchronous collaboration is that responses to others' comments and input are seldom, if ever, immediate. Responses are separated by time. Another characteristic of asynchronous collaboration is that transactions run the gamut from transactional (e.g., here is my software module), to interpersonal (e.g., a thoughtful email reply to a sensitive subject). A final characteristic is that asynchronous collaboration often involves one or more collaboration tools.

With *dynamic collaboration*, interactions occur in real time—at the same time. For example, meetings (in person and virtual), phone conversations, and problem-solving sessions involve real-time interactions. These interactions tend to be reciprocal and more personal in nature. Responses to one another are immediate and in the moment.

A Focus on Dynamic Collaboration

Each type of collaboration is important, and all are growing more important each year as business continues its shift from independent and transactional work to shared and collaborative work. Our primary interests in this book are the interpersonal aspects of all three collaboration types. However, to help simplify the discussion, we'll focus primarily on dynamic collaboration, with the understanding that this material is relevant to the other two types to the degree that they involve the interpersonal dimension. Why focus on dynamic collaboration? Because dynamic collaboration, due to its real-time nature, creates and is impacted by energy in a very immediate and significant way. It not only carries energy from the surrounding enterprise elements, which may or may not be in alignment, but it also has a dynamic relationship to the energy associated with the interactions themselves. This direct relationship can involve the creation of shared space or, on the other side of the equation, conflict. Either way, it involves the creation of an interactive momentum, which is all about energy.

In addition, dynamic collaboration permeates business affairs broadly. Consider the number of meetings, presentations, creative sessions, and customer conversations that occur every day in business. Whether dynamic collaboration is done well or poorly, it occurs at every level of the organization and in a variety of forums and formats. Therefore, improving dynamic collaboration capability in a business can have dramatic positive results with huge return on investment potential. In short, dynamic collaboration is a powerful lever of change worthy of our investment and attention. Furthermore, it is our future.

If we are to improve dynamic collaboration in our businesses, it is essential to clearly understand how it works. To do that, we must, as we have done so far in this book, look at and observe it from the perspective of energy.

The Collaboration Dynamic

The energy flow of collaboration is essentially a self-adjusting system that can work to our advantage or disadvantage, depending on the nature of the interactions. It turns out that what is being adjusted within that system, the thing that can breathe life, creativity, and power into the collaboration, is shared space. This is not theory. The presence of shared space is something we have all felt and experienced. Consider this scenario:

You are meeting with a colleague to discuss an important business problem and work out a solution. The conversation is going well. You seem to have common ground and goals. You're working together toward those goals. It seems easy. You feel a connection and a camaraderie. You get the desired results—or even better!

This is shared space in action. The more it is present during an interaction, the easier things seem to go, and the better the outcome. Shared space is an energy, and therefore it is invisible to most people. However, its effects can be seen and felt, and we are all capable of creating it through our positive interactions. We are also capable of eroding shared space and creating conflict through our negative interactions. Our goal then is to have more of the positive and less of the negative.

To do that, it is important to understand the system within which collaboration works so we can ultimately grow shared space and promote more effective collaborations. We call this system the Collaboration Dynamic. Figure 5.1 illustrates the Collaboration Dynamic at work.

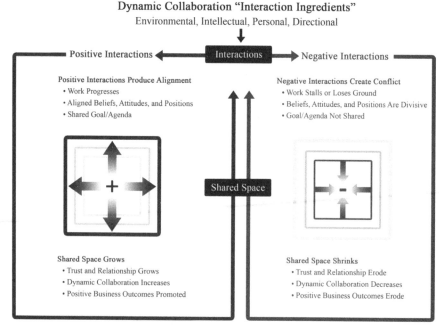

Figure 5.1 The Collaboration Dynamic

The Dynamic Overview

The ingredients of work contained in the four dimensions of energy are also the ingredients involved in our interactions. Here we refer to them as the interaction ingredients. As is the case with work, a subset of ingredients are typically the primary players in a given interaction. The short story of the Collaboration Dynamic is that we start with a set of involved ingredients as if we are baking a cake. We, as people, bring the personal ingredients to the dance, and the rest exist around us in the business environment. When the interactions begin, these ingredients come into play *as we allow them to*. Some ingredients or combinations foster positive interactions that produce alignment and build shared space. Other combinations foster negative interactions that create conflict and erode shared space.

But that isn't the end of the story. We don't have collaborations for the sake of creating shared space. We have them to create positive desired outcomes with others. So here is the connection between shared space (or conflict at the other end of the spectrum) and outcomes. Shared space and conflict are not just the result of the interactions. Once created, they also become *additional ingredients* of the interaction. Shared space makes it easier to create more shared space, and the positive outcomes flow easily. Conflict breeds additional conflict and, without intervention, can drag the entire collaboration down a rat hole. The trick to collaborations is to stay ahead of the power curve. Doing so has a host of implications for how we can promote better collaborations. We will come back to that later. First, we'll walk through the Collaboration Dynamic in more detail and relate it to experiences we have all had in order to see it in action and understand its power.

Interaction Ingredients

As shown at the top of Figure 5.1, the dynamic begins with the interaction ingredients. Again, these ingredients are the things that surround and influence the interaction as well as the personal attributes that we bring with us. We view these ingredients now within the context of interactions.

At the top of the list are the *Environmental ingredients*. These are the enterprise elements at work—organizational, operational, and individual. As discussed earlier, the ways enterprise elements are designed and developed can have big impacts on the people in the business. These impacts, positive and negative, help set the stage for the interaction. For example, if the business has a collaborative culture, that ingredient will undoubtedly give the interaction a greater chance of success. If, in contrast, the culture is more about conflict and competition, that characteristic will likely reflect in a less successful interaction.

The *Intellectual dimension* includes clarity, the degree of understanding around what the business/unit wants the person to do, and knowledge—the person's degree of knowledge and understanding associated with the work to be done. Misunderstandings about what needs to be done or insufficient knowledge to perform the work will negatively impact the interaction. A strong Intellectual capability will support positive interactions, unless it is overdone. Too much intellect without the personal and directional capacity to utilize it properly can lead to unnecessary pontification and competition to be the smartest person in the room. Having a good balance is the key.

The *Personal dimension* is composed of goals and personal agendas, personal beliefs and attitudes, and personal positions regarding things or people related to the work. This is a critical dimension when it comes to interactions because the ingredients can have a lot of energy pointed in either the same or the opposite direction of collaboration. The ingredients of the Personal dimension are outlined below as they relate to the collaboration dynamic.

- **Goals and personal agendas.** We all have goals and personal agendas. There are two types. The first type, one that may or may not be present at the start of an interaction, is a shared goal. For example, if a scheduled meeting is about planning the next executive team offsite, we may come with a shared goal of building an agenda. Having a shared goal identified up front is clearly beneficial to the interaction. But this is not the case with every interaction. Perhaps someone didn't get the email or simply doesn't agree with the goal. That can throw a wrench into the conversation. The second type of goal and agenda is personal. It would be easier if we were all robots and could leave our personal goals and agendas at the door in favor of a common goal. Interactions would tend to go much better. However, as humans, it is unrealistic to expect personal goals and agendas to disappear during interactions. They will certainly be present, but as we discuss later, what becomes important is whether and how we allow our personal goals and agendas to affect our side of the interaction.

- **Personal beliefs and attitudes.** Again, we all have personal beliefs and attitudes, and we don't leave those at the door. If I am a consultant about to meet an executive who hates consultants, I am headed for a difficult conversation. The best I can hope for is to persuade the executive that I'm not like those other consultants and find a common interest that will help build rapport. If the executive likes to bring in consultants for help with specific needs, that orientation helps open the door for a strong collaboration.
- **Personal positions.** Personal positions are our positions on issues related to the conversation we are about to have. If we are to discuss where to move our facility, and I live on the south side of town, I may have a position that the new building should be on the south side of town. If you favor the north side of town, we have a significant challenge going into the interaction. Although that doesn't mean there is no hope for agreement, it will require effort and engagement on the part of both parties to find common ground.

The *Directional dimension* consists of the skills and behaviors that we have for, among other things, conducting and participating in collaborative interactions. They will be addressed in some detail later on, but suffice it to say that these skills and behaviors can have a major effect on the quality and outcome of our interactions. Regardless of the personal stuff we bring to the table, a strong set of skills and behaviors, along with a positive intent, can go a long way toward promoting a successful collaboration.

Fixed versus Flexible Ingredients

It is important to note the different nature of the various interaction ingredients, because some are more fixed than others. Specifically, those in the Environmental dimension (enterprise elements) and the Directional dimension (interaction skills and behaviors) are essentially fixed. While they will change over time, they will not change during the course of a conversation. Conversely, the ingredients in the Intellectual dimension (clarity and knowledge) and the Personal dimension (goals/agendas, personal beliefs and attitudes, and personal positions) are subject to change *during* the conversation. In successful collaborations, this movement is usually an indication of establishing greater alignment among those involved. Therefore, adjustments in the flexible interaction ingredients are a natural part of the Collaboration Dynamic. Each ingredient starts out one way but may be quite different by the end of the collaboration. That, in turn, becomes an important part of the ultimate outcome.

For example, let's say two members of Congress are collaborating on how to draft a particular bill. One is a Democrat and the other a Republican. They start off intellectually by each representing their party lines, which means they are intellectually at odds with each other. In the Personal dimension, each has a certain mistrust and distaste for the other because they are on the other side of the aisle. In spite of these initial divides, they share information and educate each other, which helps them find common ground on an approach for the bill. As their Intellectual alignment grows and they get to know each other through their interactions, they start to build a mutual respect that begins to neutralize the "other guy" posture they both started with. Before you know it, they are shaking hands in agreement and scheduling the next steps to move the bill forward. In the course of their successful collaboration, their Intellectual and Personal dimensions shifted in a unifying direction.

It's clear that some interaction ingredients morph and change during collaborations. The cake we start to bake isn't always the cake we end up baking because some of the ingredients change right there in the mixing bowl. And that can be one of the most beautiful and even magical things about a good collaboration! We have all seen and experienced it—a better outcome than we could imagine when we started.

Given the potential for the interaction ingredients to combine with detrimental effects, though, collaboration can be difficult and elusive. Nevertheless, the dynamic also reveals a number of clues about how to have good and productive interactions.

Interactions in the Collaboration Dynamic

Now that we clearly understand our interaction ingredients, let the collaboration begin. All dynamic collaborations are composed of a series of interactions among those involved. The nature of these interactions will, to a large extent, determine the outcome of the collaboration. At the extremes there are two types of interactions, positive interactions and negative interactions. As shown in Figure 5.1, positive interactions build alignment among those involved. You see the work progress more smoothly; the beliefs, attitudes, and positions of those involved become more aligned; and your shared goal and agenda become clarified and strengthened. Beneath the surface, shared space grows. There is greater trust and relationship, dynamic collaboration becomes easier, and positive business outcomes emerge.

At the other end of the spectrum, negative interactions create conflict. You see the work stalling or losing ground; the beliefs, attitudes, and positions of those involved become divisive; and the goal and agenda that was supposedly at the center of the collaboration is not being shared by all or perhaps by anybody. Looking more deeply, shared space shrinks. Trust and relationship erode, collaboration becomes more difficult, and business outcomes are headed in a negative direction.

As a practical matter, not every interaction falls at the positive or negative extreme. Those extremes are two ends of a continuum, and the quality of an interaction may fall anywhere in between. In other words, any interaction may embody both positive and negative characteristics. However, it is the sum of those characteristics that gives an interaction its prevailing direction.

Because collaborations are a series of interactions, and because some interactions may be positive and some may be negative, the energy of collaborations may actually switch back and forth between positive and negative. Thus, the Collaboration Dynamic is indeed dynamic.

In the next section we apply the Collaboration Dynamic to some example collaborations and explore the implications of "seeing" and understanding collaboration through the lens of energy.

Applying the Collaboration Dynamic

In the previous section we discussed how collaboration works with a detailed review of the Collaboration Dynamic model. In this section we use the model to examine examples and approaches for what we can do before and during collaborations to help optimize their outcomes. Then, in the following two sections, we identify and describe collaboration skills for one-on-one and group collaborations and discuss how we can improve our own skills and/or the skills of those in a group or an entire business.

The relevance and value of the Collaboration Dynamic model comes alive when we use it to better understand and improve actual collaborations. The Collaboration Dynamic does this in several ways:

How Collaboration Works

- The Collaboration Dynamic explains how collaboration works with a model that maps the factors involved, their interplay, and how both positive and negative outcomes may occur.
- It shows us concretely why we alone cannot ensure a successful collaboration but can promote one through our interactions.

Before a Collaboration

- The Collaboration Dynamic suggests approaches to setting the stage for a more effective collaboration.

During a Collaboration

- The Collaboration Dynamic provides a tool for evaluating why and how a collaboration we are in or are observing is working and/or not working.
- It suggests possible actions to improve a collaboration that is having challenges.
- It helps us understand our contributions (positive and negative), and the contributions of others, in collaborations.

Improving Collaboration Skills

- The Collaboration Dynamic provides a context for assessing our collaboration skills as a foundation for further development.

To illustrate how all of this works, we now apply the model to two specific collaborations.

The Spiraling-Downward Collaboration

As discussed earlier, collaborations generally have a momentum that results in the growth or shrinkage of shared space. Shared space tends to promote even more shared space, and vice versa. We start with an example of a collaboration that gets off on the wrong foot and spirals downward from there, as if it were being pulled into a dark hole by a tractor beam. Here's the story.

A network technology company, Net Superior, experienced an embarrassing problem on one of its client implementation projects. The system had a major flaw that brought down the client's network for 24 hours during a critical time for the company. Similar problems had occurred on other

Net Superior projects twice during the past six months, and the CEO was concerned about this repetitive pattern. He pulled the SVP of Professional Services, Mark Watson, and the chief technology officer, Steve McMahon, into his office to discuss the problem. Mark was responsible for all of the client implementation projects, and Steve's Technology Department provided IT resources to the projects. The CEO told Mark and Steve that they needed to work together to figure out the problem and make sure it wouldn't happen again.

Mark met with his project manager in charge of the troubled project to get her take on what went wrong. She told Mark that the problem was a network design issue caused by the tech lead assigned to her project. Separately, Steve met with the tech lead for a briefing on what happened. The tech lead told Steve that the project got behind schedule and the project manager made a decision to skip the design review. When Steve asked him why the project was behind schedule, the tech lead said that, at the time, he was assigned to four different projects and just couldn't keep up.

Mark and Steve were both somewhat relieved after their preparatory meetings. The prospect that the problem originated in their areas of responsibility had them fearing for their jobs. The CEO was taking heat from the board on this issue and was known to act swiftly and abruptly. Mark and Steve scheduled a meeting for the next day for the stated reason of sitting down to collaborate on understanding the problem and finding a suitable solution. Privately, however, both men had a primary goal of protecting themselves and their jobs by pushing to get their personal positions acknowledged and agreed to by the other guy. The stage was set.

The next day, Steve and Mark walked into the conference room and sat down on opposite sides of the table. They chatted briefly about the weather and their latest golf games. The nice talk ended there. Steve opened by saying he didn't have a lot of time and there was no need to discuss the problem. He knew what it was. Mark, who could already feel the blame, responded in kind: "I know what the problem is as well, a network design issue!" "Yes," Steve said, "but it happened because your project manager cut corners and skipped the design review." Mark responded loudly, "And she wouldn't have had to do that if your guy hadn't been so far behind schedule in his design work! How many projects did you have him assigned to?"

At this point the conversation was going downhill fast. Stepping back, Mark decided to take another tack. "Steve," he said, "we're supposed to find a solution here and we can't even agree on the problem. Why don't we start over?" "Sure," Steve replied. "As long as we can agree that the problem was your project manager's corner cutting." "Really?" said Mark. "You can't see that because you haven't hired enough technology leads, the projects are shorthanded and falling behind schedule?" "Your people manage the schedules," Steve stated defensively. Seeing the futility of the conversation, Mark pushed back from the table and said, "Well, I guess we will just have to agree to disagree." With that, the "collaboration" was over.

This is obviously a fairly extreme example, but, unfortunately, it is not uncommon. Let's review what happened. How does the Collaboration Dynamic model help us understand why things went so poorly?

First and foremost, due to the circumstances and the nature of the interaction ingredients, the deck was stacked against this collaboration from the beginning. The stakes were high and fear was abundant. The business culture—the CEO's tendency and reputation for abrupt action—made this a job survival issue. There was little room for a common goal, as the survival of both men depended on making the other wrong. Both men came into the interaction with strong personal positions that were unlikely to change. Although it is possible under such conditions to pull out a successful collaboration, the odds are very low.

All of this played out as the real conversation began. Personal positions and agendas quickly took center stage. The conversation went immediately to conflict as Mark and Steve essentially fought each other for their jobs. That made them each other's enemy, so there was clearly no trust, relationship, or shared space. Mark made an attempt to rescue the collaboration when he suggested they start over. Unfortunately, the collaboration had too much negative momentum for that to work. Steve held onto his position, and Mark could see that any real collaboration was futile.

Steve and Mark remained in their positions, feuding from that point on. The CEO never figured out what the problems were because both men had plausible stories. He didn't manage the energy, he tried to manage the personalities. He kept trying to get the men to work things out. Ironically, it was the CEO who could have done more than anyone else in the story to promote a good collaboration and solve the real problems. To show how that would work, let's rerun the story with some modifications to the interaction ingredients and the interactions themselves.

The Truly Effective Collaboration

In this version of the story, we modify one collaboration ingredient, the company culture and the CEO's tendency to blame and create an environment of fear. Here we endow our CEO with a deeper understanding of how things work, a desire to get to the bottom of the real problems, and a stated position that it is OK to make mistakes occasionally as long as you learn from them and don't make the same mistakes again. When he pulled Mark and Steve into his office and asked them to collaborate, he made all of this abundantly clear. Mark and Steve knew that even if the problem originated in their areas, they would be OK as long as they fixed it. This launched a collaboration that had every chance of success.

What Mark and Steve heard from their people about the problem was the same as in the first version of this story. Mark's implementation project manager told him that the problem was a network design issue caused by the tech lead assigned to her project. Steve was told by his tech lead that the project got behind schedule and the project manager made a decision to skip the design review. When Steve asked his tech lead why the project was behind schedule, he said that, at the time, he was assigned to four different projects and just couldn't keep up. At that point Steve could see there were problems on both sides of the fence and that his insufficient supply of tech leads triggered the project manager's decision to omit the design review, a mistake on her part.

When Mark and Steve scheduled a meeting for the next day to collaborate on understanding the problem and finding a suitable solution, they had no hidden agendas. Their goal truly was to solve the problem together. Steve and Mark walked into the conference room and sat down at a corner of the table. After exchanging pleasantries and a few laughs, they got down to business. Mark opened by saying that his project manager told him the problem was a network design issue caused by a mistake on the part of the tech lead. But he qualified it by adding "With that said, I am not sure I have all of the information here, and I'd like to hear what you know." Steve replied that he received some information from his tech lead that indicates the cause of the network design issue was multifaceted. With a generous demeanor, Steve said that he believed the problem started because his tech lead was overassigned and fell behind on his work on the problem project. The project manager then decided to cut out the design review to make up lost time on the project schedule, an unfortunate decision.

Mark thanked Steve for his research and analysis. He told Steve that while he knew a design flaw was involved, he did not know the circumstances around it. Steve commented that he had been aware of the need for more tech leads and that he was having trouble recruiting for those positions. Mark admitted that his project manager should have never cut a design review and that her authority as a project manager did not include omitting essential process steps. Steve agreed and replied, "It seems we now have a good understanding of the problems. Why don't we talk about how we will correct them and make sure they never happen again?" Mark replied, "That sounds good to me."

Steve said that, first and foremost, he would work with HR to engage an outside recruiting firm to fill the open tech lead positions. "That will solve my problem right now," he said, "but it's not enough to ensure that resource shortages won't occur in the future. I need some kind of a heads-up warning system that will help me know, with as much advance notice as possible, that we are headed for shortages in a given area of expertise." Mark said, "I can put in place a process whereby my project managers notify me if they are experiencing shortages on their projects, and then I can pass that information to you." Steve liked the idea and told Mark he appreciated his offer to do that. Steve added, "But that still doesn't give me much advance notice, certainly not enough time to recruit new staff. While I think we should do it, I think what we really need is a capacity management system that looks six to twelve months out at our resource needs on the projects and translates that into needed headcount in the various functional areas." Mark said, "That's a great idea! We can propose that as a new improvement initiative." Steve agreed.

Mark next said that he would need to clarify protocols for his project managers on what they could and could not do on their projects. For simplicity, Steve suggested Mark could make a rule that the managers could not ask or pressure functional experts to cut corners on defined and approved functional processes, like design reviews. Mark agreed and said he would include that. He added that he would launch the newly refined protocols with training and communication sessions in his group. Steve liked the idea and suggested his people attend as well. Both men agreed.

Mark said, "Let me try to sum this all up and you tell me if I miss anything. You are going to work with HR to engage a recruiting firm and get your vacancies filled. I will implement a process that will notify me, and then you, when resource shortfalls occur on the projects. And we will both meet with the executive team and propose a new initiative to develop a capacity management system as soon as possible. I will clarify protocols for the project managers and roll out training and communication sessions that my people and yours will attend. Does that sound right?" "Absolutely!" Steve replied. "Let's go tell the boss we figured it out!" Both men felt relieved and energized. They shook hands and went to see the CEO.

This was a great collaboration, a far cry from the first round. The story illustrates some central points about collaboration.

- **Leadership matters.** The only difference in the starting ingredients between the first and second versions of the story was the style and position of the CEO. In the first case, he instilled a culture of fear and blame, which strongly influenced the personal agendas and positions of both men. In the second case, he fostered a culture of excellence and collaboration, which encouraged and motivated both men to hold the common goal—understanding, resolution, and prevention—as their personal goal. That made all the difference in getting the collaboration off on the right track and keeping it there.

- **Clarification of knowledge and understanding.** As discussed above in the description of the Collaboration Dynamic, some interaction ingredients are fixed while others are subject to change during the collaboration. The knowledge and understanding of the problem's root cause and solution grew throughout the collaboration. In particular, Mark's initial understanding, which was limited to the existence of a design flaw, expanded quickly as Steven explained the two factors that caused the flaw.

- **Changing intent.** Similar to the expansion of knowledge and understanding, Mark's intent changed during the interaction. He started with an intent and expectation that he and Steve would be focused on the actions of the technology lead and how to prevent people in that role from making design mistakes. As the collaboration proceeded, his intent changed as he realized there were multiple root cause issues to resolve.

- **Shared space.** You can see how shared space is reflected in virtually every interaction within the collaboration—both the creation of shared space and the boost that the existence of shared space gives the collaboration. On the side of creating shared space, Mark and Steve choose their words carefully out of mutual respect, limited their assumptions and stayed open, listened to each other and made remarks that were additive to the collaboration. Regarding the boost from shared space, you can see and feel the collaborative momentum build as the men reached a common understanding of the problems and made a string of agreements on what to do about them. The men were literally joyful at the end, and they created a beautiful business outcome that met, and probably exceeded, their goal.

As we compare and contrast these two stories, we recognize that the quality and nature of many collaborations fall between these two extreme examples. Many can go in either direction and may even flip back and forth between positive and negative. Some collaborations are saddled with issues in the Environmental and Personal dimensions, yet people can and do find ways to overcome them and achieve good business outcomes. To what do we attribute this ability to overcome adversity? Most often it is due to the power of the Directional dimension of energy.

The Power of the Directional Dimension of Energy

The ingredients of the Directional dimension of energy are the skills and behaviors that allow people in business to conduct work and collaborate. The dimension has much to do with a person's ability to create shared space while navigating obstacles and overcoming negative energy. This realization became abundantly clear after our many years of teaching consulting skills to professionals across industries. Teaching people things like empathy, how to consider the preferences and characteristics of other people, having good conversations, and building alignment within groups is all about navigating work and collaborating with powerful energy in the Directional dimension.

The many HR groups we have worked with over the years are good examples of how developing the Directional dimension can make all the difference. A popular trend in HR is to help what you might call traditional HR professionals who are used to a more transactional style of work become trusted HR business partners. HR business partners are typically assigned to a line manager and tasked with learning their part of the business and serving as a focal point for the more strategic aspects of HR. Although they may not articulate it this way, line managers think of these HR business partners as partners only if they understand their business, know their people, and, perhaps most important, have the ability to navigate complex interactions and business solutions. Line managers quickly grow tired when they are the only ones on their team who seems to be navigating complex work and collaborations. Line managers welcome skilled HR business partners who can take some of the load off.

There are many more examples in business where Directional skills and behaviors make the difference between a trusted business partner with great value and an order taker. That's why training in collaboration skills should focus on the Directional dimension with an eye toward overcoming obstacles and negative energy in the other dimensions.

We turn now to a discussion of collaboration skills, first for one-on-one collaborations and then for group collaborations.

One-on-One Collaboration

Effectively working one on one with others and providing interpersonal services ultimately boils down to the quality of our interactions. In general, if the interactions go well, the collaboration goes well. If the collaboration goes well, the work at hand gets accomplished and the stage is set for additional positive collaborations with that person. In contrast, if a conversation goes poorly, work is impeded, conflict often occurs, and future interactions with that person are burdened by the negative experience. The goal, then, is for our individual interactions and collaborations to go well. While this goal is absolutely realistic, it is formidable because there are so many ways to derail a conversation that was intended to be collaborative. We often feel an energetic shift and perceive negative cues in ourselves and others when our conversations derail. Here are some reactions to common derailers.

- You don't understand me. I don't feel like you know or care about me and my needs here.
- We don't seem to have common ground. I see that you have your own agenda.
- You talk at me, not with me.
- You seem to talk from a script, with little or no reaction to what I say.
- You tried to bully me.
- You only care about having the right answer and being the smartest person in the room. You don't budge from that role. Often I want something different or more than that.

- I see that you're trying to influence me, but it doesn't seem very relevant to me and my situation.
- I don't trust you.
- I'm not sure if I trust you.
- You don't seem to be aware of your impact on me or other people.

The question becomes this: How do we avoid such derailers and instead interact in ways that promote positive and effective collaborations? Here are some examples of reactions to the "positive" side of the collaboration equation.

- I felt like you understood me and my needs.
- You seemed to take my needs into consideration as much as your own.
- You are a good listener.
- You made me feel appreciated and valued.
- You built me up rather than shooting me down.
- The more we talked, the more I felt comfortable with and trusted you.
- I feel like we connected in our unspoken communication.

Each of these positive reactions is an indicator that we created shared space during the collaboration. We create shared space with another person when we focus on the bigger picture and the common good we can create together, not just on our own agendas. But how do we build and monitor shared space throughout the collaboration? That takes us back to the Directional dimension of energy.

Building Shared Space with Others

Some people intuitively know how to build shared space with another person during a collaboration, even if they aren't familiar with the shared space concept or term. However, if you ask them to tell you how they do it, you are likely to get a fairly general, nonspecific response. The reason for this general response is that it is difficult to describe what is often a very complex interplay. We need a way to bring it to the surface and make it explicit. In this section we use the Dimensions of Energy Model to help explain what goes on in a typical collaboration so that we can first understand and then use the model to help people collaborate more effectively. As you will see, there is both an art and a science to collaboration.

Building shared space during a collaboration requires careful communication that considers all four dimensions of energy, Environmental, Intellectual, Personal, and Directional. However, some dimensions require more focus than others. Because they are subject to change during the collaboration, we must pay particular attention to the Intellectual and Personal dimensions. Environmental factors are fixed during collaborations. Although they can clearly create obstacles and negative energy that impact interactions, or vice versa, they generally do that *through* the Intellectual and Personal dimensions in people. How do we keep an eye on these energies, process their meaning, and respond accordingly? We do this through the Directional dimension.

The trick in one-on-one collaborations is to navigate the creation of shared space from the Directional dimension to promote a co-creation that modifies Intellectual and Personal ingredients in one or both people. Take the effective collaboration story with Mark and Steve, for example. During the collaboration, both men made Intellectual adjustments as their interactions revealed a deeper understanding of the problem and identified the components of the solution. Similarly, the Personal dimensions of both men changed as they solidified a common intent to implement their agreed-upon solutions. Because of positive Environmental factors (i.e., the CEO's creation of a collaborative culture), both Mark and Steve were motivated to do their part in navigating the collaboration. Thus, a characteristic of effective collaborations is that Intellectual and Personal factors come into *alignment*.

Strong collaborators who are able to build such alignment have well-developed and powerful Directional dimensions. These dimensions have two primary parts. The first part is the Observer. As its name implies, the Observer observes everything going on in the interaction and is aware of the surrounding environment. The Observer monitors the status and direction of the conversation, including the buildup or erosion of shared space. Observers also pay close attention to the Intellectual and Personal dimensions in others *and* themselves. The ability to observe ourselves means Observers have a degree of *independence* from the other dimensions, a very important characteristic.

The second part of the Directional dimension is our Guide. Whereas our Observer watches passively without judgment, our Guide processes the information and decides how to respond. In deciding how to respond, our

Guide considers input from our Intellectual and Personal dimensions, and from those of the other person, and decides what should be represented in the next response. For example, my Personal dimension may be chattering away with "I don't like that guy, and his tie doesn't match his socks." If my Guide is reasonably well developed, it would likely filter that and not let it influence my next response. Similarly, if my Intellectual dimension is screaming "That is a stupid idea!," my Guide would not filter it but would be much more diplomatic in the presentation of that in my response, especially if my Observer was picking up that this guy really likes his idea.

Like our Observers, our Guides have a degree of independence from the other dimensions. The level of a person's independence in their Directional dimension has a lot to do with how well they are able to collaborate. For example, if I have little independence, I will have little ability to filter my personal agenda and hold it lightly in favor of a common collaboration goal. Conversely, if I have a high degree of independence, I can choose not to engage in conflict triggered by something in the Environmental dimension. Independence in the Directional dimension is a discipline that comes through awareness, practice, and experience. This independence is not about us becoming cold and machinelike. To the contrary, it is about bringing the best of our human elements to the table while avoiding those that would unnecessarily damage the collaboration. It is about building shared space, achieving business outcomes, and effectively playing our role as people.

Some people who meditate practice their ability to move into what is called the third person, a place of detachment where they are able to passively observe the chatter of their minds without engaging it. Being in the third person is quite similar to the independence and detachment ideally present in the Directional dimension. Thus, those who meditate may feel that the Directional dimension is familiar and may find that collaboration comes more naturally.

Essential Collaboration Skills

What are the essential skills and behaviors that make up the Directional dimension? What skills are needed for navigating collaborations and creating Intellectual and Personal alignment with others? While many skills may fall within the umbrella of collaboration, we focus here on the essential skills and behaviors. We can boil that down to a relatively simple recipe: Me, You, and Us. These are the basic ingredients of any interaction, so it makes sense that the essential skills fall in these three areas. Here is a summary of essential collaboration skills, which all fall into the Directional dimension.

Me

Self-awareness is essential for effective collaborations. There are two parts to this self-awareness. The first part has to do with what we bring intellectually and personally to the collaboration and how we prepare ourselves for it. We will discuss that here. The second part has to do with monitoring ourselves *during* collaborations, as we just discussed. We address specific skills associated with that in the "Us" section below.

In the Intellectual dimension, we have knowledge, ideas, opinions, and intellectual biases related to a given topic of collaboration. In the Personal dimension, we have personal goals and agendas, beliefs and attitudes, and personal positions regarding the topic of collaboration. First and foremost, it is important to know where we stand in these areas. This is especially true with regard to our Personal attributes, which have significant emotional origins. Although it may be convenient to ignore them, doing so is likely to backfire in a collaboration. Ignored Personal attributes tend to come out sideways in collaborations, often at the most unfortunate times. So the first skill in the Me department is self-awareness.

The second skill has to do with preparing for the collaboration. This has to do with our intent regarding the collaboration, as governed by our Directional dimension. Understanding our Intellectual and Personal attributes is a start, but then we must ask ourselves some fundamental questions.

- Will my Intellectual and Personal attributes, if brought to the collaboration, support what I understand to be our common goal?
- If not (i.e., I have Intellectual and Personal attributes that will work against our common goal), what am I willing to do about them going into the collaboration?

Regarding this question, there are a variety of things to consider in addition to adopting a genuine willingness to collaborate. For example, in the Intellectual dimension, if you know your ideas and opinions about the work or problem are significantly different from the other person's, you could decide to adopt the other person's ideas, try to find a middle ground, or come up with a brand-new idea that may work for both of you. In the Personal dimension, depending on where your "issues" are, you could change your goals, agendas, beliefs, attitudes, or personal positions regarding the work. Although such changes should be considered, they are not always appropriate, and often we are not willing to make them.

Fortunately, however, there is another option. If, going into a collaboration, we are unwilling to change attributes that may tend to work against finding common ground and achieving the common goal, then we can at least choose to hold them lightly. That means that while we have chosen not to change the attributes going in, we have decided to keep an open mind regarding those attributes during the collaboration. I may go into a collaboration thinking my idea is better than the other person's, but I can at least be willing to hear them out and consider their ideas. And should I see merit in their ideas as I achieve a better understanding of them, I reserve the option of adopting all or part of the ideas. If, for example, I go into a collaboration with a personal agenda that a certain line cannot be crossed or it will threaten my budget, I can at least work with the other person to see if we can find a way to cross that line while adequately protecting my budget.

The point is that we are each responsible for doing all we can ahead of the collaboration to enable a successful outcome. That doesn't mean we should just roll over. It means we should do what we are willing to do and, at the minimum, hold our potentially conflicting attributes lightly. If we allow collaboration to happen, the creative process just might help forge a path to a mutually agreeable outcome. So, the underlying skill in the Me category is to have the ability, willingness, and courage to allow for a successful collaboration.

You

The other side of the coin in our collaborations is knowing the people we are interacting with (e.g., clients, stakeholders, teammates, coworkers, etc.), so we can optimize our interaction strategy with them. In the business world, knowing a person is focused on two primary categories: their business needs and their personal characteristics. Business needs spring from the person's position and role in the business, the person's associated business goals and concerns, and the circumstances surrounding the person in the context of the matter to be discussed. These things are associated primarily with the Intellectual dimension. People appreciate it when you know something about their business, circumstances, and history. If you are meeting someone for the first time, you can find a lot of information online (e.g., company website, LinkedIn, Facebook, etc.). You can also talk with people who know the person. However you do it, try to put yourself in the other person's shoes.

Personal characteristics include the elements of what we call PLOT: their Personality, Language (both verbal and body language), Opinion and frame of reference about the work and you, and Task approach (how they like to work and communicate). These things are primarily associated with the Personal dimension, especially opinion and frame of reference.

You can use PLOT as a tool to read people and formulate an interaction strategy. For example, you are about to meet with an executive you met once before to discuss the agenda for his executive offsite meeting. He is Type A and quite serious (Personality). He talks fast and waves his arms a lot (Language). He prides himself on how much work he can get done and thinks of himself as superior to most people, including you (Opinion/Frame of Reference). He is a big-picture guy who doesn't think details are something he should get into and he likes to delegate (Task approach).

Given his PLOT, what is the best interaction strategy? He is certainly not the kind of guy who wants to spend all day brainstorming about possible agenda topics and activities. You are going into a collaboration with someone who probably doesn't like to collaborate, yet you have to find a way. You decide to meet him where he is. The meeting will be short, fast paced, and formal. He is not interested in building a relationship with you; he wants to get the meeting done and move on. You will talk fast and get to your points quickly. Instead of walking in with a blank sheet of paper, you will take a stab at framing out an agenda with options for topics and activities. That will put him in the role of evaluating and making quick decisions, things he is quite comfortable doing that reinforce his self-image. The day of the meeting comes and your strategy works like a charm. You are in and out in ten minutes, he appreciated your preparation, and you have your agenda.

This example underscores the importance of reading and knowing the person with whom you will be collaborating. What would have happened if you had walked into the meeting without a strategy to optimize the collaboration? Sometimes, in fact, we find ourselves in that circumstance. We may learn about a last-minute meeting with someone we have never met where there is no opportunity for preparation. In those cases you can apply PLOT in the moment when you meet and ask questions to find out about the person's business. That brings us to Us.

Us

As important as the Me and You skill sets are, the Us skills are probably the most important in collaboration. This is where the navigation really begins. At the heart of this skill set is the ability to *sense, process, and respond* in the moment during interactions to build shared space and alignment toward a common goal. As mentioned earlier, what is being aligned are the Intellectual and Personal dimensions of energy between you and the other person. We will address sensing, processing, and responding one at a time and then come back to how they all work together in collaborations.

Sensing has to do with monitoring the other person, ourselves, and the deeper messages of the interaction. It is the stuff of the Observer. What we are ultimately monitoring are the Intellectual and Personal dimensions of energy in ourselves and the other person. That means there is an intellectual component of the conversation and a personal component with an emotional genesis. To monitor these energies in others, we must monitor their indicators. These indicators include:

- **Words.** While it is certainly true that much of our communication happens in nonverbal ways, words remain a central form of communication. In particular, words—possibly augmented by visuals—are how you will learn about the other person's intellectual contributions to the collaboration. When people are being forthright, they may also express personal beliefs, attitudes, and positions through their words.
- **Body language.** Body language can tell us a lot about the other person's Personal dimension and reveal intellectual preferences as well. For example, if we inadvertently challenge someone's personal position about the work, we may see them push back or cross their arms. Most people read body language naturally, so we won't spend time here describing how to do it. Suffice it to say that we need to make sure we are paying attention to body language if we can actually see the other person.

- **Tone.** Even when we can't see the other person (e.g., during a teleconference), we can learn a lot about the Personal dimension and its associated emotions through a person's tone of voice and volume.
- **Generosity.** People can be generous in conversations or they can withhold information and contribute little. How generous people are to the collaboration with their engagement, willingness to listen, thoughtful ideas, and appropriate feedback can speak volumes about their intent.

Monitoring our own Intellectual and Personal energies is part two of the self-awareness equation. Intellectually, we generally go into collaborations with specific ideas and opinions about the work. As the collaboration unfolds and we are exposed to new information and ideas, our own ideas and opinions may well change. We must monitor the collaboration for things that may change us intellectually.

Monitoring our Personal energies is more difficult but essential for most good collaborations, as discussed. Remember unintentional conflict and the many things that trigger it? Well, this is the place where those triggers push our emotional buttons. At the sensing stage, we have not yet reacted and we still have a choice about how to react (i.e., do we engage in conflict or go a different way?). The important part of sensing is to be aware of when a trigger pushes one of our emotional buttons; typically this occurs when we perceive that our work survival, comfort, reputation, or level of importance are being threatened.

Not all Personal energies in ourselves and others are negative, however, and it is equally important to monitor the positive developments. For example, if the other person has a personal position about the work that was contrary to yours and decides to let that go, you will certainly want to be aware of that. If a person's level of generosity in the collaboration suddenly increases, it reflects a positive shift in the person's Personal dimension.

Processing is what we do after sensing. It is done by our Guide. Whereas sensing provides us with information, processing helps us understand what it means. Once again, there are two sides to the equation.

- **What information means to the other person.** Understanding what information means to the other person entails translating the information into how it is affecting their Intellectual and Personal dimensions and how it is affecting the creation or erosion of shared space. For example, if I throw out an idea and the other person reacts in a snippy way,

I know that intellectually she didn't like the idea and personally probably felt threatened by it. Depending on the magnitude and implications of the idea and the personal attributes of the other person, it may have also eroded trust and shared space. Conversely, if the other person likes my idea and agrees to it, I have successfully moved him intellectually. Personally, he may feel a higher degree of trust. He may feel positive emotions like relief, satisfaction, or even joy. Shared space grows.

- **What the information means to you.** Once you have the information from the last exchange, and you have arrived at what it does or may mean about the other person, you evaluate what all the information means to you in anticipation of a response. These are often your defining moments in a collaboration. For example, let's say I am easily offended by people who reject my ideas. I am offended because I am unwilling to consider other suggestions (Intellectual rigidity) and I make the rejection of my idea into a rejection of me and a condemnation of my abilities (Personal beliefs). I decide to argue in favor of my idea and to do it with some anger and righteousness; this is a clear path toward conflict.

  In contrast, I may have prepared for the collaboration by holding my ideas and personal positions lightly, as we discussed earlier. I am not offended by the rejection as I can see that the snippy component of the other person's remark was born out of fear, and I am seeing the person's human condition. I am not condoning snippy behavior; I am simply understanding what it means—something about the other person, not me. I see this as an opportunity to ask the other person for ideas, to hear what he has to say and to model the kind of collaborative behavior I would like to see from him.

These examples show us that what we make things mean to us, based on our Intellectual and Personal attributes and energies, has a huge influence on our decisions and actions in a collaboration. What we make things mean to us can send us into battle, or it can turn a negative into a positive. It also shows us a defining moment when a trigger for conflict can be engaged or left alone. Given the magnitude of conflict in our businesses today and the huge prices we pay for it, we would be well advised to develop ourselves and our people with the skills and behaviors to see things for what they are and to choose not to take things personally. Doing so would help us avoid some of the conflict triggered by Environmental factors and interactions with people who are not as adept at managing their energies.

Responding is the second part of the Guide's job. It is essentially executing the plan and decision developed in the Processing step. However, there are many options for how you can respond. We look now at four things to consider in your responses.

1. **Effective questioning.** Most collaborations include portions where people are trying to get to the bottom of things (e.g., reach a mutual understanding of the causes of a problem). During those interactions, you will likely have to ask probing questions in a way that doesn't threaten people. For example, if I were to ask the captain of the *Titanic* (had he survived), "What the heck were you thinking as you steamed at top speed across the Atlantic in the *Titanic* when you knew there were icebergs in the area?," he would have undoubtedly responded in a defensive manner. However, if I asked him, "What were the factors that night that compelled you to conclude that the risk of an iceberg collision was minimal?," he would respond quite differently and would appreciate my approach. Another aspect of effective questioning is not to script your questions too tightly in advance. Instead, let the last response, and your processing of that response, guide you in framing your next question. You will achieve an understanding more quickly this way, and the other person will know you are listening.

2. **Questions versus statements.** There are times in collaborations when you need to make a point. But many a collaboration has gone awry because when people want to make a point, they often are more inclined to make a statement than ask a question. Avoid making statements based on your opinions only. Doing so can be risky. Instead, practice the art of making points with carefully worded questions. For example, if you are concerned that the manager you are talking with will not provide enough resources from her department to make a project successful, you may say something like "I'm concerned that the project could fail because you may not assign enough people from your department to support it." That looks and feels like a direct confrontation, and it is guaranteed to close off any shared space you may have created. Alternatively, you might ask, "What is your strategy for identifying who in your department will support the project? How will you know when you have assigned enough people?" These questions are far more powerful and effective than making statements.

3. **Adjusting your role.** In our interactions we all have roles that we play, and those roles often change as the conversation progresses and evolves. For example, in the first part of a collaboration, you may be in the role

of a Strategist as you brainstorm with the other person about how to approach accomplishing a goal. Once an approach has been identified, however, the other person may want help thinking through a sticky point in the implementation of the strategy where you have had significant experience. To bring the greatest value to the collaboration, you would switch into the role of a Coach. While a thorough discussion of the collaborative roles is beyond the scope of this book, suffice it to say that you will bring the greatest value to your collaborations when you can recognize in the moment the optimal role to play and then step into it. Collaborations are severely limited and more prone to conflict when people are unwilling or unable to step out of the comfort zone of their preferred roles. While changing roles may sound mechanical, it helps to create a dynamic, empathetic, and responsive dance in the interaction. This has a tremendous effect on building shared space.

4. **Influencing others.** We are all in business to get important work done, and it is essential that we are able to appropriately influence the positions, beliefs, and attitudes of others. *How* we influence others is the key. It is best to recognize that your influence during a collaboration is constant. Even your questions have influence. As you promote adjustments in the other person's Intellectual and Personal dimensions, you can see the results of your influence. Things to watch out for include coming on too strong, which can feel like bullying, and stating opinions without ensuring they are relevant and compelling to the other person. Communicating to the other person the relevancy of our ideas to their situation is far more powerful than simply blurting out an opinion. Because this type of communication is a very thoughtful way of aligning people with our ideas, people tend to appreciate the influence as opposed to feeling pushed. And, yes, this too builds shared space.

When we put Me, You, and Us together, tremendous resolution, creativity, and innovation can happen. The acts of knowing ourselves and others, responsibly preparing for collaborations, and sensing, processing, and responding with a common goal in mind make us powerful collaborators. Looking at how all of this comes together, two overarching points about collaboration emerge. First, collaboration is best accomplished with a strong degree of independence from the Intellectual and Personal dimensions. You are observing and processing information and cues about yourself and the other person and making navigational decisions based on information. You need to be objective, especially about yourself. To do that you will want to observe and make decisions from a vantage point where you aren't taking things personally and you aren't easily insulted. This takes practice, but it can be done. Second, in your collaborations, you are ultimately reading and responding to energy. You sense these energies through the various cues we discussed. We call these cues the other conversation. The other conversation represents the bigger picture of energy. Let's look at an example.

The Other Conversation

One type of collaboration that is increasingly common in business is when a project leader interviews executive stakeholders early in the project to find out about their ideas, preferences, and issues so they can be considered in project planning and direction. We will use this type of collaboration to illustrate the other conversation. Our stakeholder's name is Jane.

The narrative part of the story below characterizes the flow of the verbal conversation. The italicized comments characterize what I call the "other conversation," where the real collaboration is happening. These comments are about what Jane and Joe are thinking and feeling, not what they are saying. Here is the story.

Joe arrives at Jane's office for the scheduled interview, having done his homework on Jane's business needs and personal characteristics.

Jane: *I hope this interview is over quickly. I have so much to do. Does this guy have a clue about my business?*

Joe: *I've done my homework on Jane and her business, and I'm going to show her that with my opening comments and questions.*
Joe opens the conversation by stating his goal of understanding Jane's preferences regarding the project so they can be considered during project planning. He then summarizes his understanding of her position and how this project might affect her operation.

Jane: *He really understands my business! He obviously took some time to get to know me. I appreciate that. Now what is his agenda?*
Jane states her appreciation for Joe's "homework" and then begins to talk about her business and concerns around the project.

Joe: *I sense she is opening up but may still have doubts about my intent. I'll show her my intent through my questions, comments, and thoughtful listening.*

Joe listens carefully and asks questions to clarify his understanding of what Jane is saying. Jane mentions that Joe asks good questions and begins to ask some of her own questions about the project.

Jane: *He seems to not just have his own interests in mind, and genuinely wants a good outcome for me and my business on this project. That's great! I'm going to do what I can to help him too.*

As this dialogue continues, the conversation becomes more open and frank. Agreements are reached on certain aspects of the project and how Jane would be given review opportunities at specific project milestones.

Joe: *I think she really trusts and appreciates what I am trying to do. She is giving me some great information that will really help me and the project!*

Jane: *Wow! His questions made me think about things I wasn't even aware of about my business. I'll have to take a closer look at those. Meanwhile, this has been a valuable conversation—time well spent. And I like this guy, Joe. I wasn't sure about him before, but I trust him now.*

By the end of the conversation, Joe has all the information he needs and thanks Jane for a pleasant and productive meeting.

This example is pretty simplistic but helps illustrate the point. The other conversation in our collaborations is real, it always happens, and it is by far more important than the surface-level conversation. The surface-level conversation is about words. The other conversation is about the dynamics of energy and the truth of the matter. You can see from the other conversation how shared space between Joe and Jane continued to open up as the conversation progressed. This led to a very successful outcome. This story and its outcome illustrate the fact that we must help people operate effectively below the surface as well as above the surface to improve their collaboration capabilities.

Not all of our collaborations are one on one. Collaborations often include multiple participants. We turn our attention now to group collaborations.

Group Collaboration

In this section we define group collaboration and then address it in two common forms. First, we dive into the collaborative group conversation, a one-time event that usually comes in the form of a meeting. Second, we look at longer-term collaborative efforts, which usually come in the form of projects.

Defining Group Collaboration

Group collaboration is when three or more people work together in concert toward common goals. All of the ingredients of one-on-one business inter- actions absolutely apply to group collaboration. The concept of creating shared space together also applies. However, the addition of people increases the complexity of the interactions and requires that we recognize group dynamics in the collaboration that contribute to and erode the creation of shared space and positive outcomes.

The Collaborative Group Conversation

Collaborative group conversations are extremely common in business and will continue to gain in both importance and frequency as the Fourth Industrial Revolution unfolds. Some of these conversations pro- duce successful outcomes; others produce just the opposite. Overall, we need to up our game. As in one-on-one collaborations, the Environmen- tal dimension can have a tremendous influence on group conversations. For example, on the negative side, anything in the enterprise that creates factions and inappropriately elevates the importance of personal agendas will detract from the collaborative group conversation. Similarly, things in the enterprise that bring up fear, scarcity, or survival issues will make the creation of shared space and positive outcomes much more difficult. On the positive side, collaborative cultures and a healthy enterprise go a long way toward promoting successful group collaborations. The bot- tom line here is that too many collaborative group conversations are doomed before they get started because of unhealthy enterprises that breed unintentional conflict.

As for the conversations themselves, collaborative group conversations have both similarities to and differences from one-on-one conversations. Like one-on-one conversations, the Collaboration Dynamic and the four dimensions of energy apply, and creating shared space is equally important. The differences have to do with dynamics within groups that don't exist in one-on-one interactions. Let's review some of the similarities and differ- ences to inject the perspective of energy onto group discussions and provide strategies for promoting effective group collaborations.

Individual and Group Alignment

We know that alignment is important in collaborative group conversations, but exactly what is being aligned and how does alignment work? The answer is that both individuals and the group as a whole are being aligned. Individual alignment is finding common ground and direction between every individual and every other individual. This occurs, for example, when two people in the group express differing opinions and then work toward alignment through their interactions. Taken literally and to the extreme, aligning everyone with everyone would require far too many individual conversations. Fortunately, that is not the end goal, nor is that the way colloboration works in group conversations.

In group conversations, there is what I call a group track that has its own consciousness and energy. This group track is born out of alignment of the group as a whole. The greater the degree of alignment at any given moment, the more powerful the group track and the greater the shared space. While many collaborative group conversations begin with an emphasis on individual alignment, especially among the more vocal members, as effective collaborations proceed, the emphasis shifts toward alignment between each individual and the group track. This makes sense from the standpoint of building shared space. The greater the shared space across the group, the more powerful that energy becomes compared with the energy of individual opinions. That's good news if you can build group shared space quickly enough and bad news if you can't.

In general, group collaborations will spiral downward if they stay too long in the energy of individual opinions, and they will be successful if the group can make early and consistent progress in building the group track. That is why it is often a good idea to identify smaller, less divisive issues that a group can agree on early in a conversation.

The Other Conversation

Just as one-on-one collaborations have their "other conversations," group collaborations have theirs. In both cases these other conversations are the *real conversation*. In group collaborations, the group track is born out of the other conversation, not the literal conversation that can be seen and heard.

People who are adept at group collaborations intuitively listen to the other conversation and monitor the evolving group track.

I have marveled over the years at how differently those who have participated in the same collaboration describe what happened afterward. After one such collaboration, a less experienced participant said to me, "We discussed the issues, heard viewpoints from most people, especially Lori and Sergio, and decided that we needed to meet again to discuss it some more." The second, more experienced person said, "Lori and Sergio were all about protecting their groups and preserving their statuses; they left no room for the creation of the new product group that intersects with both of their departmental functions."

After hearing from both people, I realized they were both correct and that their stories were not inconsistent or incompatible. It's just that the first person focused on the literal conversation while the second focused on the other conversation. If we are to improve the level and quality of group collaborations in our businesses, we must recognize that many people have a lesser awareness and ability to track the other conversations and need help developing that capability.

Cognitive Creativity

Cognitive creativity is a phenomenon that exists in the Intellectual dimension of those around the table. We have all seen and experienced it. Someone throws out a question. Another person provides a partial answer. A third elaborates on aspects of the partial answer and adds a new perspective. Someone else sees the brilliance in that even beyond the initial elaboration. He puts it out for consideration and, almost like magic, a new innovative idea is born. The group loves it. The group created it together in a collaborative process. Every comment contributes something to the process, even if we don't recognize what it contributes at the time. When this "magic" happens, you can feel an energy spike. Shared space is abundant. These are the ah-ha and Eureka! moments that get us going and give greater purpose to our working lives.

Innovation is often the child of group collaborations, which is another reason it is so important for us to collaborate well as people. Much of what is written in this book is about clearing the way and enabling this creativity to occur. We cannot overestimate or overlook the power and necessity of effective group collaborations, especially in the Fourth Industrial Revolution. It is amazing what can happen when people are free to create shared space.

Constructive Collaborators

We probably all know people who always seem to find ways to contribute to collaborative conversations. They tend to have strong interaction skills, a keen ability to monitor group dynamics through the other conversation, and a willingness to hold their personal agendas loosely whenever possible. They make a point to understand the ideas and opinions of others, to find the merit in them, and to help others see that merit. Others tend to see them as even-handed and trustworthy. Constructive collaborators are the champions of the group track and seek creative and additive alignment in virtually everything they do. Needless to say, these people are models of great collaborative behavior and are usually fun and exciting to work with. We can all learn by watching constructive collaborators in action.

Collaboration Roles

When you watch or participate in a collaborative group discussion, you often see people taking on different roles in the interaction. Some are more active, and others are more passive. Some like to provide a moral compass, and others like to be great idea adventurers. Some like to share their extensive knowledge and remind the rest how smart they are, while others play the role of more thoughtful contributors considering the needs and ideas of others.

No matter what roles people choose to play, they are all still individuals in the group with their individual energies. Therefore, everyone has an influence through their individual energy, even if they sit quietly and simply react with body language to what others say. Like many things in collaborations, taking on specific roles can be helpful or harmful to the collaboration, and what is helpful in one conversation can be harmful in another.

For example, I once worked with someone who always played the devil's advocate role. She was very good at and comfortable with that role. On several occasions she helped identify holes in our ideas that we then addressed as a group. The result was stronger solutions. However, there were some conversations where we as a group were already facing issues and objections from people outside of our team. We needed some out-of-the-box solutions, and her devil's advocate objections just felt like she was piling on. It certainly wasn't helpful to the group. What I learned from this situation is that the positives and negatives of taking on a role are situational, which is why none of us should get stuck in our favorite role.

That said, roles can be a powerful way to contribute, and when the players take on a synergistic set of roles, the results can be dramatic. We actually see this drama played out in many police/detective shows in television and films. It is essentially a formula. There is usually the wise head detective who leads the conversation and usually arrives at the big ah-has first. Then there is the forensic specialist who brings science into the conversation. Next, the guy on the case is usually the one telling the crime story and offering insights as to the criminal's behavior. And then there is the quirky cop who the others make fun of but secretly respect because she is actually brilliant. In Hollywood, the collaborations go down at lightning speed because of program time constraints and because the writers don't want viewers to get bored. Nevertheless, you can see the creativity, sometimes playful and sometimes serious, as everyone plays their roles to make unique and timely contributions to solving the crime. You get the sense that if any one of the roles had been absent from the conversation, the crime would not have been solved. All the roles are essential.

Playing roles in business collaborations can be equally dramatic and rewarding. Granted, the pace is a bit slower, the roles are not engineered, and the words are not scripted. Nevertheless, I have seen powerful results in such circumstances more times than I can count. What is most amazing to me is that people in a high-functioning group tend to find the role best suited to both themselves and to the group. They have advanced interaction skills and are extremely adept at collaborating. We need to adopt methods to teach these skills.

Influence Patterns

Most people in collaborative conversations want to have influence, and some people want to have a lot of influence. However, when you look at how that plays out in the interaction, the influence (energetic output) of any given individual often waxes and wanes throughout the conversation. Part of this has to do with the fact that there are many people who need time to speak, which limits the influence opportunity for any given individual. Another part has to do with the natural flow of the conversation and when people feel they need to jump in and say something. Sometimes people take this fluctuation to the extreme by staying quiet until the conversation reaches a pivotal point and then releasing the energy of an elephant stampede in an effort to push the group track in the direction they prefer.

To that point, I was once in a meeting with representatives from a large healthcare company. We were discussing how to implement a common IT infrastructure across the whole company, which was historically fragmented into divisions that each had its own IT departments and made its own decisions. The purpose of the meeting was to get objections out on the table so they could be addressed. For those of us who were the champions of the common infrastructure, it was like playing Whack-a-Mole. Whenever someone brought up an objection, one of us addressed it and made a case for how the objection could be addressed with the common solution. Though our whacks were gentle and professional, there was one objection after another, and they began to feel like moles popping up in the arcade.

Just when we thought all of the objections had been expressed and dealt with, one manager who had been noticeably quiet blurted out that his division could not tolerate using networking equipment from vendors other than those his division was already using. This was clearly his big issue. He didn't seem to care much about the other issues, so he saved up his guns (energy) to influence this one battle. It almost worked too, based on the shock factor and massive amount of energy released. However, the group track had grown strong by then and the option of switching vendors was preserved.

Group influence comes in many patterns. Good collaborators are watchful of these patterns. They learn to flow with the patterns and figure out the best way to interact with individuals and the group as a whole.

Factions

In group conversations, factions sometimes develop, with two or more groups polarized around one or more issues. At other times factions are formed before the conversation begins, as people bring their group loyalties and biases to the table. Whatever the reason for the factions, they are forces to be reckoned with in the group dynamics. Sometimes they can help by focusing the conversation on the divergent energies that need to come into alignment. However, just as often they can cause the collaboration to end in a stalemate with nothing resolved.

I was once in a meeting with several members of a client company. Some people had been in the company a long time, while others had recently come into the company via a small acquisition. The company that was acquired had a product my client company wanted to add to its product line. I discovered, however, that little had been done to integrate the people from the company. In the meeting, the factions quickly developed along (former) company lines. The acquired people were holding on tightly to their former company culture and methods, and the old-timers were holding on just as tightly to their culture and methods. The only thing that was certain about that conversation was that everyone "knew" they were right. Needless to say, the conversation went nowhere. I subsequently went to company executives with recommendations for immediate integration activities. These factions had overpowering energies that had to be dealt with at the enterprise level. Where factions are not so overpowering, they are best dealt with by looking for common ground and building the power of the group track.

Bombshells and Disruptive Energy

One interesting dynamic in collaborative group conversations is the tendency of some people to drop bombshells. Bombshells and disruptive energy are similar to the IT story discussed earlier in the "Influence Patterns" section. However, they differ in one fundamental way. The IT story is an example of someone trying to influence the agreed-on outcome of a collaboration. In this case, the manager wanted to continue using his preferred vendors. Bombshells and disruptive energy are more about sidetracking or blowing up the meeting so the conversation just goes away. I have seen this happen both early and late in the conversation. All of a sudden, out of the blue, someone drops a bombshell. Boom! Bombshells come in many forms. For example: "What we are talking about doing here is unethical!" or "I happen to know the superintendent doesn't like this approach," or "We will bankrupt our company if we do this."

In general, bombshells are meant to disrupt. For example, if the conversation (group track) isn't going in a direction that someone likes, the person may see a major disruption as a way of killing the conversation, at least in its current form and forum. Generally speaking, this is very damaging to the collaboration unless others in the group can expose the bombshell as opinion versus fact or somehow counter it with other evidence and arguments. Doing this preserves the group track and puts down the attempted coup. If this can't be done, it is sometimes best to put the conversation on hold while the bombshell is investigated to see if it has merit or if it was just a tactical smokescreen.

The bottom line: Learn to recognize bombshells for what they are. If they are negative efforts to disrupt, protect the group track and expose the bombshell for what it is.

Personal Agendas

As discussed earlier, one of the most important things that happens in a good collaborative conversation is adequate alignment between the personal agendas of those involved and the stated goal of the group. It is also necessary to achieve adequate alignment between the personal agendas and the group track that develops. In both cases, adequate alignment is strongly influenced by how closely and tightly the individuals hold personal agendas that run counter to the group energy. If they hold them lightly and consider alternate ideas and opinions, they may allow themselves to become a greater part of the group track, which grows the energy of the group track. If, however, they hold their agendas tightly, the only ideas they will consider are those that support their personal agendas.

Many collaborations die on the vine because of this problem. People always think they have good reasons for their personal agendas, and sometimes they do. However, when their energy and attention are focused on improving their own lot or keeping themselves safe, they leave little or no room for the larger goal or the creation of shared space. What is worse is that these people often blend righteousness and arrogance around their fixed behaviors with an attitude that they are doing the rest of the group a favor. The energy of that is bullying, but people get away with it every day because we don't look at it through the lens of energy and call them out on it. Personal agendas are a given, but they should be exposed for what they are.

The Nod and Turn

Whereas the bombshell is shocking and disruptive, the nod and turn is quiet and corrosive. It happens when someone nods in agreement with the group track and then leaves the room only to do just the opposite of that which was supposedly agreed upon. In psychology, we call this behavior passive aggressive. It gets its hideous potency because it is not only as potentially disruptive as a bombshell, it is hidden from sight, which makes it difficult to detect. It causes damage that people are not even aware of to the agreed-upon common good. Eventually, things inconsistent with the supposed agreement start to occur, but they can be difficult to trace back to the perpetrator. Some would call such covert activity a brilliant political move. Perhaps it is. But when you look at the damage and waste the nod and turn causes, it is absolutely unacceptable.

I have seen the nod and turn most often at the executive level during large change initiatives where not everybody is on board. When we level the playing field by aligning control and responsibility, those executives who believe they will lose control often resist the change. When they realize that their personal agendas for power aren't good arguments for blocking the change, they go underground with their resistance. They nod in agreement at executive meetings and then turn around and rally their people to resist the change in subversive ways. This passive-aggressive behavior is, from an energy perspective, simply aggressive. It is no less aggressive than overt aggression, and it is often more damaging. For the sake of one person's personal need for power, the entire business suffers. Business leaders need to watch for the nod and turn and deal with it decisively when detected.

Facilitating Collaborative Group Conversations

This section has illustrated many of the good, the bad, and the ugly dynamics that occur in collaborative group discussions. The bad and ugly dynamics can immobilize groups to the point where they simply cannot achieve alignment around important topics. In these cases, the only hope of achieving alignment is to bring in a neutral facilitator.

The traditional view of a good facilitator is someone who will keep the conversation fair and moving in a constructive direction toward some kind of agreement. This is all good but it is essentially an insufficient view. Looking more deeply, our energetic view of collaborative group conversations suggests that the goals and methods of a facilitator must be refined. First and foremost, facilitators need to function as champions of creativity and positive energy and guardians against negative energy whenever possible. That means they have to monitor the group track (i.e., the other conversation and how it builds and erodes shared space) as well as the energies of the involved individuals with laser beam attention. Second, they need to facilitate by encouraging constructive collaboration while calling out those who attempt the kinds of negative tactics just discussed.

Facilitation is not the work of wimps. When we call out those who are used to getting away with negative tactics, we often receive angry responses designed to intimidate. Facilitators must put down these power plays and show the group how this navigation and push-back is done.

This section is by no means an exhaustive treatment of collaborative group conversations. That could literally be a separate book. But the most important point here is to demonstrate through examples and insights how to approach these conversations as energy exchanges and, it is hoped, a co-creation of shared space with a positive business outcome. In my rowing story, I spoke of swing and the bubbles under the hull. I was recalling an exhilarating experience. As you may well know, collaborative conversations can be equally exhilarating as a group of individuals merge to create something new, innovative, and even surprising.

Having addressed collaborative group conversations, we now turn to longer-term collaborations that span many conversations and can last weeks, months, and even years.

Project-Based Group Collaboration

There are many forums for long-term group collaboration in business, but the most common is the project. Businesses launch projects to get important things done for their clients and themselves. Project types include client engagements and implementations, product development, system development, internal change initiatives, and more. The success of these projects absolutely depends on effective group collaboration throughout a variety of activities and phases.

Most business projects have a macro process that defines the project life cycle and provides a basis for planning and scheduling. For example, the waterfall life cycle model in software development is composed of requirements definition; high-level design; detailed design, development, and unit testing; integration testing; and formal testing. Life-cycle processes vary considerably according to the type of project (e.g., product development versus system development versus internal change initiatives, etc.). These processes, and the manner in which they are executed, have a significant impact on group collaboration, but we make no attempt here to address the many variations across life-cycle models. We focus instead on the common denominators present in all project-based group collaborations.

While virtually all projects involve dynamic collaboration, they may also involve institutional and/or asynchronous collaboration. For example, a software development project using the waterfall life cycle almost certainly uses a development environment/tool kit that the team can use to check in and check out software modules or units while maintaining configuration control. This is an example of asynchronous collaboration. In addition, however, the team also holds meetings and working sessions, which are all about dynamic collaboration. Although the other types of collaboration play pivotal roles on many projects, here we maintain our focus on the common denominator, dynamic collaboration.

As with one-on-one collaborations and collaborative group discussions, the four dimensions of energy are central to project-based group collaborations. To be successful, project teams must achieve adequate alignment within and among the dimensions of energy *over a period of time*. That means the alignment must be sustained, or at least renewable, and it must be developed around a host of things associated with the project: goals, problems, people, the environment, solutions, decisions, and work. In that process, each dimension has its own focus and *objectives* that, when accomplished, build alignment within the dimension and shared space within the project as a whole.

Each objective is on the list because it is an important project activity and a powerful way to build alignment. You may have done several of these activities and may view some of them as standard operating procedure for project management. Yet we discuss them here from the standpoint of energy. In doing so, these activities become more than a set of to dos. Each activity becomes a contributor to the management of energy on the project.

Working in concert, the activities align the energies of the people involved with the business and project goals to build shared space and move the project toward a successful outcome.

Some of these activities are accomplished up front during project planning to energetically set the stage for a positive work effort. Others are executed along the way as either milestones or pivot points in response to emerging project circumstances. Let's take a look at some of the more important objectives/activities in each dimension to reveal an approach for achieving project success through the management of energy.

Environmental Alignment

In the Environmental dimension, our desired alignment is between the project and the business itself, including customers and stakeholders, and the business environment that surrounds the collaborative team. Key objectives include:

- **Align with customers and stakeholders.** All projects have customers and stakeholders, whether they are internal, external, or both. We consider these to be a part of the business environment. A key goal of any collaboration is that its customers and stakeholders are satisfied with the business outcomes. But in a world where our collaborations are increasingly focused on complex solutions, this alignment can't wait until the end of the project. We must build and maintain alignment along the way to help ensure that we have alignment (satisfaction) at the end of the project. That means clearly identifying who our clients and stakeholders are and interviewing them early in the project to find out their needs, preferences, and concerns and to start building a relationship of trust with them.

  For internal stakeholders, and often for external clients as well, doing this means involving them in reviews of major work products produced as the project unfolds. And, since most projects are funded by clients and stakeholders, doing this means managing the project's scope and resources to ensure that when it's over, clients and stakeholders feel they have received adequate value for their investment. In successful projects, the team, customers, and stakeholders are all pointed in essentially the same direction, allowing the energy and shared space to flow into a successful business outcome.

Project scope management is a good example of a key alignment activity, one that many of our clients at Advance Consulting ask us to help their people with. We often hear statements like "When my project managers get requests from clients to add more work to the project scope, they tend to answer with either yes or no. Unfortunately, when they just say yes to a request for something additional on the project, they take on the work for no additional budget. And when they say no because it's not in the project scope, the client feels rejected and angry."

We teach project managers and others that having a conversation and building alignment is the way through this. Making sure that they—and clients—truly understand the *need* by engaging in interactive dialogue is usually the best way to start. Promising to price out the additional work quickly is a good place to end the conversation, which is a path toward alignment. In contrast, the "no" response is an energetic block with no alignment possible, and the "yes" response is but a temporary alignment that will lead ultimately to problems with project performance and client satisfaction. Overall, the more trust you have with a client, the easier and more effective these conversations will be.

- **Align with end users.** Many projects have end users who are not necessarily considered primary clients or stakeholders but are nonetheless an important force in the business environment. For example, users of a new system or process (internal) and consumers who will ultimately buy a new product (external) are considered end users. Ultimately, building alignment with end users can be the difference between success and failure of a project. Therefore, it is important to talk with them early in the process to understand their needs, ideas, preferences, and concerns. One-on-one interviews may not be practical when there are many end users involved, so communication forums such as focus groups can be quite effective. In addition, it is important to maintain communication with end users along the way so they are on board at the end. Like customers and stakeholders, you want them essentially pointed in the same direction as your team throughout the project.

- **Work within established boundaries.** The enterprise elements collectively define a set of boundaries that define the rules of the road for working in a business. For example, organizational structures define reporting relationships; policies and processes define how things should be done; roles define and confine the work of individuals; and systems guide people with automation. We have talked a lot in this book about how enterprise elements are often broken or dysfunctional, necessitating that people work around them to get things done. However, in general, people and teams should follow these established boundaries. For teams, following the applicable boundaries is one important way of aligning with the organization. For example, if there is a policy that any increase in the budget of an internal initiative must be approved by the chief financial officer, and a project team circumvents that policy, they are putting the project at risk because the bookkeeping will probably expose their circumvention. In summary, the energy of not working within established boundaries is conflict, which will ultimately waste project energy. Circumvent the boundaries only when they themselves are dysfunctional and stand in the way of project success.

- **Utilize available resources.** Utilizing all available resources may seem like a no-brainer, but it is interesting how often project teams complain about resource shortfalls when they haven't tapped the available resources in the business. This is a sure way to lose team credibility and raise the anger of the higher-ups receiving the complaints. For example, if there is a provision for bringing in contractors to perform specific tasks and augment teams when they are overloaded (surge capacity), a team should tap those resources if appropriate. Or, if someone in the business has been identified who can help projects that run into regulatory issues, that resource should be utilized if such issues arise rather than churning and wasting time and money. A team should not expect the business to present available resources on a silver platter. Team members should take the initiative to know them and find them. In other words, we must be careful not to ignore positive potential energy sources available to the project.

- **Overcome or accommodate limitations.** Let's face it, most projects don't have access to every resource they need when they need it. I have never seen a business that is perfect at resource management. Although major resource shortfalls are an issue at the enterprise level, project teams need to overcome or accommodate more minor and occasional limitations.

  For example, I once worked on a large system development project where various people needed access to the mainframe for different purposes. The rub was that, given the development environment, the mainframe couldn't do two things at once. Consequently, there simply weren't enough hours in a regular shift for everyone to have time with the computer. I pulled the short straw and was assigned to set up a 24/7 calendar where people came in around the clock to have their time with the computer. To my surprise, the team accepted this quickly, knowing there was no other realistic choice. Eventually, things calmed down and the team went back to regular workdays. The main point is that teams need to take control of issues where possible (positive energy) rather than sit back and be victims of environmental circumstances (negative energy). Teams are capable of vast creativity, and overcoming limitations is one place to apply it.

- **Adapt to environmental changes.** Major changes sometimes occur in businesses during the course of a project. For example, a change in executive leadership, a reorganization, or an acquisition can have significant potential impacts on a project. Such a change disrupts the field of play, which requires an adaptation on the part of the project team. If, for example, a new leader just became the project sponsor, the project manager and possibly other leads on the project should meet with the sponsor as they would meet with any sponsor at the start of a project to find out about the person's needs, preferences, sensitivities, and the like. Based on this information, the team should be prepared to do a reset on the project plan and approach to accommodate alignment with the new sponsor. While it is not always possible to adapt to environmental changes, it is important to try. Otherwise, we must live with the consequences of a misalignment, which can threaten the future of the project and/or drain its energy.

Intellectual Alignment

Aligning intellectually within a team is something that people naturally associate with projects. However, one of the very common problems we see with teams is that they focus this alignment on the "what" topics (what we will do) and give far less attention to the "how" topics (how we will do it as a team). Both are equally important, and, to help ensure a high-functioning team, both must be addressed and the resulting agreements should be documented and distributed among the team members. When teams aren't working well, it is often because they didn't align around how they would work together. That generates misunderstandings and unintentional conflict, which can literally destroy teamwork. Here are some common objectives to achieve adequate alignment within the Intellectual dimension.

- **Align around the "what" topics.** The "what" topics of a typical project address standard project management elements. Initial alignment around these topics should be achieved up front during the project planning process. In addition, as the project unfolds and evolves, changes to these elements must be clearly communicated to maintain alignment throughout the project. The "what" topics include:

- **Background of the project or engagement.** Team members need to have a common understanding of the background of the situation in order to be successful in their roles.
- **Business goals.** The expected final business results of the effort need to be understood by all who will contribute to its completion. Goals and expected outcomes need to be updated and communicated if they change or evolve during the project.
- **Scope.** People need to have a clear understanding of the scope and complexity of the project. Although project managers are responsible overall for the management of scope, they cannot do that well if those doing the work are not clear on what is in and out of scope. Performing out-of-scope work, which is typically not compensated, can be a huge energy drain on a project. Thus, creating ongoing alignment around scope is critical.
- **Deliverables/specifications.** Different parties may be responsible for different deliverables, and there may be dependencies between deliverables. All parties need to understand clearly what they are responsible for delivering as well as the specifications and interdependencies associated with those deliverables.
- **Success criteria.** Success criteria are how key stakeholders will define and measure project success. These criteria need to be clearly understood by all contributors at the outset of the project, so all know how project performance will be gauged at the project's conclusion. Individual team members may have their own success criteria, depending on the function they perform. It is critical, however, to ensure that individual success criteria roll up to achieve the overall project success criteria that key stakeholders hold as the ultimate indicator of success.
- **Schedule.** A schedule is a powerful tool for aligning project activities and energies. The team needs to have a clear understanding of the timetable and sequence of project deliverables, major milestones, and work. The degree of detail needed in a project schedule depends on the size and complexity of the project. To achieve a high degree of clarity and alignment, the schedule will identify the project tasks and, for each one, will specify who will perform it and how many labor hours are budgeted for work completion (resource loading). Ambiguities or lack of sufficient specificity in a project schedule will almost certainly lead to delays and cost issues as well as team conflict.

- **Resources required.** The team needs to consider all the human, material, and facility resources needed to meet project expectations. Human resources include project staff controlled by the team as well as outside resources that may not be under the team's control. Having dependencies on outside resources who do not have a significant stake in the outcome of the project is a risk to the project, so building alignment with those people is especially critical. In addition to the human resources, teams should identify and communicate planned material acquisitions, facilities needed, and any other resources needed to get the job done.
- **Budget.** In addition to knowing the overall budget for the project, team members should know and agree to the budget for their portion of the project work. Furthermore, should unexpected work impacts occur, team members must be prepared to communicate them and their potential effect on the project budget.
- **Risks and red flags.** The team should identify project risks and agree on plans to either avoid them or mitigate them should they actually occur. A realized risk that wasn't planned for can blow the lid off of a project's energy reserve, so it is essential to be proactive when dealing with risks.

- **Align around the "how" topics.** The "how" topics of a typical project relate to how the team works together. These topics include:
  - **Processes used to perform the work.** These are the processes used to do the primary work (e.g., agile development processes, HR business processes, etc.). These processes often need a level of customization for a particular project, so the team should be aligned around the customized process.
  - **Roles and responsibilities.** Roles and responsibilities need to be clearly defined for all team members so that all know what they are assigned to do, the roles and responsibilities others have, and what is expected from each team member.
  - **Communication/status reporting.** It should be determined how internal communication and project status reporting will take place to meet the needs and expectations of the team. The team will need to consider frequency, style, method, and content of communication and status reporting.
  - **Client communication and management process.** This process typically is used by a project manager to communicate status, discuss issues, and manage project scope with the client. This process is often based largely on the client's preferences and working style.

The objective is an ongoing alignment with the client as the project proceeds and evolves.

- **Decision-making process.** Teams often must make decisions on a variety of important matters, such as a task approach, response to an issue, a workaround, approval of deliverables, and others. To avoid arguments and conflicts downstream, the team should agree in advance on who needs to be involved in what types of decisions, the timing of the decisions, and how the decision-making processes will be facilitated when multiple people are involved. Where appropriate, team members should be empowered to make decisions relevant to their particular work if their decisions do not impact others' work. Team members should also establish in advance how they will work out disagreements, should they arise.

- **Operating assumptions.** The team should identify and agree on underlying assumptions regarding the work process, resource availability, constraints, and client responsiveness (e.g., in reviewing deliverables). A good rule of thumb is that whenever a project is dependent on an outside resource or action, the project manager and team should formulate an assumption about how and when that support will be provided. All assumptions should be clearly communicated to the team members, the client, and the outside resources.

- **Common expectations and commitments.** Teams often have problems when expectations and level of commitment are not clarified up front. For example, if some team members are working overtime to help salvage a project that is behind schedule and others are not, resentment will naturally grow. It is much better to establish expectations and commitments up front than it is to resolve misalignments after the fact.

- **Preferred work style.** Team members may have different preferences for how they like to work, they may be in different time zones, or they may work in different shifts. The preferred work styles of each team member should be communicated up front so that the team may identify the favored common denominators for the style of teamwork to be utilized on the project.

- **Achieve a common understanding of problems and needs.** Teams are often handed big problems to solve. In order to solve them, teams first must achieve an accurate understanding of what the problem truly is. Quite often, the presenting problem does not turn out to be the root cause issue. Systematic data gathering and analysis can reveal that the problem is deeper than it first appeared and that there are multiple contributors. All team members must have a common understanding of the root causes and contributors before moving to the solution phase. Without that alignment, different team members will be trying to solve different problems, making solution alignment all but impossible.

- **Align around solutions and work outcomes.** Based on a common understanding of the problem and needs, teams must then figure out the best way to solve the problems and fulfill the needs. Doing this can be a very spirited process as ideas are presented, challenged, processed, and filtered. This process can also be one of the most intellectually exciting aspects of a project. In the end, teams must align around the preferred solution or at least around solution options for the client to consider. Doing so helps establish a clear path for the team to develop and implement the solution.

Personal Alignment

As we have discussed, people bring their Personal ingredients to the table when they work. This is certainly the case with group collaborative conversations as discussed earlier. Within the Personal dimension, the difference between collaborative group conversations and project-based group collaboration is that with projects, the need for alignment spans a long period of time rather than just a single conversation. Because of this length of time, the intent of each person on the team (i.e., their goals and agendas, personal beliefs and attitudes, and personal positions regarding the work) must remain sufficiently aligned to the team and the work. This can be challenging since, as we discussed, Environmental factors can have a profound ongoing influence on the Personal dimensions of those on a team.

The story of the 1980 U.S. Olympic Hockey Team, as portrayed in the movie *Miracle*, is a great example of how divisive factors, which stemmed from the environment around the team, were ultimately overcome. When Herb Brooks, the Olympic team coach, first selected the group of amateur players as candidates for the final team, their identities and attitudes were clearly with the college teams for which they played during the regular hockey season. Old rivalries played out on the ice as what was supposed to be a team looked more like so many college factions with little interest in the larger cause (the U.S. team). Few people thought the team had much of a chance of winning anything at the Olympic Games.

Undaunted, Herb Brooks, a master motivator, purposely exposed the personal agendas for what they were, ridiculing the old college rivalries and working the team harder when they were clearly favoring their personal agendas over the larger cause. Herb knew he had to shift the team members' identification from their individual colleges to the U.S. Olympic Team. As one of his tactics, he would randomly ask players during practice, "What is your name and who do you play for?" Their answers always included the names of their colleges, until one night. Herb was working the team to exhaustion following a very lackluster, inattentive performance at an exhibition game. He was breaking down members' personal agendas and attitudes so they would realize how petty this old intent was compared with the honor and responsibility of representing their country.

Finally Mike Eruzione, who would later become team captain, got it. He stopped in the middle of the ice and shouted out with what little breath he had left, "My name is Mike Eruzione, and I play for the United States of America!" Herb Brooks, seeing that a leader among the players had turned the tide, promptly dismissed the exhausted but more enlightened and aligned team. From that point on the team came together, ultimately beat the favored Soviet Union, and won the gold medal at the Olympics. The so-called Miracle on Ice is now the stuff of legend.

You can see from this story the power of the Personal dimension on the members of a team. Misalignment in this dimension can tear a team apart, while alignment can form a bond that leads the team to unimaginable accomplishments. In the story, the team factions sprang from the college hockey environment, which encouraged the individual players to identify more with their college teams (where they came from) than with the new U.S. team. In business, functional departments and factions in the business are the equivalents of college teams. As cross-functional teams become more necessary in business, this identification problem becomes more noticeable and serious. People are drafted from their departments (where they come from) to work on cross-functional teams. They often bring the same kind of personal agendas and allegiance to where they came from that the hockey players brought to the ice. That situation, of course, leaves little room to collaborate and work as a team.

The way through this is twofold. First, the business needs to set up the Environmental factors in a way that encourages identification with the teams, not just the departments. We provided an example of this in our

Alchemy Instruments story. Second, regardless of the state of the Environmental dimension, team members must be willing to put aside and hold lightly their personal attitudes and agendas in favor of the larger team agenda and goals. Project managers can help make this happen, but, in the end, it is up to each team member to favor the larger purpose over personal agendas, beliefs, and attitudes. Each person is responsible for sustained attention to, and engagement in, the team work, and for putting forth a level of effort needed to make the project successful.

Directional Alignment

As mentioned earlier, project teams must achieve adequate alignment within and among the dimensions of energy *over a period of time* to be successful. That means the alignment must be sustained, or at least renewable. The first three dimensions of energy—Environmental, Intellectual, and Personal— each contain a number of areas where alignment is needed. Establishing and maintaining adequate alignment in these areas constitutes a set of ongoing project objectives. Achieving these objectives is where our skills and behaviors in navigating work and developing working relationships (i.e., the Directional dimension) come in. How we navigate, and the energy we bring to it, will largely determine how successful we are in establishing and maintaining alignment in the first three dimensions.

For example, if you and your teammates are skilled at one-on-one collaboration, you will tend to be successful in building alignment with others in your one-on-one interactions. Similarly, if you and your teammates are skilled at collaborative group conversations, you will tend to build alignment and shared space in your meetings and group work. Thus, if alignment is built, maintained, and renewed in all or most of the interactions related to your project, the powerful collective energy (shared space) among you, your teammates, and the project's stakeholders will essentially be pointed in the same direction, and the project will almost certainly be successful, perhaps fantastically successful.

In contrast, a team less skilled in collaboration will be more challenged in building and maintaining alignment around the key topics. There will be less positive energy and more negative energy present. There may still be enough positive energy to overcome the negative, but success will come with a higher price (lower efficiency due to the energy drain) and may be compromised in terms of final business outcomes. Worse yet, the negative energy may overtake the positive energy and start a downward spiral that leads to failure. So the importance of collaborative skills and behaviors is immense. Building these skills and behaviors will likely become a major focus area of business in the Fourth Industrial Revolution.

Although the Directional dimension is something we bring to literally everything we do on a project, there are some specific actions that we can build into project operations to help organize Directional energy and promote alignment. These key actions include:

- **Establish alignment up front.** Alignment around the topics just discussed should be established as soon as possible after project start-up. That means working with team members, clients, stakeholders, and, if applicable, end users, partners, and subcontractors. Delays in establishing alignment can easily lead to negative attitudes, the development of opposing forces, and energy drains at a time when the project needs to build momentum and positive energy.

  Many years ago I managed a mission-critical project for a large healthcare company. Although we put a great deal of effort into identifying and meeting with stakeholders from various parts of the business, we missed one—the head of finance for a major part of the company. He was quite upset about it and felt left out. I felt horrible about our oversight and was worried the man would react by somehow sabotaging the project or undermining our reputations. He was capable of both. I immediately scheduled a meeting with him, myself, and one of my teammates at his office, which required us to jump on a plane. Our immediate efforts to get there gave us an opening with him. By the end of our frank, open, and constructive meeting, we had established a good mutual understanding of his desired role as a project stakeholder and alignment around how decisions that affected the business would be made.

  Similarly, I have seen many projects that failed to align early around the team-based topics. These projects often are the ones where things just aren't working, arguments are frequent, and people seem to be going in different directions. The choice is a simple one: Either put in the effort to align quickly up front, or pay the price in obstacles and energy drains along the way.

- **Monitor alignment and reset as needed.** Once alignment is achieved on a project, it must be maintained. Why? Because various forces at work in your business, the client organization, and your team will often tend to erode alignment. Whether it is a client who changes his mind about a requirement, a teammate who decides to favor his personal agenda, or delays in meeting a deliverable date, the alignment you thought was secure is suddenly challenged. This situation tends to happen more in businesses with dysfunctional Environmental dimensions that spill into the Personal dimensions of the people involved in a project. Attention, effort, and energy are required to address problems and maintain alignment. And because misalignment invites additional misalignment, it is best to nip these problems in the bud as soon as they are detected. The reward for maintaining alignment throughout the project is success.

- **Manage communications.** Within the context of group collaboration, communication is the vehicle for monitoring and building alignment. Communications are an exchange of information. Much of what we learn through communications indicates underlying energy. Communications are essential for navigating work. They give us a way to (1) discover things relevant to the work (e.g., problems, issues, positive feedback), (2) understand the status of the work (progress against schedule and degree of alignment across the key areas), and (3) execute navigational actions that steer the work toward successful outcomes (e.g., project activities, collaborative conversations, organizational announcements).

  The "how" topics discussed in the Intellectual dimension provide structure and agreement on how we communicate within a project. In the Directional dimension, we're executing those protocols (hopefully) and navigating the dynamic situation as the project unfolds. The question becomes this: How, as a practical matter, do we manage all of those communications? How do we best manage for success? Should we do it like Captain Kirk and his team did it on the Starship *Enterprise*? Should we manage and communicate like the FBI when it's on a case? These are exciting possibilities, but there is no one answer for the best way to manage project communications. Nevertheless, however you and your team do it, there are three kinds of communications you need to address: periodic, ad hoc, and external.

  1. **Periodic communications.** Teams benefit greatly from regularly scheduled opportunities to communicate around important project topics. Often these opportunities are team meetings scheduled weekly or even daily. They can be held in person or virtually. Topics generally include project status, problems, resolutions, risk management, and decisions regarding both strategy and tactics. Ideally,

each of these topics is addressed in a collaborative fashion with the achievement of alignment marking the conclusion of each discussion topic.

Team meetings should be approached as collaborative opportunities rather than mandatory meetings driven by a checklist of topics. Well-done team meetings usually are facilitated by the project manager, who must keep the discussion on track, leverage the individual strengths of team members, champion creativity and alignment, lead the decision-making process, and delegate assignments. This complex array of activities requires a significant skill set that is not always present in project managers.

In my work building project and program management groups (e.g., in professional service groups), I have observed project/program managers who approached team meetings as if they were painting by the numbers. When this happened, the rest of the team invariably approached their parts in the meeting with the same rote method and attitude. An apathetic energy was generated where creativity was stifled and alignment became unimportant. Left unaddressed, this rote approach would have probably caused the team to hit a wall. Fortunately, once these problems were addressed, the teams came alive with enthusiasm and renewed energy.

2. **Ad hoc communications.** Ad hoc communications come in several forms, including brainstorming sessions, email, social media, texting, and phone calls. They are the day-to-day team communications that happen in between periodic team meetings. They are less formal than team meetings, more focused by nature, and they provide the daily glue that holds the team together. While I have seen teams that omitted periodic communications in favor of total ad hoc communications, I have never seen a team resist ad hoc communications. People tend to communicate this way naturally, so the issue is not *whether* to do it, but *how* to do it.

Ad hoc communications should not be overly controlled, but they can get out of hand without some structure and protocol. Collaboratively deciding on how these structures and protocols will work, which is best accomplished at the beginning of projects, was discussed earlier in this section. Now, in the Directional dimension, it is up to the team to implement the chosen structure and protocols.

For example, one communication guideline could be that ad hoc communications on any given topic are delivered only to those on the team who need them. This method avoids wasting team members' time with extraneous information. Another guideline might be that when information turns into a discussion, the discussion must be had in an appropriate forum. A violation of those protocols could occur when a team member sends an email to the entire team about a specific issue affecting only himself and one other teammate. The teammate hits Reply All and responds, which pulls others into the conversation. This unmanaged conversation has little chance of achieving alignment and wastes inordinate amounts of time. In this case, it is better to move the conversation into a more structured forum, like a meeting, involving only those affected by the issue.

Teams should be self-managing in terms of their ad hoc communications, with everyone watching for departures from the agreed-on communication structure and protocols and helping to bring things in line as needed. More important, we must remember that ad hoc communications, no less than periodic communications, are about building and maintaining alignment among team members. This is the responsibility of every team member.

When I see a team that isn't working well, problems with ad hoc communications are either a symptom or a cause, but they are always present. Either way, the problem boils down to a lack of alignment among the team members, which usually coexists with a lot of conflict and emotion. There is no single correct way to manage ad hoc communications. However, if you decide as a team how they will work and then self-manage toward those protocols, your efforts will be rewarded with greater team alignment and cohesion.

3. **External communications.** External communications are with people outside of the project team, including clients, stakeholders, and end users. They are a hybrid between periodic communications (e.g., client status meetings) and ad hoc communications (e.g., informal conversations and emails). Without specific agreement about how these communications will work, teams can face significant risks.

For example, I once took over management across a group of external client-facing projects. These projects were composed of cross-functional teams with our people interacting daily with client peers. The whole thing was way out of control because there had been no discussion and agreement about how external communications would work. Commitments to take on extra scope without adjusting the budget were being made by virtually everyone during casual conversations with client peers. Disagreements among our team members were aired to client staff, who became inappropriately involved in the debates. The situation essentially invited clients to pit our team members against each other to get what they wanted. A great deal of damage was being done, and a lot of energy was being drained from the projects.

The interesting thing is that this problem was not that difficult to fix. We agreed on the external communication protocols and then held to them. Project managers were the only ones who could commit the projects to additional scope, which usually came with commensurate budget. Disagreements among team members were worked out in internal meetings, and the aligned decisions were then communicated with client staff. Although some clients no longer got everything they wanted without paying for it, our overall alignment with them was dramatically improved.

- **Review and reflect at project completion.** One final Directional activity that can add significant value to the growth and maturation of a business is to review and reflect at project completion. Project teams learn and innovate a lot during projects, and that information can benefit future projects and the enterprise as a whole. For example, the information can result in changes to process and policy, can spawn system modifications, and can seed new product development initiatives. Reviewing and reflecting can take different forms. Perhaps the simplest form is the after-action review. Developed initially by the army to debrief soldiers coming off the battlefield, after-action reviews ask four questions: What was supposed to happen? What actually happened? What did you learn from that? What will you do differently next time?

  This simple yet powerful process can be done on a whiteboard with teams at the completion of a project, ideally while the information is still fresh. Teams should have a way to submit the results to the broader organization for consideration and possible action. This final form of alignment works across projects and throughout the enterprise to build customer focus and foster business excellence.

As we have discussed, project-based group collaboration requires that we build alignment on our projects up front and then maintain alignment throughout the project's life. As with individual work and one-on-one collaborations, alignment on projects involves all four dimensions of energy: Environmental, Intellectual, Personal, and Directional. Understanding this model (and reality) gives us a strategy and set of concrete objectives for achieving success on any project. Now that we have the clarity that comes from understanding the hidden energy of projects, we can better utilize the unique talents of people to accomplish amazing things as part of the Fourth Industrial Revolution.

Chapter 6

Managing People

I've observed many managers over the years and talked with several about their views and experiences regarding the management of people. Depending on whom you ask, managing people is everything from a rewarding privilege to a necessary evil. Some love the power of management while others say that people are just one big string of problems. I've seen equal diversity in leadership and management styles. For example, autocratic managers are prone to quick decisions and inclined to bark out orders. This tends to work in cop shows on television. At the other end of the continuum are consensus managers who won't make a move unless everyone agrees. But mostly I see managers who don't fit neatly into a box with a label. They display an array of eclectic management characteristics. Some are more effective than others.

The question that all of this raises for me is: What serves as our compass when it comes to leading and managing people? People, groups, and circumstances are all variable, so one size does not fit all. That which works in one situation may be disastrous in another. An interaction approach with one person may cause another to run out the door, and a leadership style that is effective with one group may backfire with another. Leadership and people management courses, which many managers have attended, can only take us so far. Eventually the cookbook runs dry and we are left in uncertain territory. For that reason, this chapter is not a recipe on how to lead and manage people. Rather, it is an attempt to provide you with the elements of a strong compass. The common denominator of these elements is the observation and management of energy—in individuals, in groups, and in ourselves—and the alignment of those energies toward common goals.

Machiavelli Was Right and Wrong

The term "Machiavellian" has been vilified and is used most often to describe ruthless, cunning people. Before all of that, however, there was a brilliant author with deep insights that help us set the stage in this book for our discussion on leading and managing people.

What Drives People

Centuries ago, Niccolò Machiavelli wrote his political treatise, *The Prince* (2014, originally published 1513). Many would agree that his book is the foundation of modern political science. It is also about what drives and motivates people. *The Prince* is a deeply insightful piece of work, based on Machiavelli's direct observations of princes, principalities, and power. I remember first reading it as part of my MBA program. The core message was that the best way to motivate and drive people was through fear. My reaction was twofold. First, I could see the truth in what Machiavelli was saying. People are, in fact, motivated and controlled by fear. Second, I was disappointed by that fact and could not completely accept it as the whole truth. Thus began my search for the rest of the story. It is my hope that this book provides at least a glimpse into the next chapter of that story.

We have talked a lot about positive and negative energy. Fear is negative energy. There is nothing positive about it. The motivation that fear provides comes from our desire to avoid it. Fear is strongly attached to our desire to survive, a driving instinct that exists at the deepest and most primitive level of all human beings. Fear served us well over the millennia by helping us survive. But as we began to form what in Machiavelli's time were called principalities, leaders used our survival instincts to align, organize, and control us. Today, the principalities are governments and companies.

And, unfortunately, many of our common business practices still rely on the use of fear to align, organize, and control people

For example, I saw fear clearly at play in our recent work with a federal government agency. In the agency, a strong culture of fear had the effect of keeping people in their places and, in some cases, virtually immobilized them. Risk taking was out of the question since employees generally felt that any significant failure put their jobs at risk. For the most part, employees were order takers. Their creative spirits and desire to take initiative had been broken. The risks were simply too high. When we encouraged leaders to go to their bosses and make some suggestions to solve significant issues, they were unwilling to do so. They never said no; they just didn't do it. In their culture, bold suggestions were too risky.

In this agency, being at fault was like playing musical chairs and being the one without a chair when the music stopped. No one ever wanted to be left standing. This orientation provided an automatic motivation for people in the agency to throw each other under the bus, which happened quite a lot. "Better him than me" was the rationale. That's what you do when you are focused on survival. And then there was the dreaded budgeting session that happened at least once a year. During these periods, people were afraid that their jobs would be cut. This fear motivated them to behave just the way the agency wanted them to behave: Do what you are told. Keep your head down. Don't stand out or rock the boat. Protect your leaders. Then you might be able to keep your job. With all of that fear, which constituted negative energy working against the forward progress of work, people were inherently inefficient.

No one person created this culture and management style. A collection of many leaders and business norms over the years created and sustained it. But this fear-based culture and management style doesn't have to be this way, and in fact it shouldn't be. We don't have to rule the people in our companies, agencies, and schools by fear. We don't have to use negative energy to align and control people. There are ways to lead people that encourage creative and productive behaviors instead of forcing them into a nonproductive, fear-based, order-taking allegiance. To lead in this way, we must appeal to a different part of people and stop pushing their survival buttons. The promise of this type of leadership is that by removing the negative energy of what we might call Machiavellian leadership, we can harness much more positive energy in our people so that they perform the work of the business more effectively and efficiently. And we can have a much happier and healthier working environment.

Appealing to the Best Part of People

Given our circumstances in business, education, and government, with chronic conflict and a pressing need to work differently in the Fourth Industrial Revolution, we need an alternative to leading and managing people through fear. Fortunately, people are motivated by things other than fear. In his book, *Drive: The Surprising Truth about What Motivates Us*, Daniel Pink (2009) asserts that the secret to high performance and satisfaction at work are the deeply human needs to direct our own lives, learn and create new things, and do better by ourselves and our world. Artists are a good example of people who live out of these more creative and altruistic motivators in a more visible way than perhaps most of us do. Although such motivators are not the exclusive drivers of human behavior, they seem to coexist with the survival-based motivators discussed earlier. In fact, all people have what I call an *intrinsic essence* that spawns these deeply human needs. This essence is about positive energy. It is inherently the best part of us. In the expression of this essence, we are naturally motivated to create shared space in our work with other people.

You may be thinking that you know people who don't seem to have an ounce of intrinsic essence within them. I know such people as well. But I have also seen these people turn around and tap into their reservoirs, so to speak. The truth is that we never lose our intrinsic essence, but we can cover it up and choose not to operate from it. Two primary drivers can lead to this cover-up. First, in many businesses, the environment encourages this path. For example, the culture and management practices in the government agency had the effect of moving people away from their intrinsic essences and encouraging them to operate out of their fear-based instincts. Any individual could, of course, try to resist that pressure. However, such resistance is very difficult to sustain over time. Tribes (e.g., businesses) have a way of either bringing outliers into the fold or booting them out.

The second path that can lead to people covering up and ignoring their intrinsic essences starts with a personal orientation and intent toward survival at all cost. Doing work and the outcome of work are important only to the extent that they support this goal of survival, (i.e., keeping my job, status, and income). That orientation, in turn, drives fear-based behavior (through the Directional dimension). In other words, this second path has to do with what we, as individuals, bring to the table and how what we bring affects our work. For example, if my intent at work is to survive and stay safe, I hold that agenda tightly, and I consistently give it a number-one priority. I give little if any consideration to my intrinsic essence, or to any motivations that may stem from it. They simply are not a priority. Doing what I have to do to stay safe and prevent others from perceiving that I am at fault are much more important to me than doing good for my business or the world.

In the end, it is up to the people to choose their path in work. However, managers and leaders can influence which path people choose by the way they design their enterprise elements and the way they manage people. These things can push people either toward their intrinsic essences or toward their fear-based instincts. Again, the need to tap into the intrinsic essences of our people and help them work from that orientation is becoming more essential. Collaboration and interpersonal services are easily tainted by fear and personal agendas. People need a clean playing field to operate at the level we need them to, less unencumbered by negative energy. The people themselves are part of the solution, and managers and leaders are the other part.

In managing people, we need to *appeal* to their intrinsic essences. We need to engage and ignite the deeply human needs that Daniel Pink identified as key motivators. To effectively engage the intrinsic essence of our people, management itself must be viewed as an interpersonal service. In other words, every interaction a manager has with one of their people is a collaboration with a goal of optimizing the person's performance, the performance of the business overall, and the intrinsic satisfaction the person receives by performing the work. As with all collaborations, these management interactions involve the four dimensions of energy.

To appeal to the best part of people, we must be thoughtful, aware, and attentive to our contributions to each of these dimensions and the affects they have on the other person. We cannot approach management as a one-directional activity where we give the orders, they do the work, and all of the motivation comes from us. Instead, people are largely responsible for their motivation, and we are responsible for facilitating an ongoing process that helps them engage their internal motivations and apply them toward meeting or exceeding the goals of the business.

In my career I have had many different bosses. They ran the gamut from awesome to horrible. As I reflected on the best versus the worst bosses, I recognized some common differences, including these:

- The worst bosses tended to view me as one would, let's say, an ox pulling a cart. Their only interest was to get the ox to work harder and pull the cart faster. This felt like domination, distrust, and devaluation. In contrast, the best bosses recognized my intrinsic essence and related to me primarily through that essence. Those interactions felt much different. They were not dominating, they were partnering and guiding. These bosses trusted me and opened the door for me to build on our trusting relationship. And they valued me for who I was, what I could do, and my partnership with them.

- The worst bosses wanted too much intellectual involvement in, and control over, my work. If I wanted to brief them on my progress on a project, they would grill me for details and get way down into the weeds, which made me feel as if they were usurping my project in an attempt to prove that they were smarter than I. If I pushed back with alternative ideas, they were easily insulted and often reacted by giving me direction (orders) to show that they were still the boss. Conversely, the best bosses had a sense of shared space and understood the importance of building that with me. They did nothing to take away from the responsibility they had given me but sought to help me with it. They listened to and respected my ideas and invited healthy debate. And they gave direction reluctantly, urging me instead to tell them what I was going to do next.

- The worst bosses were either completely closed off about sharing their own situations, experiences, and motivations at work or they wouldn't stop talking about them in a negative way. When they didn't share at all, there was no room for partnership, no way for me to put myself in their shoes and find solutions that would work for them. It was a constant guessing game in which I felt a sense of failure whenever I guessed wrong. My experience with bosses who incessantly complained about the company and their work was that they were useless to the cause and cared only about themselves. The best bosses knew what to share and what not to share; most important, they knew when to share and how to share it. Their sharing was motivated not by what made them feel good but by what I needed to know to build shared space with them. If they had information that needed to stay at their level, they would tell me as much as they could without getting into details. If they had a personal experience that was relevant to what I was experiencing, they shared it, even if it didn't paint the perfect picture of a boss. I respected them even more for that and felt a strong professional camaraderie.

You can see from these examples that the worst bosses crushed my internal motivation while the best bosses engaged, fed, and guided my intrinsic essence. But we must allow for the fact that not everyone is like me. While I am all about working from my intrinsic essence, other people are not. They are not automatically bad people for that, but they are somewhere else on the continuum between intrinsic essence and fear-based instincts. As much as I would like to say we should abandon all management techniques that involve fear in favor of the intrinsic essence methods, I cannot. I cannot say that because people who operate more toward the fear-based end of the continuum, either in a particular situation or chronically, cannot be reached without a dose of fear. That's why Machiavelli was both right and wrong. He was right because some people will only respond to fear. And he was wrong in that his answer was incomplete. There is another way to lead people that many will respond to.

I once had a program manager on my staff who managed a large program on a very important account. I'll call her Alice. I "inherited" Alice when I took my position. Soon I began to hear complaints from the client staff that Alice had said things and done things that they felt were disrespectful. When I asked Alice about the incidents, she always had a rationalization for doing what she did, such as "That client always wants something for nothing." In fact, her stories were more often true than not, but that didn't excuse her unkind and unprofessional interactions. Furthermore, Alice painted herself as a victim of both the client and the company we both worked for. This was her way of not taking responsibility. I coached Alice and tried to appeal to her intrinsic essence, the part of herself that got her into this company and industry in the first place. I talked with her about all the people her large program served and the opportunity she had to make a difference in their lives. I talked about it being an honor to serve and even told a story about King Arthur and the Round Table. Nothing worked. She kept up her disrespectful behavior. The complaints got worse, and the account was in jeopardy. I had no choice but to operate from the fear-based side of the continuum where Alice was entrenched. Along with HR I gave her a verbal warning, hoping that her fear of losing her job would be enough to turn her around. But she didn't budge. I went to a written warning, which also didn't motivate her. Ultimately I terminated her.

This kind of situation is an unfortunate reality in our workforce. Some people are beyond influence when it comes to moving them in the direction of their intrinsic essences. A colleague of mine calls these people the "uncoachables." Managers and leaders generally have little or no effect on entrenched Personal characteristics that people bring with them to work—and to life in general. Impacts are possible but much less likely, and are far from a sure thing in any individual. For this reason, appealing to the best part of people who have rendered their intrinsic essences inaccessible, to themselves and others, is either impossible or not worth the major energy required for what will likely generate a low return. Only the person can impact these personal characteristics, and some people are unwilling to do so.

For managers and leaders, the message here is simple. If you are interested in tapping the intrinsic essence of your workforce, you need to understand who you can help and who you can't help. Then you need to understand that if you keep people around who are entrenched in the fear-based side of the continuum, they will continue to operate out of their personal agendas because it is their orientation. They may have tremendous Intellectual gifts, but the value of those gifts to the business will always be compromised by their personal agendas. Furthermore, keeping these people around sends a message to everyone else that you condone personal agendas at the expense of the business. At best, doing so will make you look hypocritical. At worst, your efforts to move people in the direction of their intrinsic essences will fall apart.

Most people will fall somewhere in the middle of the motivational continuum, and most businesses have Environmental characteristics, poorly designed enterprise elements, that breed conflict and competition and push people toward the "dark side." This negative environmental influence complicates things because someone who exhibits negative behaviors in one company may behave quite positively in a company with a healthier environment. Therefore, it is important to evaluate people in the context of their environment, and it is important to take action on negative Environmental factors while you are asking your staff and managers to undergo their own transformations.

In the next section we discuss how leaders can ignite and harness the intrinsic motivations of people to achieve the important goals of the business.

The Energy of Leadership

Whereas management is about managing individuals, leadership is about managing the collective. The collective may be a platoon, a department, a school, a corporation, or any other defined collection of people in business or government. Much has been written about leadership. The many books and articles addressing the topic provide suggestions and insights on things like what makes a good leader, the most important leadership skills, why leaders fail, and tasks that good leaders do every day. Although this advice is valuable, leaders can get lost in it. This chapter is unique in that it provides a perspective on leadership from the standpoint of energy. This perspective gives us a simplifying framework and approach, unified by a single theme—the systematic management of energy to achieve desired business outcomes.

On the path of energy management, being a good leader is about knowing yourself, your people, and your surroundings, identifying and communicating a vision and direction, and engaging the hearts and minds of the people toward achieving that vision. It's all about energy. As with all types of work, leadership involves the four Dimensions of Energy in a collaboration between the leader and the collective. Similar to the management of individuals, leadership is about connecting to the motivational forces within people and then working across the dimensions to align their energies with the direction and energy of the business. This section provides a leadership path and checklist for how to align personal and business energies.

Align Your Personal Dimension

As a leader, your intent (i.e., your goals, agendas, personal beliefs, and attitudes) will be under a microscope and watched by all whom you lead. Your intent will play out in how you lead and in ways that may even surprise you. Your power will be significant, and you will want to find the best blend between your Personal dimension and the interests of the business and its people. Therefore, it is a good idea to check your intent to find the sweet spot and make sure you are committing to the job for the right reasons.

You may ask, Why should I need to check my personal intent? I'll just keep that stuff to myself. Nobody has to know my secret beliefs or agenda. Technically that would be correct. However, as a practical matter, you need to understand your personal intent.

If you enter a leadership position with a significant disconnect between your intent and the interests of the company, it is unlikely that you will be able to keep that a secret. Under the pressure of daily leadership, you will probably find yourself saying and doing things that expose your true goals, agendas, personal beliefs, and attitudes. As we sometimes say, it comes out sideways. As you become more exposed, the disconnect can lead to major problems.

For example, let's say you come in saying that you are going to improve the working environment and are later heard to say that revenue growth trumps people and the environment is good enough. Word will spread like wildfire, and you could become instantly unpopular. You may find a way to set the record straight, but you may well end up exposing yourself again in some other way. The point is, leading with a significant disconnect between your goals and those of the business will waste a lot of energy, your risk of exposure is high, and the consequences are even higher. Perhaps the larger point is that leadership is about service. If you lose sight of that service orientation, or never engage it in the first place because you are more focused on your own agenda, you will likely fail as a leader because your people will follow you right into their own personal agendas. For these reasons, it is worth your while to resolve as much personal misalignment as possible before you start down the leadership path. Doing so will help you set the stage for your sustained attention, effective engagement, and maximum effort in performing the functions of a leader.

Know the Environmental Dimension

As a leader, it is important to know and understand the business environment, the playing field upon which you will lead. It is also important to know the people with whom you will be working. This knowledge comes over time as you gain experience with the business, but it is good to have at least a high-level view when you start a new leadership position. One way to approach this is to use the Enterprise Elements Model as a checklist of areas to investigate. For senior executives and business leaders, your investigation will focus across the business. For mid-level leaders, your focus will be on your part of the business, but you should also have a general idea of the business as a whole.

Another view of how the business works can be had by mapping the flow of money, as we discussed in chapter 3. It follows, of course, that you will want to know, in general, where the business is "broken." Look for chronic conflict and misalignments of control and responsibility. Keep in mind that this is the environment your people work in every day. Your job as a leader will almost certainly include making the environment better in support of the people and your overall business direction. As a leader, you are responsible for the use and conservation of the collective energy. If dysfunctional elements in your environment are draining energy, you are going to have to plug some holes.

Understanding the business culture is also key. Cultures are about "the way we are in this business." They are composed of many things, including norms, expectations, protocols, and stories. For example, every business has what I like to call the unwritten book of rules that are tacitly agreed upon within the collective over time. These rules are usually about how to keep each other safe, when and how to promote self-interest over company interests, and underground channels of information flow. In my experience, people usually are more loyal to the unwritten rules than written policies and procedures. These rules are not written down because, if they were, people would have to admit to them, and they are not the kind of rules people want to acknowledge. In addition, if the business has defined values, they are worth a careful review, but look at them as more of an aspiration than a fact. Often the declared values of a company and the values of the people are in stark contrast.

If you have an adequate understanding of culture, you will be more immediately trusted and respected by the collective, and you will also be in a better position to change the culture as needed.

Finally, there is the matter of knowing the people and how they work. People you lead want to be seen, known, heard, and involved. Forming and nurturing business relationships is essential for successful leadership. And don't just give this lip service. People know when you are insincere and when you are genuine. As you get to know people, they will get to know you. Show them who you are, let them touch you with their words and experiences and learn from them. In the words of Chinese philosopher Lao Tzu, "To lead people, walk behind them."

Establish the Energetic Direction

The overall goal of leaders is to lead the movement of the business in a direction where it will better serve customers, achieve its business goals, and provide returns to its investors. In doing this, leaders are growing and maximizing the collective energy of the business. The growth in collective energy is essentially the return from the efforts invested to move the business. An obvious early step in this process is to establish the desired direction. That clarity then provides a set of targets for applying the collective energy. Establishing too many targets will diffuse the energy and risk them all. Too few targets will result in wasted time and a lesser performance in the marketplace. Thus, leaders must choose their targets wisely, and they should do so with a sense of how much energy their business has available to invest in achieving new targets. If, for example, the current state of the business is quite dysfunctional, with work less efficient and draining energy, the leader should be aware that the energy available to do new things is quite limited.

There are essentially two types of targets: business and environmental. Business targets are what you would expect, and have to do with the business as it relates to the outside world. Leaders at the highest levels of business target things such as increased market share, product line expansion, and increased revenue. Mid-level leaders target such things as production increases, improved capability, and functional talent development. Environmental targets, of course, have to do with improving the environment (i.e., the collection of enterprise elements). Environmental improvements are often necessary to support specific business targets and the business as a whole.

For example, the Alchemy Instruments case earlier in the book showed us a company that had to create a new sales paradigm to support its desired increase in revenue, a major business target. Because external business initiatives often require complementary internal initiatives, it is suggested that business and environmental targets be established simultaneously.

Align the Environment

The stage has been set in your leadership collaboration. You have aligned yourself with the business, you know your environment, you know the people with whom you will be working, and you have clear targets for the business. Now it is time to aim the energy gun, so to speak. Doing so begins with the environmental changes needed to hit your established environmental targets.

We discussed an approach for making environmental changes and creating shared space in chapter 3. All of that applies here. As a leader, you are redesigning those aspects of the environment that create energetic obstacles to people doing what you want them to do and/or removing energy drains that rob energy from the desired activities. You are thereby facilitating the work you want people to do by making things easier. People appreciate that support, and it will begin to move the needle on their intellectual and personal alignment.

Align People Intellectually and Personally

With the environmental alignment under way, it's time to align the collective with you and the business targets. Initially, doing so means aligning the people within their Intellectual and Personal dimensions (i.e., engaging the concurrence and support of their hearts and minds). Leaders do and say a multitude of things that move people toward alignment; there are just as many that erode alignment. Therefore, leadership is as much about what not to do and say as it is about what to do and say. The message here is to be careful about everything you do. It is much easier to erode alignment through a careless statement or inattentive behavior than it is to build it.

Intellectual alignment is getting people to know and understand where the business is going, why that direction is important, what they can expect from the business, what is expected of them, and what's in it for them in their jobs. Intellectual alignment is accomplished by the flow of explanatory information along with interactive dialogue for questions, clarifications, and feedback to ensure an adequate level of understanding. There are many ways to communicate with people and no one "right" way to do it.

You should consider every method of communication and the communication preferences of individuals. For example, I started texting so I could communicate more with my daughters. It helps to meet people where they are, and it helps to have information available in ways they prefer.

The indicators of energy that signal the degree of alignment in the Intellectual dimension tend to focus on evidence of understanding and of confusion. At the individual level, a simple conversation will usually tell you how clearly a person understands something. At the collective level, it is more useful and pragmatic to look at behaviors and listen to what people say. Internal survey results can also serve as good indicators of where people are in their understanding of key points and messages. There will undoubtedly be adjustments and refinements to the targets along the way, so plan on Intellectual alignment being an ongoing endeavor. The most important thing is that you establish and maintain an adequate degree of Intellectual alignment. If you are watching the indicators, you should have a strong sense of whether you are in the adequate range.

Personal alignment is about connecting with the people on a more emotional level, one that inspires them and engages their motivational forces. Personal alignment is accomplished primarily through the relationship that people have with the leader, the business overall, and themselves. That, of course, doesn't mean that a CEO has to know everybody in the company by name. The relationship does not require that kind of contact. However, it does require a personal connection.

The energy of a personal connection fires off when people feel elements of their Personal dimensions (i.e., their goals, agendas, personal beliefs and attitudes, and personal positions regarding their work), being acknowledged and supported. This is an emotional energy born of our human need to survive. The elements of our Personal dimensions are simply products of this survival energy playing out in the workplace. It is perhaps an unfortunate truth that the way to get many people to follow you is to do things and say things that make them feel you will help them survive. Every time you say or do something that encourages people's goals and agendas, agrees with their personal beliefs and attitudes, and supports their personal positions at work, you are speaking to them at an emotional level and telling them that you will help them survive.

Now, about the darker, more Machiavellian side of leadership. If you want to crank up the emotional gain and exploit survival emotions to control people, first tell them their survival is in jeopardy and then tell them you will help them survive if they follow you. I mention this not because I condone this leadership behavior, but because I want to be thorough. As we discussed in the last section, this kind of leadership comes with a price. Fear among people will get in the way of them doing their best and most productive work. Conflict among people will take its toll on them and the workplace and will ultimately erode the customer experience. The bottom line is that every leader has to decide how to engage the emotional side of the people. Calming their fears and helping them survive is one thing; stoking their fears to generate self-serving power is another.

The other way to fire off the energy of a personal connection is by engaging the intrinsic essence of people. This is a more altruistic energy than the survival-based emotional energy just discussed. It is much more about the larger goals of the business and how those will help people than it is about personal agendas. It is about the greater good, not about the individual good.

Earlier we discussed engaging the intrinsic essence of people as a motivational approach. Using that approach can go a long way toward motivating people to follow you. The other way to engage is to share how your vision for the business is connected to your own intrinsic essence. For example, "Our business is to help homeless people. I believe that every person deserves a hot meal and a safe and comfortable place to sleep." Or "We make the fastest cars in the world. People don't really need them, but they touch a spirit of adventure and excitement in me and others. That feels like magic." These statements are inspirational. Even if someone is not as passionate about taking care of homeless people or generating feelings of magic, they can relate to the statements; these messages touch their own intrinsic essences. If people believe in and appreciate your intrinsic essence, they are likely to believe in and follow you. At the very least you will have added to the Personal alignment among those in the workforce.

For several reasons, it is more difficult to gauge the degree of Personal alignment among your people at any point than to appraise Intellectual alignment. First, feelings and emotions are less tangible than knowledge and are more difficult to detect. Second, people tend to keep their Personal dimensions private and share only with those whom they trust. Third, even if you ask people about their Personal dimensions, they can talk only about the parts they are conscious of, and a large part of the

Personal dimension is unconscious in all of us. While it is good to talk with people about their feelings directly, it is often more informative to watch their behaviors.

For example, I took on a leadership position in a company division where the previous leader tended to blame and punish. I explained to the people my general position on making mistakes—avoid them but, if you make one, learn from it, don't make that mistake again, and move on. I made it clear that if people didn't make a mistake once in a while, they weren't trying new things, and I was not about punishing those who took measured risks for the sake of the business. After that little speech, I hoped my people would begin to engage more in the kind of innovative behavior I was looking for. But I kept seeing the same risk-averse behavior. I realized that even though I told the people that we wouldn't punish them for intelligent failures, they hadn't had enough time with me to see proof of that in my behavior, nor had I built an adequate level of trust. In other words, they did not yet trust that I would help them survive after they made a mistake. With more time together and some purposeful actions on my part to display the desired behaviors, the trust was built and my people became much more innovative and willing to take risks.

This is one small example of how the behaviors of people serve as indicators of Personal alignment. There are many more, so many that you won't see them all yourself. To help provide a more comprehensive view, you probably will want to engage your trusted network in helping you watch for the indicators. One final point is that the Personal dimension also includes the attention, engagement, and effort of the people. These things are somewhat more tangible and should definitely be included in the list of indicators to watch for.

Align People Directionally

All of your efforts to this point ultimately culminate in Directional alignment, where people are actually doing what you want them to do in concert with each other and you. The achievement of Directional alignment is not typically a single event. It usually happens in layers over time, ideally with each successive layer representing a deeper level of alignment. However it happens, it can be quite exciting. Energetically, it can be like reaching points of critical mass that result in the release of (or, more accurately, the receipt of) massive energy. This energy comes from the achievement of your targets and often comes in the form of revenue and profit. But it comes in many other forms as well, and certainly stokes the fires of your intrinsic essence as well as the intrinsic essences of your people.

Your daily work is guided by your Directional dimension, which ideally is focused on building and maintaining alignment across all of the dimensions. This is the work of a leader. You must plant seeds and tend to the garden before achieving a bountiful harvest. Over time, various aspects of the business start to become misaligned. That is the nature of things. A strong leader watches for those misalignments and corrects them as quickly as possible, knowing that one misalignment can beget another and another. You stop the leaks when they occur, and you work to avoid energy drains.

By pointing, marshaling, focusing, and applying energy in specific directions, amazing things happen. As I mentioned earlier, this is not a cookbook on how to be a good leader. Rather, it is a leadership approach for accomplishing great things by collaborating with your people through the management of energy. When your focus is on energy, your focus is on the things that will, collectively, achieve the large returns you are looking for. And furthermore, by conserving and focusing the energy you invest in achieving your targets, you will minimize your required investment. That makes the returns all the sweeter and gives you extra energy to accomplish other things.

Reward and Celebrate

As your business achieves success, don't forget to celebrate and reward it. Rewards are both intrinsic and tangible. Use them all! Celebrations are rituals that touch the deepest parts of people and reinforce their motivations and behaviors. Reward and celebration position you and your people for the next round of achievement. Give some energy back to the people. If it weren't for them, you wouldn't be successful. Your gifts back to them will go a long way toward positioning you for your next success.

Avoiding Negative Behaviors

In this final section on managing people, we address some of the most common negative behaviors at work. We are all capable of engaging in these behaviors, but some do so more than others. These behaviors are extremely damaging and take a huge energetic toll on businesses, especially during times of change. By creating negative energy, they push against forward progress. The penalty is fourfold. First, the person who exhibits the negative behavior wastes energy. Second, the negative energy created counteracts positive energy created by others. Third, the negative energy taints the outputs of the company, including its products and services. And fourth, the negative energy hurts the people in the business and their working environment. Although they are difficult to measure, these negative behaviors add up and can be a major drag on business.

At the end of this section we discuss how organizations, managers, and individuals can identify, avoid, and deal with negative behaviors. We have compassion for people who exhibit these behaviors because we know what drives people toward these behaviors. However, that doesn't mean we have to accept chronic negative behavior in the workplace. We can unlock and reclaim a lot of energy, and improve our working environments dramatically, by limiting these behaviors.

Putting Me First

As we have discussed, we all bring to our work a Personal dimension of energy. Within that energy we have personal goals and agendas, beliefs and attitudes, and positions regarding our work. The nature of that energy tends to affect the attention we give a particular task, how we engage others in doing the work, and the amount of effort we put into that work.

Putting me first happens when people give their own personal agenda a higher priority than the larger business goal and the interests of the business. In practice, putting me first is not an absolute. It comes in degrees based on the relative priority people place on their own agendas versus the needs of the business. At the extreme, there are people who seem to live by their personal agendas, which essentially means they often work at cross purposes with others and the business. Let's look at two examples.

I once worked with a marketing manager who seemed to believe that she was entitled to be taken care of but wasn't receiving the appropriate care. Therefore, she would rationalize the prioritization of her own agenda as a way of getting what she "deserved." In meetings her comments were seldom constructive. Instead, she tended to criticize other people, their ideas, and the company. She had a holier-than-thou attitude that was designed to make others feel inferior so she could get what she wanted. She didn't produce much original work, and most people (except her closest allies) didn't really like working with her. Her managers knew there was a problem, but she seemed untouchable. She knew how to do just enough to protect herself from negative personnel actions. She knew how to cloak her negativity with supposedly positive remarks and hide that negativity altogether when her managers were present. She got away with her destructive behavior for a long time, until I coached her managers on how to appropriately deal with it. Part of my coaching was to help the managers recognize how they were enabling her behavior by feeling responsible for taking care of her. In other words, they had, to some extent, bought into her premise.

Earlier in my career I encountered another example of putting me first. I worked with a man, a fellow manager, whose put-me-first behavior had a more competitive premise. His premise boiled down to this: "I work hard for this company and I need to be recognized and rewarded over my peers. No one else will look out for me but me. I'm just playing the game." The deep issue here is that this attitude can be used to justify all sorts of actions that hurt others and the business. And this man did just that to look out for himself. Such a person may work hard, but we must question how much of that work is for the business and how much is for himself.

Whatever the source of their personal agendas, me-first people spread considerable negative energy as they operate out of their own self-interests. They generally do a lot of damage and know how to survive so they can continue spreading negative energy. In my experience, it is amazing how often, and how well, me-first behavior works for chronic users. But it only works if managers aren't looking for it, don't see it, and don't take appropriate action to stop it.

Engaging in Conflict

Conflict, as it is defined in this book, is never good. People engage in conflict for different reasons. As we discussed, dysfunctions and misalignments in the business environment can provide an ongoing source of triggers that invite people to engage in conflict. But people still have a choice to engage in conflict or handle the situation in a different way. People also engage in conflict to further their agendas. These agenda items can include everything from being right, to protecting a faction, to making someone look bad, to getting something from someone. Throwing someone under the bus is a form of conflict that often occurs as an escalation of an ongoing conflict.

It is probably impossible to be in a business without engaging in conflict from time to time. Life is not perfect, and neither is business. However, in business, there are some people who are involved in conflict frequently. They look for it, start it, and sometimes seem to enjoy it. They appear to have little motivation to walk away from a potential fight and may view doing so as weakness. In general, men are more prone to overt conflict than women. It is the nature of men, in general, to just have it out. It is male DNA to fight, and men have been going to war for millennia. But that doesn't make it OK for a man or a woman to chronically engage in conflict within a business. Conflict, as we have discussed, constitutes a huge energy drain on a business. When unintentional conflict escalates and when conflict becomes intentional and premeditated, it needs to be addressed.

Men also engage in covert conflict, yet women have a greater tendency to engage covertly, more often with other women than with men. Women compete with each other for attention and recognition, among other things. Much of the time men don't see these battles. They become aware only when the conflict becomes a factor in conducting business. For obvious reasons, it is difficult to see how much time and energy is being expended on covert conflicts. Nevertheless, they take a toll.

Whatever the cause of conflict, people who *chronically* engage in conflict drain the energy of business. If they are not dealt with, they continue to drain energy, and their behavior is being tacitly condoned. Managers must consider the environment and any role it may be playing in triggering conflict, but they also must deal with chronic offenders appropriately, once they are recognized, or the business will pay the energy price.

Resisting Change

People who resist change most often do so because they are afraid of the unknown, don't trust the company or its leaders, aren't sure if the change will be good for them, perceive a possible loss of power or status, and/or are more comfortable with the status quo. Everyone experiences some of these feelings. Change can be difficult and uncomfortable. But there are those who resist change as if they are on a crusade, most often an underground crusade. The activities happen in private conversations behind closed doors. They happen at parties where only certain supporters are invited. In short, the leaders of these unofficial groups organize the resistance and use tactics from negative PR and misinformation, to smear campaigns, to active recruiting. Many resisters are less involved and dramatic than that, yet they resist in a variety of ways including nonresponsiveness, negative comments, and continuing to do things the way they have always done them.

We acknowledge here that not all changes, as designed, will be good for a business. We spend considerable time discussing that problem and ways to solve it in chapters 2 and 3. However, assuming the desired change is good for the business and something it needs to do, resistance to change is born out of personal agendas, beliefs, and attitudes. Most people resist change at some point in their careers, and companies and change leaders have learned to anticipate this common reaction and deal with it through effective dialogue and other change management techniques. However, when people chronically resist for their own personal benefit at the expense of the company, that is a different matter. Chronic resisters can waste a tremendous amount of energy and can cause a change initiative to fail. As a change leader, I have often commented that it takes about one-tenth the amount of energy to move an initiative backward with resistance than it took to move it forward in the first place. Therefore, those who resist change substantially or chronically are in a position to do great damage to the business.

Resistance to change is largely a covert affair. The challenge for leaders and change agents is that it is difficult to track covert activity, and if you can't identify resistant behaviors, you can't deal with the involved people. However, I have found two ways to be effective in revealing the covert operators. First, people talk to people, and tapping your trusted network can give you a lot of information about the resistance. Second, covert activity tends to result periodically in some kind of overt challenge. The beast tends to surface when it feels powerful. In doing so it reveals at least some of the people involved in the resistance and gives management a chance to deal directly with the problem. Look for the indicators of resistance, such as people not behaving in the new ways wanted by the company, rumors designed to discredit the change and the people involved, and political maneuvering. Above all, identify the ringleaders and chronic resisters and deal with them directly.

Bullying

Bullying isn't restricted to the schoolyard. It happens all the time in business. The energy of bullying is an overpowering force designed to intimidate and make others afraid so the bullies get their way. Bullies are often managers with a level of positional power, but they can derive their power from other sources as well. For example, a company I worked with had a CEO who was known to play favorites. Several of his favorites used that status to bully others and get what they wanted. People were afraid of any kind of bad press with the CEO so the bullying usually worked. Some bullies get their power from personal characteristics, such as their physical size or ability to verbally intimidate. Whatever the source of their power, bullies know how to use it to move people toward submission.

The problem with bullying is that is serves a personal agenda at the expense of other people and the business. Furthermore, it takes an emotional toll on those who get bullied. It is one thing to get forceful once in a while. It is quite another when people consistently take on the mantle of the bully to get what they want, be more powerful than others, and create a fear-based mechanism for controlling others. Sometimes bullies seem to be born that way; other times they are latent bullies who get activated by certain situations. For example, I have seen a fairly consistent phenomenon in companies with multiple functional departments. Almost always, one department and department manager is the bully. This department usually has the most people and the biggest budget. It is as if the people's positions in the biggest departments impel them to become bullies. This use of power may be hard to resist.

Generally speaking, men most often bully men, and women most often bully women. Conquest is in the primitive nature of men. Left unmanaged, bullying can become an expression of that nature, where behavior essentially is a game of King of the Hill. Women seem to bully for similar reasons, but I have seen several examples in groups with a preponderance of female employees and a male boss where women bully each other to gain favored status from the boss. Quite often the male boss hasn't a clue about the bullying and the competition among the women. Worse, if the female bully is the boss's favorite, he may be unknowingly and tacitly giving her at least some of her power to bully. Her message to the other women is something like "I am the boss's favorite and I have his ear. Don't cross me or I'll smear you with him." The boss unconsciously invites her to bully, and she goes ahead and does it. Both are problems to be solved.

The actual behavior of a bully can take many forms. One form is to rob others of the credit for their accomplishments. Another common form of bullying is when a bully breaches the boundaries of another person's position or turf. The bully tells the person what they should or shouldn't do, usurps their resources, and steps into their business as if they own it. Perhaps the most common form of bullying is when the bully simply makes it clear, in a meeting, for example, that they expect to get their way, with the full force of their intimidation behind it.

Bullying is also done in gangs. In a business, such bullying may not be on the same scale and intensity as Al Capone's gang, but it can be quite effective and destructive nonetheless. In business, gangs are factions with a common agenda and a will to achieve it through the use of bullying tactics. There is almost always a ringleader and a set of loyal followers. The dynamics are basically the same as any gang. People join the gang and promise to be loyal to it in exchange for being taken care of by the gang.

I saw an example of this behavior in a fast-growing small company that was going from start-up to grow-up. Its informal practices were no longer sufficient or appropriate for a complex company of its size. A new CEO was brought in who launched a major initiative to formalize operations while preserving the character of the company and the "things that made it great in the first place." Unfortunately, not everyone agreed with that goal, including a senior manager who rallied the troops and formed an informal gang to resist the change. People who favored the informal practices they had

212 The Energy Equation

enjoyed for years quickly and, at first quietly, jumped on board. They soon made the CEO the bad guy who "didn't understand the company." They spread misinformation and false rumors about the CEO and his new initiative. Before long the CEO was spending a lot of time trying to set the record straight and was losing support even among those who were initially on board with the changes. By the time the CEO figured out who was leading the resistance, the senior manager, a longtime employee, had opened a covert dialogue with some board members, who had heard that there were problems. Public opinion of the CEO at the board level deteriorated as the senior manager spun the information in a negative light. Ultimately, the board removed the CEO for failing to accomplish his goals and sold the business to a rival company. That is the power of a gang. I often wonder where that company would be today if the gang had not blocked its efforts to grow up.

There are plenty of other forms and tactics of bullying, and they are all ugly. Regardless of who does it, bullying robs energy from the business and other people involved and can take a business off track as it serves the bully's agenda instead of its own. Whether the bullies are men or women, people need to stand up to them. Managers, in particular, need to show them that bully behavior is unacceptable and will not be tolerated.

Playing the Victim

Playing the victim is a common act in business. In general, women make more credible victims than men because they are often viewed as more vulnerable. Nevertheless, men play the victim too. Playing the victims can be extremely powerful, as the victims' energy is almost entirely negative. They pour buckets of negative energy into the business and often go undetected or undiagnosed.

People learn to play the victim by watching others do it. As far as I know, there is no victim cookbook or training class. People observe and practice the various victimization strategies and behaviors and learn how these ingredients work together to create what can be a very damaging role. This development process is probably more unconscious than conscious. In any event, people have a choice about playing the victim or not. Unfortunately, playing the victim is often effective and creates considerable power for the individual at the expense of others and the business. The reason it works so well is that unless you understand the victimization formula, it is difficult to identify and discuss concretely. Here is a summary of the victim's recipe.

- The people adopt a premise and an orientation that they have been, and continue to be, a victim to the business and those who work there. Perhaps they are victims of other life circumstances as well. Therefore, the business owes them a large and undefined consideration.
- These victims tacitly communicate their victim status and the large unpaid consideration due them to others in the company with whom they interact, eliciting feelings of sympathy and guilt. After a period of consistent victim communication, other people begin to think of the people as true victims (i.e., victimhood becomes part of their identity).
- The victims use their victim status in meetings and other interactions with coworkers as leverage to get things and avoid work assignments and responsibilities. They use spoken or unspoken messages, such as "I'm already being dumped on by this company and don't see how I could take on any more. You all know I am overworked and under-paid, right?"
- These victims often complain and criticize others in order to reinforce their victimhood, to shift attention away from their responsibilities and performance, and to blame others—often for things they have done or not done. Doing this helps keep the victims unaccountable and safe.
- Should anyone challenge these victim tactics, the victims will lobby support from others in the business (often other victims) to mount propaganda campaigns designed to protect them and discredit the "attacker."

What all of this boils down to is that people who play the victim are unaccountable, produce little value for the business, live by a different set of self-serving rules, damage the reputations of others, and threaten attack and retaliation upon anyone who threatens to expose them and their tactics. Victims feign innocence as a cover for their destruction. The irony is that the energy of victims is very much like the energy of bullies, only it is less honest and more covert. The threat to, and intimidation of, others is formidable. Victims paint themselves as the victims of bullies, yet they are bullies themselves. This is the secret that victims never want you to know.

When you recognize this fact, victims' cover is blown. It's time for managers to wise up, expose victims for what they are, and recognize the immense damage they cause.

Gossiping

In his 1998 book, *Grooming, Gossip and the Evolution of Language*, Robin Dunbar discusses the evolution of human language. He argues that between 30,000 and 70,000 years ago during the so-called Cognitive Revolution, our unique human language evolved as a means of sharing information about the world. Because the most important information that needed to be conveyed was about each other, our language evolved as a way of *gossiping*. Reliable information about who could be trusted, and who couldn't, allowed small tribes to expand into larger tribes, and people to develop more sophisticated types of cooperation. Today, these larger tribes include businesses. This tribal element in organizations suggests that gossip plays an important role in business as a tool promoting the cooperation of those involved.

Based on the fact that gossip actually plays a useful role in companies, you may be asking why we included gossiping in our list of damaging behaviors at work. Clearly it serves a purpose. The answer is that there are two ways to cross the line in gossiping that make it damaging. Gossiping for the purpose of information exchange as a way to promote the interests of the business is fine. However, when the agenda behind the gossip is personal and self-serving at the expense of the company, it crosses the line into damaging behavior. Second, when the amount of time a person spends gossiping becomes unreasonably high, significantly detracting from their work, it crosses the line.

As a practical matter, monitoring gossip and identifying when it crosses one of the lines is difficult, since gossip typically happens behind the scenes. Nevertheless, gossip usually goes public within the business, and when it does, we can sometimes trace the information leak, untrue rumor, attack, or misinformation back to its source. In addition, chronic gossipers tend to reveal themselves through indicators such as poor productivity. In either case, damaging gossipers waste the energy of the business. And when their personal agendas are involved at the expense of the business, they hurt others and the company. When you add it all up, damaging gossip can rob a business of a whole lot of energy.

Addressing Negative Behaviors

Of course there are many more types of negative behaviors than those addressed in this chapter. However, the six behaviors covered here are some of the big ones in terms of their frequency and degree of damage. Putting a dent in these behaviors has the potential to make a big difference in the energy and performance of most businesses. But how do we go about addressing negative behaviors to help prevent them and to deal with them when they do occur? We suggest an approach that includes action at three levels: organizational, managerial, and individual.

Organizational Actions

Many businesses seem to believe that if they don't talk about a particular kind of behavior, everyone can ignore it and even pretend it doesn't exist. That seems to be the easiest and most comfortable thing to do. But there is a price to pay for this response. Inaction condones the behavior and it essentially becomes part of the company culture. At that point, the damage is done, day in and day out. Instead, it is better to get these behaviors out into the open.

The suggested approach is to first communicate with employees about these behaviors to raise awareness and give them a language to talk about people. Identify and talk about the desired collaborative behaviors discussed in this book at the same time you discuss the negative behaviors. Together they cover both ends of the spectrum and help give employees a compass with which to navigate their work and behavior.

In my experience, having conversations about behaviors (as we have done at Advance Consulting for over two decades) is much more impactful than the more typical business conversations about core values. First, people don't tend to change their values just because their company claims to have adopted some new ones. Second, people are usually left with a vague notion about how to implement core values, so they seldom make much progress toward real adoption. Behaviors, in contrast, are much more concrete. Certain behaviors are encouraged while others are discouraged. Part of the equation is to be very specific in descriptions and examples of behavior. We don't want to make the same mistake we made in our vague definitions of sexual harassment. If we do, people may be afraid to come out of their offices for fear that they might do something negative. To that point, the other part of the equation is to approach this learning and adjustment period firmly, but with some compassion and tolerance. A heavy-handed enforcement of behaviors will backfire. A safe developmental environment will allow people to make mistakes, learn from them, and get better at avoiding negative behaviors.

Addressing both negative and positive behaviors will help move the business toward a new culture, a culture of collaboration, excellence, mutual respect, and responsibility. It also sets the stage for behavioral activities at the other two levels.

Managerial Actions

Managers, along with the HR department, are the ones who must deal with chronic behavior problems in a business. They are the ones who condone these behaviors when they don't take appropriate action to address them. Appropriate action includes behavior identification, communication, coaching, and enforcement.

When managers observe or become aware of a person's chronic negative behavior, they must first ensure that they have enough objective information about the behavior to have a constructive conversation with the person. He says, she says is weak. Direct observations and documentation are much stronger. Gathering relevant and factual information sets the stage for the conversation. A simple yet powerful three-part method for feedback conversations includes observations, implications, and suggestions.

- **Observations.** It is amazing how often feedback conversations go awry because people start with their opinions and suggestions. Without a context for the conversation grounded in fact, people tend to argue with opinions and suggestions. So, as a manager, you can't start with those topics. Instead, you begin by communicating what you objectively know about the negative behavior in enough detail to reveal the underlying behavior. It is important to stay on the observation step until the person acknowledges the truth of your observations and/or appropriately corrects any misunderstandings or misinterpretations.

- **Implications.** Once the conversation is grounded in fact, you can move to the next step. This is where you describe the implications of the person's behavior. For example, "Jim, your repeated bullying is causing disruption and dysfunction in the team, it is intimidating and hurting your teammates, and it certainly isn't helping your career." It may be necessary to elaborate and provide examples of the implications. Once again, it is important to stay on this step until the person understands and acknowledges the implications of his or her behavior.
- **Suggestions.** Now, with the necessary level of understanding and agreement established by the first two steps, it is time to offer your suggestions. "Jim, I'd like you to stop your bullying altogether. Let's talk about how that's going to work. What ideas do you have for how to approach that?" This kind of suggestion is designed to co-opt the person into the development of a solution and approach instead of just telling them what to do. This helps to create buy-in and ownership for the solution. It also opens the door for a deeper dialogue around the person's drivers, not just his or her behaviors. In such a dialogue Jim may reveal, for example, that he feels a lot of pressure to perform and he justifies bullying when he thinks things have to go his way or the team will fail. This response becomes fertile ground for working with Jim to adopt more appropriate influence skills and techniques. It also promotes a new and improved relationship between Jim and you, his manager.

When addressing negative behaviors in others, you should also examine your own actions to see if they are in any way encouraging, enabling, or reinforcing those negative behaviors. In some cases, managers are part of the dynamic and the problem. This is a good time to figure that out and make some adjustments if needed.

Individual Actions

At the individual level, we each have opportunities to flag negative behaviors and offer constructive feedback. There are two aspects of negative behavior at the individual level: negative behaviors expressed by others and negative behaviors expressed by ourselves. When negative behavior is expressed by others in your presence, and it impacts you negatively, it is not your job to make the person change his or her behavior. You can communicate what and how much you are willing to tolerate, but forceful and judgmental demands to change behavior often backfire. Only the negative people can decide to change their behavior. Instead, you can actually use an abbreviated form of the feedback model described above. Focus on communicating what you see, how it impacts you and makes you feel, and what you would like to see happen now and/or going forward (in that sequence). Be willing to look at anything you may be doing to encourage more positive behavior. While you don't have the power to change their behavior, you do have the power to communicate, and that just might help others decide to make some changes.

As individuals we live with our Personal dimensions in every moment. We are in a better position than anyone else to witness firsthand our imprint and drivers and how they tempt us to employ negative behaviors. Frankly, our Personal dimensions, left unattended, make us prone to negative behavior. Our beliefs, attitudes, and personal agendas run the show in that dimension. Fortunately, however, we all have a Directional dimension as well. This dimension is somewhat independent of the other dimensions and is the final authority on choosing our behavior. Those who are adept at not living out of their imprints and avoiding knee-jerk reactions to conflict triggering events usually have well-developed skills in the Directional dimension. At the other extreme, some people appear to be almost completely driven by their Personal dimensions, giving way to every personal agenda item and emotion that springs up. These people tend to have poorly developed skills in the Directional dimension.

The power and importance of skills in the Directional dimension cannot be overstated. These skills are not acquired through an online course. They are acquired through practice, and the practice is never over. In the Fourth Industrial Revolution, robots and AI will get better and better at doing things that people do now. At some point they may approximate or even surpass the abilities of the average knowledge worker. They will not be prone to the influence of ancient imprints like people are and will easily avoid engaging in wasteful and damaging human dynamics. This will make robots and AI very attractive options and may render many people obsolete if we aren't careful. If anything can prevent human obsolescence, it is skill and diligence in the Directional dimension. We must push ahead with the evolution of how we live and how we work.

In the next chapter we discuss how people and other enterprise factors often make business change and transformation difficult but how the management of energy can significantly improve our chances of success.

Chapter 7

Business Transformation, Health, and Agility

In the movie *The Karate Kid*, Mr. Miyagi agrees to teach karate to Daniel, a local teenager. Daniel is tired of being beaten up by local boys from a dojo where they are taught to be aggressive and merciless. Mr. Miyagi insists that karate is about something deeper and more important than that. Daniel's training begins with a series of seemingly irrelevant menial tasks like waxing cars. Mr. Miyagi instructs him, "Wax on, wax off," making circular motions with each hand. Daniel is not at all pleased with this course of training as it didn't involve the punches and kicks he associated with karate. After several days, Daniel blows up, accusing Mr. Miyagi of taking advantage of him. In response, Mr. Miyagi let out one of those loud guttural sounds that karate people sometimes make when they challenge someone to fight. Daniel faces him. Mr. Miyagi throws a punch with one hand, and Daniel automatically responds with a motion that blocks the punch. The motion strongly resembles the wax on-motion. Mr. Miyagi throws a punch with his other hand and, again, Daniel automatically responds, this time with a wax-off motion that again blocks the punch. By the time the fight is over, Daniel is shocked and realizes that through seemingly unrelated tasks, he had learned and had ingrained within himself some of the most important fundamentals of karate.

This chapter is similar to that moment of revelation. You learned the fundamentals and techniques of managing energy in the first six chapters. Now chapter 7 reveals the power of integrating and applying what you have learned to move your business forward. Specifically, you will see how these fundamentals and techniques can become your tool kit for pursuing three critically important goals: managing change, creating organizational health, and achieving business agility. For each of these goals I offer deep and somewhat revolutionary insights about what they are, what success looks like, and how to achieve it.

Making Transformation and Change Initiatives Successful

One of the most difficult things leaders must do is move their businesses through formidable business transformations and major change initiatives. It is one thing to manage a business. It is quite another to change one. In spite of the major attention that has been given to this area in both business and academia, we still don't have a very good track record. By most estimates, approximately 70% of change initiatives fail or significantly underdeliver. Many would argue that the number is even higher. Despite the fact that successful change has become essential for most companies, we really haven't been improving much. We need to understand why that is the case and use that insight to adjust the way we approach business transformations.

The Top Ten Real Reasons Why Change Initiatives Fail

There are hundreds, if not thousands, of books and publications on the management of change. Many provide their lists of the top reasons why change initiatives fail and cite reasons like poor planning, resistance, and leadership issues. Getting the list right is the Holy Grail of change management, but it is difficult to declare any given list right or wrong. I would agree, for example, that poor planning, resistance, and leadership issues contribute to the change management problem. Practically every list I have seen contains things that contribute to failed change initiatives, so who could call them wrong? Yet business leaders and academics keep coming out with new lists, perhaps hoping that their list will be the right one, the one people finally agree to. What have we been missing?

The answer is that we have been looking at why change initiatives fail from the standpoint of what change leaders did or didn't do in their initiatives. We have been searching for a recipe for change instead of looking at it from the context of how change occurs and doesn't occur. Fortunately, energy gives us that context. Change is a shift in energy. There can be no change without an energetic shift, and to create an energetic shift, we must apply a sufficient amount of energy in the right places and in the right directions until *sustainable shift* occurs. Based on this understanding, there is really only one reason why change initiatives fail.

Change initiatives fail because they run out of energy before they cross the finish line (i.e., before they reach the point of sustainable change).

It's really that simple. The list of things that cause initiatives to fail is the list of things that cause initiatives to waste and leak energy. When enough energy is wasted and leaked, initiatives die, and things generally slip back into status quo. Sometimes initiatives die a quiet death. It's as if people sneak away in the night and move on to something else. Other initiatives, especially high-stakes initiatives with large budgets, go up in flames, along with the careers of some people associated with them. Either way, it's an unfortunate failure.

Many things cause change initiatives to waste and leak energy. We can't plug every hole, so it's best to focus on plugging the big ones. Here is our top ten list of things that cause waste and leakage and lead to the failure of change initiatives.

1. **Misaligned enterprise.** The enterprise has so much misalignment, conflict, and fragmented energy that it is almost impossible to build adequate alignment and energy for *any* initiative to succeed. There are too many energy drains in the field of play. Most of these drains are caused by environmental factors that breed misalignment among people. People who work in substantially misaligned companies often refer to change initiatives as the flavor of the month. They come and they go, but not much changes. These companies need major surgery.

2. **Enterprise element leaks.** The initiatives do not adequately consider or address the *involved* enterprise elements that negatively impact the new/improved function/activity/capability. In chapter 3 we discussed the need to define the footprint of a change initiative by identifying all of the involved enterprise elements. Many change leaders don't do this. They go in with tunnel vision and focus only on the core change. Others are aware of the involved elements but are restricted by the company's tunnel vision and inadequate budgets. Left unattended, the

involved yet unrefined enterprise elements drain too much energy. As a result, the initiative starves for energy and has little or no impact. Remember our Alchemy Instruments example in chapter 3? To create the sustainable shift to a team selling model, changes were required in ten enterprise elements. Had we arbitrarily ignored half of them and called them optional, their ongoing negative impact, and the resulting energy leakage, would have almost certainly killed the initiative.

3. **Lack of personal alignment.** Alignment between the Personal dimensions of the affected people (e.g., their intent, attention, engagement, and effort) and the overall change itself does not occur. While there is effort to bring people on board, the needed shift in the Personal dimensions is not achieved because the business and/or change leader does not recognize the importance and magnitude of aligning this dimension. Said differently, the energetic ingredients of the Personal dimension are not understood and, therefore, are not specifically or fully addressed as part of the change. When the Personal dimension of energy is not aligned with the initiative, there can be no substantial change, since the aligned and consistent involvement of people is needed to achieve real, sustained change. This blockage happened consistently in the company discussed in chapter 4 where the veterans were all about maintaining the status quo. They knew how to nod their heads in apparent agreement but, all the while, had every intention of resisting and sabotaging any substantial change that came along.

4. **Artificial success.** Initiatives are declared successful too early. Apparent success is achieved, due primarily to an initially large amount of management attention focused on the change. This energy and attention partly and temporarily affects the Personal dimensions of energy in those involved, making it appear as if the change has occurred. When company leaders declare victory and remove their energy and attention (leaving the project team to finish up), the intrinsic Personal energies of those affected shift back as well and are not sufficient to sustain the change. Close but no cigar.

5. **Inaccurate diagnosis.** Surface-level diagnostic methods are applied that do not identify the deeper root causes of problems in the business. Consequently, change leaders solve the wrong problems and fail to impact the overall issue significantly. Energy is misdirected and wasted, and the real problem persists. This happened the first time around in our Alchemy Instruments example.

6. **Poor design.** The design for the new function/activity/capability does not create alignment among the four dimensions of energy sufficient to drive and enable a sustainable change. This design issue can take

many forms, including an inappropriate operational model, an incomplete design, misalignment among involved elements, and poor design of individual elements. Without the perspective of energy, your vision is limited and the art of design is hit or miss. When designing a business process, for example, you may focus on making it lean but inadvertently create a breeding ground for conflict.

7. **Mixed messages.** Leadership transmits conflicting messages about the initiative, leaving people confused, frustrated, and personally unaligned with it. For example, when people are aware that there are big enterprise obstacles to an initiative that leaders are not addressing, they are put into conflict. It is unclear to them if the status quo or the new initiative is more important. Thus, alignment with the Personal dimension is not possible, and people do not take the initiative seriously. Energy invested in the initiative is blocked and diffused by the unaligned Personal dimension and the obstacles in the way of the change. I've seen this happen in many companies. It is a close cousin with, and often a companion to, the enterprise element leaks discussed in item 2. Nothing turns people off faster in a change effort than leaders pretending obstacles/leaks don't exist or aren't something they need to worry about.

8. **Inadequate resources.** Energy applied to the initiative, usually in the form of people, money, and management attention, is insufficient to drive change to the point of sustainability. This situation is like starting a road trip with a quarter tank of gas. Poor planning, which leads to an underestimation of the initiative scope and resources, is often the culprit here. However the shortfall occurs, the result is that all of the resources and energy applied to the project, however insufficient, are wasted, and the initiative fails.

9. **Piecemeal implementation.** Implementation of the revised elements involved with the change are implemented serially over time rather than quickly in parallel. As the initial implementations occur, elements associated with the unimplemented changes continue to leak energy. The initiative becomes energy starved, creates negative reactions among those involved, and either dies on its own or is killed by the people. Companies and change agents often think they are being careful and responsible with a multiphase, drawn-out implementation approach. Too much change too fast is not good, they reason. Ironically, with significant changes, just the opposite is more often the case. As we discussed in chapter 3, business transformations are vulnerable to the mischief of people during their implementation periods. The sooner we can establish and reinforce the new desired behaviors and eliminate opportunities to persist in old

behaviors, the sooner we stop the leaking of energy in the involved enterprise elements and the more likely success will be achieved.

10. **Poor visibility.** Change leaders and "change experts" who operate and analyze at the surface level are not adept at managing the energy of business, nor do they know the techniques for doing so. Consequently, they have a partial view of the involved elements and energies at play. This partial view often leads to guesswork, inaccurate assumptions, and erroneous conclusions that send initiatives down paths that cannot succeed. Many well-meaning change agents have done the best they could with limited surface-level visibility and understanding, only to see their initiative fail for reasons that they often don't understand. How could they understand with such limited visibility and perspective?

When initiatives run out of energy before they cross the finish line, it is generally because significant energy is applied to the wrong things and/or not applied to the right things and/or not applied in sufficient quantities for a long enough period of time. Now that we know how change initiatives fail, the question becomes, how do we optimize their chances of success?

Managing the Energy of Change

Much of the answer for how to manage change initiatives to optimize their success has been discussed in previous chapters of this book. When we bring these pieces together, they collectively provide a set of tools and an overall approach for driving change in a business. They serve as the guideposts for managing the energy of change. The remainder of this section is devoted to knitting these pieces together to reveal a more enlightened approach for managing change.

As discussed in chapter 1, any business transformation happens within the current system of the business, which includes the environment, the people in it, and all of their associated energies. If we are to make any significant change, we must first understand that system and how it works so that we can make intelligent and informed adjustments. To do that we need to learn the language of energy through its many indicators. Chapter 1 provided the fundamentals of "seeing energy" and understanding its messages in the way we look at the behaviors of people, misalignments, and the flow of money. Learning and practicing this language is the starting point for managing change.

As chapter 2 explained, unintentional conflict is a huge problem in businesses today. Caused by misalignments at the organizational, operational, and individual levels, unintentional conflict can drain a business of a large portion of its vital energy. Change initiatives need to correct these misalignments, but they also need to view them as threats. If an initiative involves misaligned enterprise elements, it is subject to the conflict and energy drain that spews from those misalignments. Change leaders must be aware of these landmines and either steer around or eliminate them.

Chapter 3 explained that the creation of shared space is an antidote for unintentional conflict and a conscious way to fix broken business functions. We offered models for diagnosing problems, designing shared space, and implementing the solutions in an expeditious manner. We also offered a number of strategies for creating shared space in the enterprise. Together, these models and strategies form the backbone of any significant business transformation or change initiative.

In chapter 4, we defined the four dimensions of energy in work (Environmental, Intellectual, Personal, and Directional) and discussed their involvement in three types of work streams (Individual, Common, and Collective). These concepts and their associated tools provide meat for the bones discussed in chapter 3, in terms of both diagnosing problems and designing solutions, to optimize the outcomes of work streams. Change initiatives typically involve common work streams (e.g., a new business process or system) and collective work streams (e.g., the project planning and execution associated with the initiative). We discussed important relationships among the dimensions, such as the profound effect the Environmental dimension can have on the Personal dimensions of the affected people. In guiding a business through change, it is essential to understand and consider how these relationships may affect the success of the initiative. Finally, we discussed the notion that we must align the energies across the four dimensions to promote successful work and initiative outcomes. To achieve sustainable change in a business, the four dimensions must be adequately aligned. To gauge progress in a change initiative, one of the primary things we look at is the degree of alignment, which we strive to maintain throughout the project.

In chapter 5 we began our discussion of people and how we can create the kind of alignment discussed in earlier chapters. We addressed the increasing demand for effective collaboration and the emphasis on dynamic collaboration today and as we move forward in the Fourth Industrial

Revolution. The Collaboration Dynamic explained, at the level of energy, the ingredients of collaboration and how they work together to form both positive and negative alignment and outcomes. We covered the skills and methods for having effective one-on-one and group collaborations and characterized projects, including change initiatives, as ongoing group collaborations. These models, skills, and behaviors are important to change initiatives for two primary reasons. First, they help the change agent/project manager develop a high-functioning team with a high degree of alignment to drive the needed change. Second, the collaborative techniques and methods will ideally permeate the entire population of people performing work in the business and be reinforced by the designs of the various enterprise elements. There is no time like the present to begin this development and transition toward a higher level of collaboration in the business. All current and future change initiatives should support this shift as a common goal and strive to bring it about within the footprint of the particular initiative.

Continuing our discussion of people, in chapter 6 we covered the intrinsic essence within people and the two primary motivators that managers and leaders can tap into. We then provided a systematic path for leaders, including change leaders, to align the energies of the people and the business to create sustainable change. Whereas chapter 5 focused on alignment at the micro level, this chapter focused on alignment at the macro level. We then discussed some of the most significant and common negative behaviors that can quickly sap the energy of any change initiative. Change leaders should strive to be aware of these negative behaviors when they occur and address them appropriately whenever possible. Chronic resistance to change is perhaps the biggest enemy of any change initiative.

Strategy and Tactics

Overlaying these building blocks for managing change is an energy-based change management strategy. As stated earlier, initiatives fail because they run out of energy before they cross the finish line. All of the ingredients discussed are designed to help build and maintain energy throughout the initiative so that it makes it to the finish line. However, we must recognize that, in practice, the level of energy in any change initiative fluctuates over time. Energy drops as it is used to drive change and overcome obstacles and as it leaks in the various ways described earlier. However, energy is also renewed by outside assistance, such as a boost in the initiative's budget or special positive attention from senior management, or from the initiative's wins along the way. For example, achievement of a milestone, completion of a pilot, or endorsement from a key manager or constituency will give an initiative an energetic boost. Refilling the gas tank along the way is probably the most important job of any change agent and team.

Ideally, initiatives are planned so that they come out of the gate with some momentum and refill their gas tanks at planned milestones along the way. However, while a good plan and strategy are essential, change initiatives are far from predictable. They become very tactical affairs as problems and obstacles present themselves and the team works to overcome them before they rob too much energy. Things can get political and downright nasty at times. Nevertheless, change leaders can optimize their chances of success by employing the strategies, tools, and techniques discussed in this chapter and in this book as a whole.

By managing the energy of change, we create an advantage and give ourselves a much greater power to create and implement the critical changes that businesses so urgently need to make. But driving change doesn't have to be so difficult. In the next section we look at business agility and organizational health and why they make change a whole lot easier.

Creating Business Agility and Organizational Health

One of the most powerful things that managing energy reveals to me is the true nature and importance of business agility and organizational health. We start this section with an overview of the business imperative driving the substantial conversation around these two topics.

The Business Imperative

Companies are very interested in achieving business agility. Gone are the days when we could rest on our laurels and do things the same way year after year. Advances in technology in the Fourth Industrial Revolution continue to accelerate, customers increasingly expect a good and more informed customer experience, and the management of supply chains is more complex, geographically dispersed, and dynamic than ever. These factors and many others add up to a business environment in a constant state of flux where the need for agility is a matter of survival.

Organizational agility has been defined as "the capability of a company to rapidly change or adapt in response to changes in the market. A high degree of organizational agility can help a company to react successfully to the emergence of new competitors, the development of new industry-changing technologies, or sudden shifts in overall market conditions" (Business Dictionary.com 2019).

Similarly, organizational health is increasingly sought after as research-based evidence mounts that "healthy" companies significantly outperform their peers. For example, a 2017 *McKinsey Quarterly* article by Chris Gagnon, Elizabeth John, and Rob Theunissen reported that publicly traded companies scoring in the top quartile of their Organizational Health Index (OHI) delivered roughly three times the returns to shareholders as those in the bottom quartile. In addition, data suggest that benefits can be realized rather quickly. In response to the traditional notion that companies have to sacrifice some short-term performance to achieve long-term health, the authors add: "Companies that work on their health . . . not only achieve measurable improvement in their organizational well-being but demonstrate tangible performance gains in as little as 6 to 12 months. This holds true for companies across sectors and regions, as well as in contexts ranging from turnarounds to good-to-great initiatives."

Clearly organizational agility and organizational health are essential capabilities and competitive enablers in the Fourth Industrial Revolution. However, opinions vary significantly on exactly what constitutes a healthy organization and an agile business. For example, in his 2012 book, *The Advantage: Why Organizational Health Trumps Everything Else in Business*, Patrick Lencioni suggests that creating a *healthy organization* involves four primary efforts: build a cohesive leadership team, create clarity, overcommunicate clarity, and reinforce clarity. From the perspective of energy as we have developed it here, Lencioni's model is focused primarily on building alignment but doesn't answer questions about how to codify the capabilities of a healthy organization so they don't slip away over time. In contrast, McKinsey's OHI focuses its definition of a healthy organization on management practices and broad organizational outcomes in nine specific areas. The dozens of management practices are a blend of business characteristics, capabilities, and aspirational goals that roll up into nine broad buckets representing the blend at a higher level of detail. McKinsey's model is research-based and makes an important contribution. However, the conceptual difficulty here is in translating this blend of characteristics, capabilities, and goals in the McKinsey model into actions and assets that create organizational health. Although both the McKinsey and Lencioni models have pluses and minuses, the models are quite different in their constructs.

Definitions and approaches for *organizational agility* are equally divergent. For example, the Project Management Institute (2012) suggests that organizational agility is best achieved by improving practices for change management, risk management and portfolio, project, and program management. These are very important capabilities, but such a laser focus on projects limits the breadth of the model for a business enterprise. Using a different model, researchers at the University of Northern Colorado present an organizational agility framework that is grounded on ten pillars: a culture of innovation, empowerment, tolerance for ambiguity, vision, change management, organizational communication, market analysis and response, operations management, structural fluidity, and a learning organization (Harraf et al. 2015). These capabilities and characteristics cover a much wider swath, but we again face the challenge of translating them into actions and assets to create an agile organization.

Each of these publications contains valuable insights. However, the differences between them suggest that, while we use the terms "organizational health" and "organizational agility" freely, there is little agreement on exactly what constitutes them. The problem has more to do with the fact that researchers and authors are looking at different parts of the "elephant" and viewing them from different perspectives. That leaves business leaders and change agents grasping for clarity. They need a deeper view, perhaps one that explains how various viewpoints and models fit into the larger, more integrated, whole—one that provides an organizing principle enabling actionable paths toward sustained health and agility.

A Well-Oiled Machine

At the surface, organizational agility and organizational health appear to be two different things. However, the deeper perspective of energy suggests they are actually achieved by doing the same things within the business. How can that be? Agility and health seem like such different outcomes. Surely the journeys to achieve these two major goals must have different paths. Actually, however, they don't. Agility and health are simply two different characteristics of what we will call here a high-functioning business, which is the real goal. We have been talking about high-functioning businesses and, in turn, organizational agility and organizational health, throughout this book. Both are achieved by managing the energy of the business and creating an enterprise that is, to use an old expression, a well-oiled machine.

Let's take the opposite extreme to help make this point. We have looked at examples of businesses that have significant dysfunction as well as pervasive conflict created by that dysfunction. The conflict and dysfunction slow work down, block progress, create great difficulty, wear people down, waste huge amounts of energy, and ultimately lead to the failure of most change initiatives. A business simply cannot be healthy or agile under those conditions. How do you respond quickly to a changing business environment when you can't respond quickly to anything? How can you be a healthy business when everything you do flows through conflict and is forced to pay an energy toll as it passes through the gates of dysfunction, or sneaks around them, each step along the way? A great Zen story captures the essence here:

> A Zen student approached his master one day, concerned about his progress. He said, "I have been working on my practice for years now and my progress has been painfully slow. Why does all of this take so long?" To which the Zen master replied, "Because it has to go through you!"

Such is the case with business. Whether we are doing work for customers or working to change our business, the work has to flow through us. The more we can create our business to stay out of our own way, the healthier and more agile the business will become. "Staying out of our own way" means minimizing the negative energy our business creates relative to the positive energy it creates. Therefore, it is the *ratio* of positive to negative energy over time that determines how high functioning, healthy, and agile a business is. If you want your business to be high functioning, healthy, and agile, manage the energy.

To explain exactly what that means, let's look back to some of the models and concepts introduced earlier to see how they connect to these goals. Specifically, there are four primary components for creating a high-functioning business (aka a well-oiled machine) that is both healthy and agile: robust enterprise elements, engaged and capable people, effective leadership and people management, and collaborative self-management. In general, the first two, enterprise elements and people, are assets. They are where information, knowledge, and culture are stored, and we engage them to do the work of the business. The last two, leadership/people management and collaborative self-management, have to do with the conduct of work. They are about actions and movement.

This distinction between assets and actions is important. A primary criticism of the organizational health and organizational agility models was that the path for implementing characteristics, capabilities, and goals was nebulous and the approach for sustaining the changes was unclear. The clarity of assets and actions solves this problem. It provides a framework for implementing any characteristic, capability, or goal and sustaining the change.

For example, take role clarity, one of McKinsey's management practices in its Organizational Health Index. Whether you view that as a characteristic, capability, or goal, it involves both the creation/development of assets and consistent actions associated with the management and conduct of work. Assets would likely include an organizational chart plus policies and procedures guiding the creation of such charts and job descriptions. These assets would help ensure clarity of responsibility and prevent unnecessary overlap in roles, especially among managers. The assets may also include a training course or tutorial for all who write job descriptions and manage people. This course would serve as a tool for developing the human assets involved in these matters. On the action side, managers will enforce appropriately the boundaries of roles as they have been defined to avoid damaging conflict and turf wars and to promote teamwork. The people will be responsible for managing themselves to stay within appropriate boundaries of their roles. With this framework, the assets serve as the "memory" and codification of role clarity, while the actions execute and enforce it. This combination of assets and actions makes the role clarity aspect of organizational health sustainable.

Next let's review the four primary components of creating a high-functioning business as they relate to models and concepts developed in this book. In this view we focus on the broad characteristics of the components, not on the creation of individual capabilities, such as role clarity.

Robust Enterprise Elements

The Enterprise Elements Model presented in chapter 2 lays out the building blocks of the enterprise at the organizational, operational, and individual levels. How well these elements are designed, developed, implemented, and integrated is a huge factor in creating a high-functioning business. When enterprise elements are poorly designed or insufficient for their purpose, they trigger unintentional conflict, which wastes energy and slows down work streams flowing through them. We discussed several examples of how poorly designed enterprise elements can trigger unintentional conflict in chapters 2 and 3. Unintentional conflict creates negative energy that works against business agility and organizational health.

When enterprise elements are well designed, sufficient, and integrated, however, they help create shared space where work can proceed quickly, efficiently, and harmoniously. This environment sets the stage for both organizational health and business agility. It puts the organization in a position to perform the work of the business efficiently and effectively and to transform rapidly in response to the changing business landscape. For either type of work, operational or transformational, the work streams must flow through the enterprise elements. The journey through the elements can be either long and painful or expeditious and orderly. Thus, a robust set of enterprise elements is the first primary component for creating a high-functioning business.

Engaged and Capable People

Any business needs people who are capable of doing their work effectively and who remain motivated, over time, to do it. The capability part is usually pretty clear. Most businesses focus on capabilities when they interview job applicants and supplement workers' capabilities through employee training and development programs. However, the motivational part is at least as important and is more difficult to evaluate in an interview and maintain over time. We often use the term "employee engagement" to represent the collective level of motivation across employees. In general, hiring is about bringing an asset into the business. Everything else is about engagement.

Increasing engagement is, perhaps, the Holy Grail of the Human Resources department. The problem is that engagement is everyone's business, and HR can't do it alone. The good news is that people in high-functioning businesses tend to be more highly engaged. They generally have good working environments, well-defined jobs, supportive bosses, and challenging work. They don't have to deal as much with dysfunction in their organizations; they can focus instead on meaningful work and accomplishments. Thus, creating a high-functioning business is a path toward higher engagement.

However, this game is not all about offense. On the defensive side, we must also be attentive to, and protect against, detractors of engagement, such as conflict-oriented interactions among people in the workplace and the common negative behaviors discussed in chapter 6. Better to take the offense and focus people on adopting the collaborative interpersonal skills and behaviors discussed in detail in chapter 5. With such a focus, we can more fully utilize the talented human assets in our businesses instead of letting them go to waste on dysfunctional behaviors and a general lack of engagement.

Effective Leadership and People Management

All businesses need a clear direction and a set of leaders who communicate, inspire, and manage others in moving toward their stated goals. In chapter 6 we discussed key aspects of this broad capability including leadership and motivational style, the path of leadership, and the nature of people. At the end of the day, leadership and people management is about aligning the people in the business around a common vision and managing them to optimally support the business in achieving that vision. In concert with the Environmental dimension of energy stemming from the robust enterprise elements (discussed above), leaders and managers *guide* the movement of people in desired directions by also aligning their Intellectual, Personal, and Directional dimensions. This alignment of energy is not static. It is renewed repeatedly in an ongoing relationship between leaders and people as the direction of the business evolves over time. The ability to align indicates organizational health, and the ability to align quickly indicates organizational agility. But leaders and managers can take this alignment only partway. It is the people themselves who must carry the ball across the finish line.

Collaborative Self-Management

In chapter 4 we discussed individual work streams as they relate to the dimensions of energy. While each of us benefits from a robust set of enterprise elements (i.e., the Environmental dimension), we are responsible for our individual work streams and for aligning our energy to optimize work outcomes. Similarly, as we engage and participate in common work streams (e.g., complex business processes) and collective work streams (e.g., team-based projects), we are responsible for our part of the work and for aligning our energies with others involved and with the goals of the work.

In chapter 5 we looked in depth at how to work collaboratively with individuals and groups by building on the shared space created by the environment to create work-specific shared space. In that shared space we create, innovate, and accomplish by aligning with one or more people around a common cause. It is through this collaborative self-management that most work actually is accomplished. This collaborative self-management makes teams work, and it creates the capability to execute, which is characteristics of high-functioning, healthy, and agile businesses.

Moving Toward Health and Agility

There is no single way to move your business toward greater health and agility. Your options run the gamut from a sweeping enterprise overhaul to the development of a series of individual capabilities. The framework discussed in this chapter enables many optional paths for improvement, giving your business the flexibility it needs to accommodate its particular priorities and circumstances. Yet the framework also provides a stable context that facilitates the ongoing build and integration of each improvement within the overall enterprise architecture. As a practical matter, most businesses do best with an incremental approach toward health and agility through a series of change initiatives. Here are a few things to keep in mind:

- **Leverage all initiatives.** To move toward health and agility, make sure all of your initiatives contribute to the whole. That is, strive to have complete initiatives that address all of the affected enterprise elements, and make sure the contributions the initiatives make to the enterprise elements move the elements along their individual paths toward becoming what they ultimately need to be. No matter what the topic of a change initiative may be, it is an opportunity to move the enterprise forward. Leverage this opportunity.

- **Architect your enterprise.** To provide a stable context for incremental change, assign someone to be your enterprise architect or, if your business is large enough, hire a chief transformation officer who will spearhead change and own the enterprise architecture.

- **Prioritize.** Identify what is most important and urgent, but also identify your quick wins. Remember to design your overall path of change with milestones that refill your gas tank along the way with needed energy.

- **Plug energy leaks.** Just as you would plug leaks in a rubber raft before crossing a lake, consider plugging some of your energy leaks before starting a major initiative. You can begin this process with an enterprise energy assessment or an assessment of a problem area within your business. Alternatively, start in areas with chronic conflict, identify the root causes, and plug the energy leaks.

- **Use technology.** Technology can be a great way to automate and codify new capabilities. Similarly, systems can be quite effective in promoting compliance with policies and procedures. Use technology appropriately to help with change, but be careful about leading with technology. It's better to start with clarity around your business model and how you want people to work within that model.

- **Use the tools and techniques.** The tools and models discussed in this book can help virtually anyone make positive changes in the business. In addition, the powerful techniques, such as following the money and looking for the misalignment of control and responsibility, will serve you well. Use the tools and techniques to help you on your path.

- **Rethink strategic initiatives.** What you have learned from reading this book will help you rethink your strategic initiatives from the perspective of energy. It may change your entire approach to an initiative. Give yourself the latitude to take a fresh new look below the surface.

- **Start with the work.** Remember that virtually everything you do to improve your business is about making work happen better. In your design of any change, start with your vision for how you want the work to go, and then design everything to support that.
- **Involve people appropriately.** Develop your managers and people with the skills they need to be a part of your team, and then engage them in the change itself. However, be careful not to overinvolve people. You need buy-in, but transformations are not democracies.
- **Use a scorecard.** Measuring progress not only proves that progress was made, but it gives people something visible to celebrate. Making change visible can be a great source of energy.
- **Align, align, align.** Align in the beginning, align along the way, and make sure you are aligned at the end.

In summary, organizational health and agility are essential capabilities in the Fourth Industrial Revolution that enable competitive advantages and produce financial dividends. They are by-products of high-functioning businesses, which combine well-designed and developed assets with aligned management activity to effectively accomplish work effectively and evolve the business. High-functioning businesses create significantly more positive energy than negative energy as they minimize conflict, avoid work blockages, and adeptly leverage the productive potential of their people. The concepts, language, and tools presented in this book provide an actionable framework for creating and sustaining a high-functioning business through the management of energy.

Chapter 8

Start Your Journey

Don't believe what your eyes are telling you. All they show is limitation. Look with your understanding. Find out what you already know
and you will see the way to fly.
— Richard Bach, *Jonathan Livingston Seagull*

This book is about a new topic, a new approach to business management and the management of ourselves at work. But is your understanding of energy new, or did this book give you a language and approach for
accessing what you intuitively understood? Either way, it's now up to you to
decide if you will put your understanding, along with the tools and strategies offered in this book, into practice in your business. We've been living
under the limitations of surface-level management for a long time. There is
a way to surpass those limitations, if you choose it.

As we come to the closing chapter of this book, I am reminded of the
opening story about my early encounter with energy while rowing with
my crew team in college. To me, rowing is a perfect metaphor for business.
We all have an oar to pull. The better we pull our oars, and the more aligned
we are in our motions and energy, the faster our boat goes. The sound of
bubbles under the hull as the boat lifts and hydroplanes is exhilarating, but
no more exhilarating than being part of an aligned team in business that

is much greater than the sum of the individual team members. If we pay attention to energy, much can and will happen.

Working collaboratively is the future work of people in the Fourth Industrial Revolution. This may be our chief domain and our place of unique human contribution among robots and AI. As we have seen, there is much more to collaboration than meets the eye. We must build our businesses to create collaborative environments. We must develop our people with deep collaborative skills and encourage them to make collaboration a lifelong practice. And we must continuously seek the alignment of people and energy that is the hallmark of effective collaboration.

The benefits of managing the energy of business are potentially huge. Imagine less conflict, greater harmony, increased efficiency, expanded innovation, better productivity, business growth, and a jump in financial performance. All of these things, and more, are possible. Managing energy is not a business fad. Whether people choose to apply it or not, energy will continue to flow in business and in life. Whether we choose to unlock energy or ignore it, the truth of energy will remain.

In this book we've focused on how to help make businesses and the people in them work better and prepare for the future. But there is an even deeper aspect to this that I've held back on until now. Perhaps it is obvious, but it needs to be said. Managing energy is a kinder and more loving way to build, run, and participate in business. While that motive may or may not be your cup of tea, many are eager to help move business, and the world, in that direction. As Dr. Masaru Emoto (2005) showed us in his research on messages in water, the energy around us, and within us, has a significant effect on our well-being. We are affected by our environment and by those around us, and we, in turn, affect them. Just as water grows into beautiful crystals when exposed to loving energy, people at work blossom when the energy is positive.

As people in business, we have great responsibility. Companies, governments, and schools run most of the world. We have the opportunity to set an example for others. The rest of the world watches and waits for what we will do. Each of us alone will decide how we will manage ourselves and our parts in the business. We're on a collision course, but there is a way out, a way that can truly make a difference in the world. We are at the dawn of a new era. Let's fly!

References

Aon Hewitt. 2017. *2017 Trends in Global Employee Engagement*. https://www.aon.com/unitedkingdom/attachments/trp/2017-Trends-in-Global-Employee-Engagement.pdf

Baker, Greg. 2009. "Don't Throw People Under the Bus." Accessed May 30, 2019, at https://www.advanceconsulting.com/blog/dont-throw-people-under-the-bus/

BusinessDictionary.com. 2019. Definition of "collaboration." Accessed May 30, 2019, at http://www.businessdictionary.com/definition/collaboration.html

BusinessDictionary.com. 2019. Definition of "organizational agility." Accessed May 30, 2019 at http://www.businessdictionary.com/definition/organizational-agility.html

CPP Global Human Capital Report. 2008, July. "Workplace Conflict and How Businesses Can Harness It to Thrive." 1–32. https://shop.themyersbriggs.com/Pdfs/CPP_Global_Human_Capital_Report_Workplace_Conflict.pdf

Dana, Daniel. 2005. *Managing Differences: How to Build Better Relationships at Work and Home, Fourth Edition*. Prairie Village, KS: MTI Publications.

Davenport, Thomas, and George Westerman. 2018, March 9. "Why So Many High Profile Digital Transformations Fail." *Harvard Business Review* (Digital Article).

Drucker, Peter. 1957. *Landmarks of Tomorrow*. New York: Harper & Brothers.

Drucker, Peter. 1999. *Management Challenges for the 21st Century*. New York: Harper Collins.

Dunbar, Robin. 1998. *Grooming, Gossip and the Evolution of Language.* Cambridge, MA: Harvard University Press.

Emoto, Masaru. 2005. *The Hidden Messages in Water.* New York: Beyond Words Publishing.

Gagnon, Chris, Elizabeth John, and Rob Theunissen. 2017, September. "Organizational Health: A Fast Track to Performance Improvement." *McKinsey Quarterly* 1, 3. https://www.mckinsey.com/business-functions/organization/our-insights/organizational-health-a-fast-track-to-performance-improvement

Gunther McGrath, Rita. 2014, July 30. "Management's Three Eras: A Brief History." *Harvard Business Review* (Digital Article).

Harraf, Abe, Isaac Wanasika, Kaylynn Tate, and Kaitlyn Talbott. 2015, March/April. "Organizational Agility." *Journal of Applied Business Research* 31, no. 2: 675–686. DOI: https://doi.org/10.19030/jabr.v31i2.9160

Hiscox. 2015. "The 2015 Hiscox Guide to Employee Lawsuits." 1-10. https://www.hiscox.com/documents/The-2015-Hiscox-Guide-to-Employee-Lawsuits-Employee-charge-trends-across-the-United-States.pdf

Kabcenell Wayne, Ellen. 2005, May 9. "It Pays to Find the Hidden But High Costs of Conflict." *Washington Business Journal* (Digital Article).

Lencioni, Patrick. 2012. *The Advantage: Why Organizational Health Trumps Everything Else in Business.* San Francisco: Jossey-Bass.

Machiavelli, Niccolò. 2014. *The Prince.* Los Angeles: Millennium Publications. Originally published 1513.

ManpowerGroup. 2017. "The Skills Revolution: Digitization and Why Skills and Talent Matter." (July): 1–7.

Pink, Daniel. 2009. *Drive: The Surprising Truth About What Motivates Us.* New York: Riverhead Books, Penguin Group.

Project Management Institute. 2012. "Pulse of the Profession In-Depth Report: Organizational Agility."

Russell, Stuart. 2017. "A Glimpse into the Future: Widespread Artificial Intelligence." World Economic Forum podcast. Posted May 19, 2017.

Slaikeu, K., and R. Hasson. 1998. *Controlling the Cost of Conflict.* San Francisco: Jossey-Bass.

Thomas, Kenneth W., and Ralph H. Kilmann, 2009–2019. "An Overview of the Thomas-Kilmann Conflict Mode Instrument (TKI)." Accessed May 30, 2019, at http://www.kilmanndiagnostics.com/overview-thomas-kilmann-conflict-mode-instrument-tki

WebMD. 2005–2019. "The Effects of Stress on Your Body." Accessed May 30, 2019, at https://www.webmd.com/balance/stress-management/effects-of-stress-on-your-body

About the Author

Greg Baker is president and CEO of Advance Consulting Inc., a management consulting and professional development firm serving corporate and government clients in the United States and abroad. Advance Consulting specializes in the transformation of people, teams, and organizations, helping clients adapt and thrive in the turbulent and challenging global business environment. Mr. Baker is a strategic and visionary leader with demonstrated experience growing and transforming businesses across multiple industries. He shares his experience by providing executive coaching to business leaders who are themselves leading significant change and innovation.

Since 2005, Mr. Baker led the transformation of Advance Consulting from a specialized training company into a management consulting and professional development company serving the needs of clients undergoing major business transformation. He directs company strategy and operations toward achieving its mission:

> To partner with our clients to achieve sustainable change in how their people and businesses operate, delivering strategic growth and profitability, and serving the broader evolution of the global community.

Advance Consulting's clients represent virtually every major industry and functional area. Primary clients are typically CXOs, business unit leaders, department heads, and functional area leaders (e.g., information technology, human resources, finance, professional services).

Mr. Baker was formerly an executive with CTB/McGraw-Hill, where he was vice president of Programs and Business Transformation. Prior to CTB/McGraw-Hill, he was a vice president at Science Applications International Corporation (SAIC). He currently serves as chairman of the board at Learning for Life Charter School. Throughout his career, Mr. Baker's focus has been on growing and transforming businesses across a variety of industries.

Mr. Baker holds an MBA in Management from San Diego State University and a BA in Psychology (Honors Program) from the University of California, San Diego. He is a Registered Organizational Development Consultant with the International Society for Organization Development and Change. Awards and honors include the SAIC Founders Award for outstanding success in business development and a Top Ten ranking in the International Business Plan Competition hosted by college MBA programs around the world.

Mr. Baker is launching his career as an author with this, his first book.

Index